Justification in a Post-Christian Society

CHURCH OF SWEDEN

Research Series

꧂

Göran Gunner, editor
Vulnerability, Churches and HIV (2009)

Kajsa Ahlstrand and Göran Gunner, editors
Non-Muslims in Muslim Majority Societies (2009)

Jonas Ideström, editor
For the Sake of the World (2010)

Göran Gunner and Kjell-Åke Nordquist
An Unlikely Dilemma (2011)

Anne-Louise Eriksson, Göran Gunner, and Niclas Blåder, editors
Exploring a Heritage (2012)

Kjell-Åke Nordquist, editor
Gods and Arms (2012)

Harald Hegstad
The Real Church (2013)

Carl-Henric Grenholm and Göran Gunner, editors
Justification in a Post-Christian Society (2014)

Carl-Henric Grenholm and Göran Gunner, editors
Lutheran Identity and Political Theology (2014)

Justification in a Post-Christian Society

Edited by
CARL-HENRIC GRENHOLM
AND GÖRAN GUNNER

◐PICKWICK *Publications* · Eugene, Oregon

JUSTIFICATION IN A POST-CHRISTIAN SOCIETY.
Church of Sweden Research Series 8

Copyright © 2014 Trossamfundet Svenska Kyrkan (Church of Sweden). All rights reserved. Except for brief quotations in critical publications or reviews, no part of this book may be reproduced in any manner without prior written permission from the publisher. Write: Permissions, Wipf and Stock Publishers, 199 W. 8th Ave., Suite 3, Eugene, OR 97401.

In cooperation with the Department of Theology, Uppsala University, Sweden

Pickwick Publications
An imprint of Wipf and Stock Publishers
199 W. 8th Ave., Suite 3
Eugene, OR 97401

www.wipfandstock.com

ISBN 13: 978-1-62564-889-1

Cataloging-in-Publication data:

Justification in a post-christian society / edited by Carl-Henric Grenholm and Göran Gunner

xii + 258 p. ; 23 cm. Includes bibliographical references.

Church of Sweden Research Series 8

ISBN 13: 978-1-62564-889-1

1. Justification (Christian Theology)—History of doctrines. 2. Christianity and culture. I. Title. II. Series.

BT764.3 J87 2014

Manufactured in the U.S.A.

New Revised Standard Version Bible, copyright 1989, Division of Christian Education of the National Council of the Churches of Christ in the United States of America. Used by permission. All rights reserved.

Contents

Contributors vii
Abbreviations xi

1   Introduction: Remembering the Past—Living the Future—Carl-Henric Grenholm and Göran Gunner | 1

PART ONE: *Justification, Atonement, and Reconciliation*

2   Promise and Trust: Lutheran Identity in a Multicultural Society —*Christoph Schwöbel* | 15
3   The Experience of Justification—*Christine Helmer* | 36
4   Atonement in Theology and a Post-Einsteinian Notion of Time —*Antje Jackelén* | 57
5   Healing as an Image for the Atonement: A Lutheran Consideration —*Cheryl M. Peterson* | 72

PART TWO: *Lutheran Theology and Ethics in a Post-Christian Society*

6   Law and Gospel in Lutheran Ethics—*Carl-Henric Grenholm* | 91
7   Outside Paradise: Renegotiating Original Sin in Contemporary Lutheran Theology—*Eva-Lotta Grantén* | 107
8   Lutheran Spiritual Theology in a Post-Christian Society —*Karin Johannesson* | 121
9   Lutheran Theology and Dialogical Engagement in Post-Christian Society—*James M. Childs, Jr.* | 137
10 Physicality as a New Model for Lutheran Ethics in a Multicultural Global Community—*Richard J. Perry, Jr.* | 155

PART THREE: *Reformation as a Model for Interpretation of the Present*

11 Incarnate vs. Discarnate Protestantism: Martin Luther and the Disembodiment of Faith—*Niels Henrik Gregersen* | 173
12 Contra Philosophos: The Lutheran Reformation as Critique of the Rationality of Modernity—*Knut Alfsvåg* | 192

13 Priesthood of all Believers as Public Opinion: An Unexplored Link between the Lutheran Reformation and the Enlightenment? —*Urban Claesson* | 207
14 Luther's Interpretation of the *Magnificat* and Latin American Liberation Theology—*Elina Vuola* | 222
15 "Satis est" (CA 7): The Confessional Unity of the Church and the Augsburg Confession Today—*Henning Theißen* | 241

Contributors

KNUT ALVSVÅG is a Professor at the School of Mission and Theology, Stavanger, Norway and at Kobe Lutheran Theological Seminary, Japan. His main research interest is the history of Christian thought with particular emphasis on the philosophical and methodological implications of the understanding of God. He has published *What no Mind has Conceived: On the Significance of Christological Apophaticism* (2010) and several articles on the theological significance of the Reformation.

JAMES M. CHILDS, JR. is Joseph A. Sittler Professor Emeritus of Theology and Ethics. After serving in the parish ministry and teaching in both college and university he has been at the Trinity Lutheran Seminary, Columbus, Ohio, USA, since 1978 where he also served as Academic Dean for 22 years. Recent books: *Ethics in the Community of Promise: Faith, Formation, and Decision* (2006), *The Way of Peace: Christian Life in the Face of Discord* (2008), edited and updated George Forell's 1966 *Christian Social Teachings* (2013).

URBAN CLAESSON is Doctor in Church History and Researcher at the Church of Sweden Research Unit. His main areas of research are the emergence of Pietism in Sweden during the seventeenth century and the nation building processes during the nineteenth and the twentieth centuries in relation to the Nordic Folk Churches. He has published *Folkhemmets kyrka. Harald Hallén och folkkyrkans genombrott* (A Church for a Social Democratic Nation. Harald Hallén and the emergence of the Swedish Folk Church, 2004). He has also published articles on the Nordic Folk Churches and on early Swedish Pietism.

EVA-LOTTA GRANTÉN is Associate Professor of Ethics, Uppsala University, and Director at the Diocese's office in Lund, Sweden. Her main research areas are contemporary Lutheran ethics, and the interplay between theology and the natural sciences. Her publications include *Patterns of Care: Relating Altruism in Sociobiology and the Christian Tradition of Agape* (2003) and

Utanför Paradiset: Arvsyndsläran i nutida luthersk teologi och etik (Outside Paradise: Original Sin in Contemporary Lutheran Theology and Ethics, 2013).

NIELS HENRIK GREGERSEN is Professor of Systematic Theology at the Faculty of Theology, Copenhagen University, Denmark. His main research areas are contemporary Protestant theology, and the relations between theology and the biological sciences. His publications include *The Gift of Grace: The Future of Lutheran Theology* (2005), *Information and the Nature of Reality* (2010), *Lutherbilleder i dansk teologi 1800–2000* (Luther in Danish Theology 1800–2000, 2012), and *Den bevægelige Ortodoksi: Konflikt og kontinuitet i kristendommen* (Orthodoxy in Transition: Conflict and Continuity in the Christian tradition, 2014).

CARL-HENRIC GRENHOLM is Senior Professor of Ethics at the Department of Theology, Uppsala University, Sweden. His main research areas are ethical theory, Christian social ethics, work ethics, ethics and economics, and theological ethics. He is the leader of a research project on Lutheran Theology and Ethics—in a Post-Christian Society. Among his publications are *Protestant Work Ethics* (1993), *Teologisk etik* (Theological Ethics, 1997), *Bortom Humanismen* (Beyond Humanism, 2003), *Sustainable Development and Global Ethics* (2007), and *Etisk teori: Kritik av moralen* (Ethical Theory, 2014).

GÖRAN GUNNER is Associate Professor in Mission Studies, Uppsala University, and Researcher at Church of Sweden Research Unit, Uppsala. Dr. Gunner is also Senior Lecturer at Stockholm School of Theology, Stockholm, Sweden. His research areas include religious minority situations in the Middle East and issues related to human rights. He is also the editor of Church of Sweden Research Series. Among his publications are *An Unlikely Dilemma: Constructing a Partnership between Human Rights and Peace-Building* (co-authored with Kjell-Åke Nordquist, 2011) and *Genocide of Armenians: Through Swedish Eyes* (2013).

CHRISTINE HELMER is Professor of Religion and Professor of German at Northwestern University, Evanston, USA. Her research areas include the theology of Martin Luther, the philosophy and theology of Friedrich Schleiermacher, biblical theology, and philosophy of religion. Her most recent publications on Luther are three edited volumes: *The Global Luther: A Theologican for Modern Times* (2009), and together with Bo Kristian Holm, *Transformations in Luther's Theology: Historical and Contemporary Considerations* (2011), and the forthcoming *Lutherreanaissance: Past and Present*.

Her new book *Theology and the End of Doctrine* is published 2014, and she is currently working on a monograph on Schleiermacher.

ANTJE JACKELÉN is the Archbishop of the Church of Sweden. Dr. Jackelén is also an Adjunct Professor of Systematic Theology/Religion and Science at the Lutheran School of Theology at Chicago, USA, where she taught and was director of the Zygon Center for Religion and Science 2001(3)–2007. From 2008–2014 president of the European Society for the Study of Science and Theology. Author of *Time and Eternity: The Question of Time in Church, Science and Theology* (2005), *The Dialogue between Religion and Science: Challenges and Future Directions* (2004), *Gud är större* (God is greater, 2011) and numerous articles, published in various languages.

KARIN JOHANNESSON is Lecturer in Philosophy of Religion at the Faculty of Theology in Uppsala, Sweden. Her research concerns primarily philosophy of language, the realism-debates, and spirituality. Her main publications in English are her doctoral thesis, *God pro Nobis: On Non-metaphysical Realism* (2007) and "Concept of God in Contemporary Philosophy of Religion" in *Encyclopedia of Sciences and Religions* (2013). Since 2008 she has been involved in the research project Lutheran Theology and Ethics—in a Post-Christian Society, writing a study (in Swedish) entitled *The Philosophy of Sanctification: On Spiritual Training within Lutheran Tradition*.

RICHARD J. PERRY, JR. is Professor of Church and Society/Urban Ministry, Lutheran School of Theology at Chicago, USA. An ordained ELCA pastor, he joined the faculty of LSTC in 1996. His research interests include bioethics, African American Lutheran history and thought, Lutheran and African American social ethics, and environmental justice. His publications include editing *Catching A Star: Transcultural Reflections on a Church for All People* (2004), chapters in books on Lutheran ethics, and various articles on stem cells, genetics, and race and genetics. He is completing a manuscript on African American bioethics.

CHERYL M. PETERSON is Associate Professor of Systematic Theology at Trinity Lutheran Seminary, Columbus, Ohio, USA. Her main research areas are ecclesiology, pneumatology, and Lutheran theology. Among her publications are *Who is the Church? An Ecclesiology for the Twenty-First Century* (2013) and "Spirit and Body: A Feminist and Lutheran Conversation" (2010).

CHRISTOPH SCHWÖBEL is Professor of Systematic Theology and Philosophy of Religion in the Protestant Theological Faculty of the University of Tübingen, Germany. He is Director of the Institute for Hermeneutics and the Dialogue of Cultures. Before coming to Tübingen in 2004 he held appointments at King's College London, the University of Kiel and the University of Heidelberg, where he was also Director of the Ecumenical Institute. His publications include: *Gott in Beziehung. Studien zur Dogmatik* (2002), *Christlicher Glaube im Pluralismus* (2003) and *Gott im Gespräch. Studien zur Gegenwartsdeutung* (2011).

HENNING THEIßEN is Assistant to the Chair of Systematic Theology at the University of Greifswald, Germany since 2007. He wrote his Ph.D. thesis on nineteenth century Protestant eschatology and Judaism (2002) and his Post.Doc. thesis on the fundamentals of Protestant ecclesiology (2011). In 2012 he was awarded Hanns Lilje Prize and Oberlin Innovation Prize. His main research interests are united ecclesiologies and the ethics of adoption. Among his publications are *Die evangelische Eschatologie und das Judentum. Strukturprobleme der Konzeptionen seit Schleiermacher* (2004) and *Die berufene Zeugin des Kreuzes Christi. Studien zur Grundlegung der evangelischen Theorie der Kirche* (2013).

ELINA VUOLA is Academy Professor at the Faculty of Theology, University of Helsinki, Finland. Her research interests are Latin American liberation theology, gender, sexual ethics, and Virgin Mary. Her dissertation *Limits of Liberation. Feminist Theology and the Ethics of Poverty and Reproduction* (2002) is also published in Spanish with the title *La ética sexual y los límites de la praxis. Conversaciones críticas entre la teología feminista y la teología de la liberación*. Her current research project Embodied Religion. Changing Meanings of Body and Gender in Contemporary Forms of Religious Identity in Finland is funded by the Academy of Finland (2002–2017).

Abbreviations

BEThL	Bibliotheca Ephemeridum theologicarum Lovaniensium
BEvTh	Beiträge zur evangelischen Theologie
BHTh	Beiträge zur historischen Theologie
CA	Confessio Augustana
DB	Die Deutsche Bibel
DBW	Dietrich Bonhoeffer Works
DiKi	Dialog Der Kirchen
EKD	Evangelical Church in Germany
ELCA	Evangelical Lutheran Church in America
EvTh	*Evangelische Theologie*
HUT	Hermeneutische Untersuchungen Zur Theologie
LD	Luther, Martin. *Luther deutsch: Die Werke Martin Luthers in neuer Auswahl für die Gegenwart.* Stuttgart: Ehrenfired Klotz Verlag, 1957.
LKW	Lutherische Kirche in der Welt
LW	Luther, Martin. *Luther's Work's.* 55 vols. Philadelphia: Fortress Press; St. Louis: Corcordia, 1955–1986.
LWF	Lutheran World Federation
MJTh	*Marburger Jahrbuchs Theologie*

NZSTh	*Neue Zeitschrift für Systematische Theologie und Religionsphilosophie*
QD	Quaestiones disputatae
RPP	Religion Past & Present
TEH, NF	Theologische Existenz heute: [n.F.]
WA	Luther, Martin. *Werke: Kritische Gesamtausgabe.* 65 vols. Weimar: Hermann Böhlau Nachfolger, 1883–1993.
WABr	Luther, Martin. *Luthers Werke: Kritische Gesamtausgabe. Briefwechsel.* Weimar: Verlag Hermann Böhlaus Nachfolger, 1930–1985.
WA DB	Luther, Martin. *Werke. Kritische Gesamtausgabe.* 7 vols. *Die Deutsche Bibel.* Weimar: Herrmann Böhlaus Nachfolger, 1906–1931.
WA TR	Luther, Martin. *Werke. Kritische Gesamtausgabe. Tischreden.* Weimar: Hermann Böhlaus Nachfolger, 1912–1921.
ZThK	*Zeitschrift für Theologie und Kirche*

1

Introduction: Remembering the Past—Living the Future

CARL-HENRIC GRENHOLM & GÖRAN GUNNER

Lutheran tradition has been of immense importance not just within the churches in quite a lot of countries worldwide but also for society and culture in general. Ideas within Reformation theology have in various ways influenced education, health care, attitudes to work, economy, and politics. This impact of Lutheran tradition has been based on particular theological positions that have been developed in different ways. Some of these positions are the doctrine of justification by grace alone, the idea that the Bible has a particular role as a source for theological reflection, the doctrine of original sin, the idea of a sharp difference between law and gospel, and the doctrine of the priesthood of all believers.

The Reformation Jubilee in 2017 will give an opportunity to celebrate the importance of Lutheran tradition within the churches and in the society. It is an opportunity to remember what happened 500 years ago and to analyze the meaning of Reformation, its main theological ideas, and its societal consequences. However, it is also an opportunity to make a critical evaluation of Lutheran tradition. How are different theological positions within this tradition to be evaluated today? What role can the Reformation predict for the future? What would be a reasonable Lutheran position in a multicultural and post-Christian society?

Lutheran tradition emerged in a sharp opposition towards the Catholic Church. The theological and ethical reflection of Martin Luther and Philip Melanchthon is characterized by their critique of certain positions within

Catholic theology. An alternative interpretation of Christian faith was developed in a society where the Church had a considerable political power and where the impact of Christianity on culture was immense. Theological disagreements were important, and they were taken seriously by those in political power.

After the Reformation in the sixteenth century, Lutheran tradition has had a great impact on culture and politics in many societies. This is particularly true in Germany and the Nordic countries, where the political power has been allied to the Lutheran Churches. These churches have often been state churches, which mean that they seldom have developed a critique of those in political power. At the same time Lutheran churches had a great impact on personal faith as well as on basic moral conviction. Within some societies almost all of the citizens were members of the Lutheran church, and its interpretation of Christian faith was mostly taken for granted.

Today, society is quite different. In many Protestant countries in the Western hemisphere the secularization is apparent and it is often adequate to argue that it is a post-Christian society. There has been a separation between church and state in many countries, and the position of Christianity in culture and society is rather weak. Only a minority of citizens today would say that they share a Christian belief. At the same time the society is multicultural, which means that different cultures exist in a close relationship in the same community, often as a result of migration. In this multicultural society there is an obvious religious and moral pluralism, which means that there is no longer a shared system of beliefs and values.

How should we evaluate Lutheran tradition in today's multicultural and post-Christian society? Is it possible to develop a Lutheran theological position that can be regarded as reasonable in a society which involves the considerable weakening of the role of Christianity? What are the challenges raised by cultural diversity for a Lutheran theology and a Lutheran ethical position that makes claims to adequacy? Is it possible to develop a Lutheran identity in a multicultural society, and is there any fruitful Lutheran contribution to the coexistence of different religious and non-religious traditions in the future?

These questions were discussed at an international conference in Uppsala during October 8–10, 2013, on the theme "Remembering the Past—Living the Future. Lutheran Tradition in Transition." The conference was hosted by the Church of Sweden Research Unit and the Department of Theology at Uppsala University. During the conference almost two hundred participants from all parts of the world discussed issues concerning the interpretation and relevance of Lutheran theology and ethics today and in the future. Lectures were given and papers presented on eight different themes:

(1) Lutheran theology and ethics in a post-Christian society, (2) the Bible in Lutheran tradition, (3) Lutheran identity in a global world, (4) Reformation as a model for interpretation of the present, (5) Lutheran theology and politics, (6) atonement, reconciliation, and forgiveness, (7) Lutheran tradition and tolerance, and (8) Lutheran tradition and gender.

It is important to note that this was not a conference on Luther and his theology. Rather, it was a conference on Lutheran tradition and its possible relevance today. Some of the papers presented at the conference did analyze the theological positions of Luther himself. However, most of the papers dealt with later developments within Lutheran theology. When Luther's theology was discussed, the purpose was not to recapitulate his ideas for a credible theological position today. On the contrary, the purpose was to give a fair interpretation of his ideas and then to make a critical evaluation of his theology. It is obvious that there are ideas in Luther's theology that we can learn from today, but it is also obvious that we have to criticize many of the theological positions developed in his writings.

During the Luther renaissance in Germany and the Nordic countries, one hundred years ago, the idea was to get a thorough understanding of the theological positions of Luther himself, behind the later development in Lutheran tradition that often was criticized. At the same time the idea was often that it is possible to give a constructive contribution to a reasonable theological position through an interpretation of Luther's theology. Today it is necessary to make a strict distinction between the task to give a fair description of ideas within Reformation theology and the constructive task to elaborate a Lutheran theology that can be regarded as reasonable in a multicultural society.

This means that in celebrating the Reformation Jubilee there is a need not only to remember what happened in the sixteenth century. It is also necessary to make a critical evaluation of the past and discuss what would be a reasonable Lutheran position in the future. This implies a critique both of Luther himself and some positions in later Lutheran tradition. Today, Lutheran theology is interpreted in different ways in various cultural and social contexts, and sometimes it is hard to determine what a Lutheran identity stands for in a global world. Therefore, it is urgent to evaluate this tradition and try to find out what a tenable Lutheran theology would look like in a post-Christian society.

The conference in Uppsala on "Remembering the Past—Living the Future" has resulted in two volumes based upon some of the lectures and papers presented. The volume on *Lutheran Identity and Political Theology* deals with the issues of Lutheran identity in a global world, Lutheran tradition and gender, and the possibilities to develop a Lutheran political theology. In this volume on *Justification in a Post-Christian Society* three main problems are discussed. How should we today interpret the doctrine of atonement and justification by grace alone? What would be a fruitful formation of Lutheran theology and ethics in today's post-Christian society? How has the history of Reformation been interpreted and how can narratives about Reformation be used to justify modern beliefs and attitudes?

JUSTIFICATION, ATONEMENT, AND RECONCILIATION

The first theme of this book concerns the doctrine of justification by grace alone. This is often understood to be the central doctrine in Lutheran theology and the heart of Lutheran identity. At the same time the signing of the *Joint Declaration on the Doctrine of Justification* (1999) has created a vivid discussion on different interpretations of this doctrine today. Is a "forensic" interpretation of this doctrine tenable or does the justification imply a union with Christ that renews the believer by making her righteous? How should we today understand the Reformation formula that the believer is simultaneously righteous and a sinner (*simul iustus et peccator*)?

Various interpretations of the doctrine of justification are often related to different understandings of atonement, reconciliation, and the role of the death of Jesus on the cross. Some interpretations of atonement seem to be rather controversial in theology today. Is it reasonable to argue that the love of God presupposes the suffering and the brutal death of his beloved Son? Should atonement be understood in terms of a theory of satisfaction? Does the atoning activity of God in Christ presuppose total passivity on the human side? These problems concerning our interpretation of atonement are in Lutheran theology related to different understandings of the doctrine of justification.

Chapter Two, written by Christoph Schwöbel, takes as its starting point the challenges that Lutheran churches are confronted with in a multicultural society. How should we understand Lutheran identity in a society where different cultures exist in a relationship of coexistence? Schwöbel argues that important for understanding Lutheran identity is the emphasis on God's word, God's work, and God's being as promise. God's justice as the justice by which God makes sinners just means a communication of grace. God's promise connects creation, redemption, and sanctification, and it can be understood as gift, address, and enablement to cooperate with the promises of God.

In Lutheran theology promise and trust are inextricably linked, according to Schwöbel. He argues that humans are trusting animals and that faith can be understood as radical trust in God. Justification is possible through faith alone, and faith is contrasted to everything human beings can achieve on the basis of their own powers. This understanding of God's promise and trust is central in Lutheran theology, and it also constitutes the Lutheran contribution to life in a multicultural society. Its implication is that the identity of human persons is not established by their differences from other people. Human identity is rooted in the relationship of God to particular persons, which has the form of the promise of enduring identity in all the changing situations of life.

The next chapter, which is written by Christine Helmer, gives a critical analysis of some important interpretations of the doctrine of justification in Lutheran theology. The basic question in this chapter is if experience and justification is a category mistake. Helmer discusses why Lutheran theology has lost the notion of experience in relation to justification. This is done by a careful analysis of the understanding of justification on the writings of three influential theologians in the beginning and the end of the twentieth century, namely Karl Holl, Oswald Bayer, and George Lindbeck. Helmer's conclusion is that there is a shift in the Lutheran theological concept of experience. Holl introduced Luther scholarship to the possibility of constructing a concept of religious experience. However, at the end of the century religious experience is generic and unarticulated, and antithetical to linguistically articulated doctrinal truth.

Against this background Christine Helmer discusses possibilities for thinking anew how justification can be experienced. Her thesis is that we need new insights into what counts as religious experience, and more accurate appreciation of the religious dimension of experience. According to Helmer, a Lutheran theology of justification much work out a more complex dialectic between faith and experience that makes room for the religious development of the self. It must also move beyond a restricted semantics of justification to experiential dimensions of the self, such as emotions, physical postures, relationship with the divine. Human experiences cannot be immune to the divine work of justification.

Different interpretations of the doctrine of atonement are in focus in Chapter Four, written by Antje Jackelén. She mentions some of the obstacles that have been identified for a consistent presentation of the atonement in a contemporary global context. One is the idea that the love of God is expressed in the brutal death of his beloved Son. Another is the complete denial of the human potential to do good that seems to be presupposed by the theory of atonement. A third obstacle is the idea of Christ substituting for depraved humankind, which seems to imply a strange kind of human passivity and collectivism.

Antje Jackelén argues that post-Einsteinian notions of time may contribute to the theological attempts to cope with some of these obstacles. Einstein's theories of relativity gave a new perspective on the relational character of time, which was quite different from Newton's conception of absolute time. An adoption of post-Einsteinian notions of time would according to Jackelén be productive in several areas of theology. It can inspire theology to focus on the comparative and relationally instead of looking for the absolute and correct superlatives. This post-Einsteinian theological approach would also make it easier to deal with some of the problems concerning atonement theory.

Cheryl M. Peterson argues in Chapter Five that healing can be a fruitful image for the atonement. In Lutheran tradition a forensic interpretation of the doctrine of justification has been dominant, and the atonement has been interpreted in a similar way. However, these interpretations have ignored the personal nature of forgiveness and a relational view of salvation. Considering healing as an image for the atonement would, according to Peterson, better address the human predicament in more relational and transformational ways. The language of healing as an atonement image would also be adequate in our context today, both in the west and in the global south.

Cheryl M. Peterson gives a critical analysis of different atonement theories in the past and the present. She clarifies the problems related to the Latin view, the subjective view, and the classic patristic view. Her thesis is that atonement theories have always been contextual. In a new cultural context we need images and metaphors that are more appropriate. The language of healing could be such a possibility, and it can help bringing together the objective and the subjective aspects of atonement. In Lutheran theology, Peterson argues, it would be possible to affirm healing as a metaphor for the doctrines of justification and atonement, if healing is understood relationally.

LUTHERAN THEOLOGY AND ETHICS IN A POST-CHRISTIAN SOCIETY

The second theme of this book concerns the understanding of Lutheran theology and ethics in a post-Christian society. This theme is related to a research project at Uppsala University that has studied important ideas in Lutheran theology. One aim has been to analyze some main theological and ethical positions that can be found in Martin Luther's own thought. Another purpose has been to analyze how these ideas have been further developed in later Lutheran tradition. A third objective has been to critically assess different positions in Lutheran tradition and to constructively tackle the question as to what a fruitful formation of Lutheran theology and ethics could look like in today's post-Christian and multicultural society.

It is quite obvious that theological and ethical positions in Martin Luther's thought have been developed in various ways in later Lutheran tradition. This tradition contains a variety of interpretations and is by no means uniform. Today we have to critically evaluate these different positions anew from the perspectives of a post-Christian and multi-cultural society. Is it possible to formulate Lutheran theological and ethical positions that can be considered reasonable in a society that involves the considerable weakening of the role of Christianity? What would be a reasonable Lutheran approach in a multicultural society where it is necessary to establish a dialogue with a large number of different religious and non-religious traditions?

In Chapter Six Carl-Henric Grenholm argues that the sharp distinction between law and gospel should be challenged within a Lutheran ethical reflection in a post-Christian society. He gives a critical analysis of the ethical theories that are elaborated by three influential Lutheran theologians, namely Paul Althaus, Helmut Thielicke, and Gustaf Wingren. All of them argue in favor of an ethical theory that is primarily based on reason and the doctrine of creation. The gospel and the conception of God's love in Christ are not regarded to give any new substantial contribution to the contents of ethics. This position is combined with a political ethic which is uncritical towards the existing political power.

Grenholm argues that a more tenable ethical theory in Lutheran tradition should be based not only on creation but also on Christology and Eschatology. This means that the opposition between law and gospel should be challenged, as far as it means that the gospel does not have any implications for the content of ethics. The doctrine of the two kingdoms should be abandoned in such a way that the conception of God's love and the idea of human equality, which are important in the gospel about Christ, become relevant also within political ethics. Thereby, Lutheran ethics could be an inspiration for social critique.

In the next chapter Eva-Lotta Granténdiscusses what a reasonable Lutheran understanding of original sin would be today. Is it possible to defend a doctrine of original sin in a society where a scientific world view is widely accepted? Her thesis is that a post-Christian and pluralist society challenges Lutheran theology to renegotiate its understanding of original sin. One challenge is raised by the historical critical method in biblical exegesis. Old Testament scholars unite in describing the Eden narrative as a myth that does not give a historical account of something that really happened. Another challenge is raised by evolutionary theory. From this perspective the fall is not a historical event, and there is no clear point in history where sin entered.

According to Grantén, Lutheran theology can learn from Reinhold Niebuhr and Ted Peters how to renegotiate the content of original sin. Niebuhr gives a clarifying analysis of the ambivalence in the human situation as finite freedom, connected to a condition of anxiety and lack of meaning. From this perspective it is possible to develop an interpretation of original sin that is compatible with modern biblical exegesis and insights from evolutionary theory. At the same time a reasonable Lutheran doctrine of sin today should be able to connect to people's experience, and it should be true to its heritage.

Karin Johannesson discusses in Chapter Eight the possibilities to develop a Lutheran spiritual theology in a post-Christian society. Spiritual training seems to be controversial in Lutheran tradition, since Luther fought forcefully against the belief that human undertakings such as spiritual exercises can strengthen a person's relationship to God. However, there are interpretations of Luther's understanding of sanctification that make it possible to encourage some kind of spiritual training. Johannesson gives an analysis of three such interpretations, namely those put forward by Tuomo Mannermaa, Arvid Runestam, and Rudolf Hermann.

According to Mannermaa, the leading idea in Luther's theology is his insistence on Christ's real presence in faith, and his conception of sanctification is corresponding to the notion of *theosis*, that is divinization. Runestam argues that Luther understands sanctification as a certain extension of the freedom of a Christian, and from this perspective he emphasized the value of asceticism. According to Hermann, Luther understands sanctification as a time-concept, which means that it is a process of increased dialogue with Christ in prayer. Johannesson argues that the position of Hermann is the most fruitful, since there are vital flaws in the other two alternatives. From this perspective it is possible to maintain that spiritual training in the form of praying to Christ can contribute to the believer's growth in faith.

Two chapters deal with the question how to elaborate a reasonable model of Lutheran ethics in a post-Christian and multicultural society. James M. Childs, Jr. starts with an analysis of what it means that society is post-Christian. He refers to Charles Taylor, who has provided an important account of the impact of secularity upon the status of religion in Western society. For some this points to a post-Christian society where people are leaving the faith. For others, like Jürgen Habermas, it is a post-secular society in which religion still flourishes but in an atmosphere of societal indifference. All agree that it is a post-Christian and pluralistic society.

Childs argues that a vital theologically grounded Lutheran ethic in this context is one of active solidarity with human needs and those of the planet itself. This is Bonhoeffer's "church for others" following the Christ who was the "human for others." The posture of servanthood in the spirituality of Luther's theology of the cross can speak dialogically across the gap between the traditional language of the faith and the multiple voices of pluralism. Lutheran theologians like Helmut Thielicke and Gustaf Wingren have, according to Childs, corrected the quietism of earlier generations. He also argues that eschatological theologies such as Pannenberg's have further paved the way for engagement with the world as central to the church's vocation.

Finally, Richard J. Perry, Jr. argues that physicality can be a new model for Lutheran ethics in a multicultural global world. This is a model for articulating Lutheran ethics that has been developed by some African and European American elders, who carried their bodies from the sanctuary of their churches to the street where God was also active with demonstrators for justice. Physicality means the act of intentionally placing one's body into public spaces as a means of expressing concerns for justice in the world. It emerges out of the lived experiences of poor and marginalized people, and it renews our contemporary and future witness for racial justice and equality.

Perry reflects on the fifteenth anniversary commemoration of the Birmingham Civil Rights Movement. The movement developed a method for seeking racial justice in society, from which Lutheran ethics today can learn a great deal. Perry describes the practice of physicality by some Lutheran elders at this time, namely Andrew Schultze, Jospeh Ellwager, and Will Herzfeld. Participating in public actions against racial segregation they developed a model for articulating Lutheran ethics, which can be of great importance in a global multicultural world.

REFORMATION AS A MODEL FOR THE INTERPRETATION OF THE PRESENT

The third theme of this volume concerns Reformation as a model for interpretation of the present. What we now call the Reformation comprises a large number of disparate narratives, constantly reinterpreted for different purposes. In keeping with present-day demands and challenges, these stories can be used to justify beliefs, attitudes, behavior patterns, power, and communities. This means that Reformation can be interpreted differently, depending upon the perspectives and intentions of the interpreter. Ideas within the Reformation can also be used to support opposite positions.

How has the history of Reformation been used and how is it constantly transformed? In what ways have the Middle Ages been constructed as an antithesis to the modern era that began with the Reformation? How should we understand the relationship between Luther's theology and the modern project of secularization? In what ways have his ideas been utilized both to legitimize power and to criticize a system with an autocratic ruler? Can Lutheran tradition give a constructive contribution to the controversies about the values of modernity that are so typical of pluralist societies today? These are some of the questions discussed in this theme.

In Chapter Eleven Niels Henrik Gregersen discusses the contemporary status of religion in everyday life by referring to Charles Taylor's analysis of different meanings of secularity. A typical phenomenon today is the "discarnation of belief," especially in Protestant countries. The disembodying of spiritual life, "excarnation," is a point of departure for everyday secularity. In this society an important question is if Protestantism should define itself as the archetype of disembodied faith. There is without doubt a Protestantism without blood and flesh, in which faith is understood primarily as an individualized attitude of faith and inner freedom vis-à-vis church and society.

However, Gregersen argues, there is also a Protestantism of blood and flesh which knows that faith, hope, and love can only thrive in and through social forms of embodiment. This is a Protestantism that knows that faith can never be a purely private affair. Gregersen argues that this Protestantism of flesh and blood is expressed in Martin Luther's theology of creation as well as in his Eucharistic theology. Luther interprets the Christian faith as thoroughly embodied in the three life-circles of the human person, the social realm, and the wider drama of creation. From this perspective faith is always lived as emerging from tradition, as environmentally sensitive, as socially embedded, and as psychosomatically embodied.

Knut Alfsvåg argues in the next chapter that a substantial critique of late medieval *via moderna* was an important part of the intellectual development of the young Luther. There are contemporary scholars, like John Milbank and Alasdair MacIntyre, who have criticized Luther for having expressed his theology by grace alone in a way that either implies a kind of philosophical vacuum or anticipates the modern project of secularization. Alfsvåg argues that this interpretation of Luther is wrong, and that there are clear parallels between the critique of modernity in Luther, Milbank, and MacIntyre.

According to Alvsvåg, Luther is well aware of the philosophical implications of a theology of grace and explores them in detail. One may argue that the young Luther is much better at deconstructing the contradictions of *via moderna* than in presenting a consistent alternative. This changes, however, with Luther's evangelical breakthrough, which gives his thought an incarnational depth that informs even his theology of creation. The work of the mature Luther should therefore not be read as an anticipation of the modern idea of the secular. Alfsvåg argues that there are two important theologians who in the context of modernity repeat Luther's Christologically informed double emphasis of the limit and reliability of human reason, namely Johann Georg Hamann and Dietrich Bonhoeffer.

In Chapter Thirteen, Urban Claesson argues that there are possible links between the Lutheran theology and later ideas of the Enlightenment, and that one of these links is the doctrine of the priesthood of all believers. Claesson explores the conflict between the Swedish state and the priest Jacob Boëthius that came to surface in 1697, when Luther's teaching of the priesthood of all believers gained providence for formulating critique against a system with an autocratic ruler. According to Boëthius' perception of this Lutheran doctrine, all Christians had to criticize and admonish each other in order to help each other living holy lives. For Boëthius this also included the right to criticize the king.

As a way to institutionalize the priesthood of all believers within the political system Boëthius suggested a new form of national meeting. The king ought to be responsible in front of this national congregation and its opinions. Claesson argues that this model anticipates later and secularized versions of forming public opinion and establishing national parliaments. This means that this interpretation of the priesthood of all believers can be seen as a link between Lutheran theology and ideas of Enlightenment. Luther's theology was not only used by states to legitimize power—it also provided tools for critique of those in political power.

Luther's commentary on the *Magnificat* is analyzed in a chapter by Elina Vuola. She compares this commentary with contemporary interpretations of the Virgin Mary in the writings of some Catholic Latin American liberation theologians. There are two reasons to make this comparison. First, the silence about Mary and her absence in the Lutheran tradition need to be rethought in relation to Luther's own texts. A critical reflection on Luther's Mariology can make his theology more relevant for contemporary discussions about gender and social justice. Secondly, theological reflection on Mariology can be a contribution—and not an obstacle—to ecumenical relationships.

According to Vuola, Luther both agrees with pre-Reformation ecumenical Mariology and has Mariological interpretations of his own. The latter is especially clear in his commentary of the *Magnificat*. The double emphasis on Mary as the ordinary, even "lowly," woman and as the paragon of faith can be found in both Luther and liberation theology. Even if there are some differences between Luther and liberation theology, there are important similarities that may point to the possibility of an ecumenical

Mariology, which starts with the experiences of ordinary Christians, especially the marginalized and oppressed.

The final chapter in this volume is written by Henning Theißen. He offers a relecture of the ecclesiological key article of the *Augsburg Confession*, preceded by some reflections on why present day theologians consider the confessional writings from the Reformation period meaningful for their work in the early twenty-first century. Theißen gives a perspective on recent debates on Reformation theory, and then he gives a careful analysis of CA 7 and its concept of the true unity of the church. The purpose of the chapter is to transfer some fresh ideas from historiographical Reformation theory to dogmatic ecclesiology.

According to Theißen, particularly Thomas Kaufmann's concept of a Lutheran "confessional culture" seems apt to embed the doctrinal approach to church theory into a broader framework of religious, social, and political values. The main thesis of the chapter is that this confessional heritage enables present day Lutheranism to make a constructive contribution to the controversies about the values of modernity that are so typical of the pluralist societies most Lutherans find themselves in today. These controversies over values require exactly that kind of communication Lutherans are perfectly acquainted with due to what Theißen has identified as the freedom of conscience in Protestant ministry. This means that Lutherans have a particular expertise in "unity in reconciled diversity."

PART ONE

Justification, Atonement, and Reconciliation

2

Promise and Trust

Lutheran Identity in a Multicultural Society

CHRISTOPH SCHWÖBEL

MULTICULTURALISM AND ITS CHALLENGES

It is a commonplace that today we live globally—and often locally as well—in a multicultural society where different cultures coexist, oscillating between cooperation and competition. These multicultural settings are the result of various factors, from the migration movements of large groups of people caused by economic necessity, war, oppression, displacement, and the search for better opportunities for shaping one's life. If one wanted to write a diachronic history of the genesis of most multicultural societies, one would come across the most grievous aspects of modern history, racism, nationalism, ethnic strife, exploitation, and religious oppression, leading to the banishment from one context of life to the attempt at settling in another. These external factors are always accompanied by internal factors, affecting both those who have to find a new place in a hitherto foreign setting and those who have to accommodate people with different practices, beliefs and values in their midst. Because of their history, multicultural societies carry the burden of multiple memories of a past of injustice, conflict and suffering and are challenged to develop a common vision of a better life for all of their participating communities and individuals in order to achieve a state of peaceful coexistence and just cooperation.

In most cases a multicultural situation arises as the result of a transition from a monocultural situation. Typical of such a transition is the loss of common ground in terms of shared values and beliefs, informing the practices, conventions and ideals of a society, entertained by a majority of members of that society, which is replaced by a plurality of belief systems and values held by various minorities within the same society. If we understand culture in its most rudimentary sense as a system of signs for interpreting reality, which serves as a framework of meaning for all interactions with reality in a society, we find that multicultural scenarios are characterized by pervasive differences in symbolic communication. It is typical for a monocultural situation that most of the shared beliefs and values, which form the common ground of society, can remain implicit. They form a tacit consensus and rarely become the subject of explicit debate. In a monocultural situation beliefs and values are ingrained in the texture of society, part of the way everyday life is conducted in all areas of life, and they are only explicitly mentioned on occasions of public remembrance of the formative events in the history of society or in times of crisis when the very foundations of society seem to be called into question. The implicit common ground is more appealed to than argued for.

This changes with the transition to a multicultural society. The implicit consensus of society concerning its most fundamental values is replaced by a plurality of value and belief systems, which necessitates explicit debate on the values and beliefs that structure the lives of different people and communities in society. In such a situation it becomes clear that cultures are primarily a system of signs, creating universes of meaning, because the plurality of cultures and the conflicts between different cultures often appear as a clash of meanings, as a dispute concerning the way different communities read the world and act according to that reading. The differences in symbolic communication make apparent the problems of the relationship between different communities and point to the importance of translation as a primary technique for living together in a multicultural society, for common deliberation on the good of society, and for cooperation, but also for dissent. It is here that criticism of multiculturalism finds its primary targets: can the common ground claimed by the majority of a society, be replaced by a diversity of different grounds, occupied by different minorities? Does the loss of common ground in a multicultural situation automatically lead to a pervasive loss of trust in the institutions of society and to the eclipse of altruism across cultural boundaries?[1] On the other hand, it is also evident that

---

1. For a discussion of the risks of multiculturalism, including most significantly the loss of social capital, cf. Putnam, "*E Pluribus Unum:* Diversity and Community in the Twenty-first Century."

in a multicultural situation any attempt to claim a position of dominance for "majority culture," i.e. the former common ground, appears as little less than a claim to hegemony in the world of values. Would it make sense in such a situation to give up trying to establish common ground and instead look for common aims, defining the common good of society, which could be achieved on the basis of very different grounds but by complying with common rules?² Can multicultural societies have a vision of the promise of a common future?

Since in many cases cultures are rooted in a *cultus*, expressing the center of meaning and being of the symbolic system of a culture, multicultural societies are shaped by a religious and ideological pluralism.³ Scenarios of religious and ideological pluralism are characterized by the coexistence of groups and individuals holding diverse religious or ideological basic orientations, which claim ultimate significance for the lives of their adherents. The different pluralizing tendencies, which have been at work in Western societies since the Reformation, reach their most radical stage in religious and ideological pluralism which represents the interior view of a multicultural society. Multicultural societies with a belief and value system characterized by religious and ideological pluralism often live in a state of uneasy coexistence, which can result in either a falling apart of society into several self-segregated communities or in open, potentially violent conflict between different cultures with different religious beliefs. Multicultural societies present their members with the need to define their identities, both in order to express what makes them different from others, and in order to enable members of society to address the different communities and individual people in terms of their respective identities. Religious identities sometimes define the "hard core" of cultural identities, the non-negotiable element in cultural interaction. Religion can thus provide the identity markers in multicultural, pluralistic scenarios.

The identity politics which are to be found in multicultural and religiously as well as ideologically pluralist societies have a high potential for conflict, which is often focused on the symbolic identity markers of religious identities.⁴ The headscarf of Muslim women and the conflict over the caricatures of Muhammad are but two of the most strident examples of symbolic conflicts relating to identity definition. While it is important to see how easily religious identities can be exploited to serve other purposes, be

---

2. Cf. Schwöbel, "Talking over the Fence. From Toleration to Dialogue."

3. Cf. Schwöbel, *Christlicher Glaube im Pluralismus. Studien zu einer Theologie der Kultur.*

4. Cf. Sen, *Identity and Violence: The Illusion of Destiny.*

they political aims or economic interests, it is nevertheless safe to assume that for religious believers religious reasons are strong reasons for resisting the abuse of religion in the name of other interests. Moreover, while it is plausible that all our identities are bundles of the different functional roles we play and identities we assume in different contexts, it seems nevertheless true that religious beliefs determine the combination of identities. However, in multicultural settings characterized by religious pluralism, identity issues are often connected with problems of justice.[5] Are we with our distinctive identity treated fairly and justly in society? Neither distributive justice, focusing on the just allocation of goods in a society, nor corrective justice, establishing liability for rectifying the injustice inflicted by one party on another, seem to address the underlying question of justice in multicultural settings. Even the capabilities approach, focusing on what people are able to do in order to achieve wellbeing,[6] seems to touch the deepest layer of justice issues, which seems concerned with the recognition of what people are fundamentally to be in terms of identity and otherness and in those patterns of reciprocity that are already presupposed in other theories of justice.

The problem of justice, often hidden in issues of identity politics, is exacerbated by the tendency that most societies have had in recent years, which is to undergo a process of extending the market logic of supply and demand and of the calculus of costs and gains to all spheres of society, from education, politics, health care, and culture, even to include religion. If the economic paradigm is extended to the relationship between cultures, it seems that the potential conflicts of multicultural societies are intensified because there is only one currency in which the value and dignity of cultural and religious identities is negotiated. With the development of a market economy to a market society, the underlying view of what it means to be human becomes normative: humans are what they do, their value is dependent on "what they are worth," and their merit relative to their market value.

Lutheran churches are confronted with the challenges of multicultural society in many different ways, whether in the past they were part of the majority in a monocultural setting, or whether they were tied to ethnic minorities from the beginning. The Lutheran churches are tied in so many ways to the rise of pluralism, which received a considerable impetus from the Reformation, that they are called upon to contribute to a critical and constructive shaping of the situation of religious pluralism in multicultural

---

5. Cf. Schwöbel, "The justice of God and justice in the world."

6. Cf. Sen, *The Idea of Justice*; Nussbaum, *Creating Capabilities: The Human Development Approach*.

societies. The challenge does not consist in contrasting the "Lutheran identity" to other forms of Christian identity or to other religious identities, perhaps in order to place themselves to best advantage in the marketplace of religious possibilities. This would be to misunderstand the situation. The Lutheran Reformation was not intended as the foundation of a new church, but as the reformation of the Catholic Church. Furthermore, the formative insights of the Reformation are not meant to apply only to a subsection of humanity but are meant to be gospel, the promise of freedom, to the whole of humanity. The task consists in applying the basic insights of the Lutheran Reformation to shaping the situation of multiculturalism. Undertaking this task acquires a particular urgency since the multicultural situation raises so many problems, which belong to the core problematics of Reformation theology.

A PROMISING GOD

If one looks for an element that unites the different theological and ecclesial aspects of the Lutheran Reformation and is therefore of paramount importance for understanding Lutheran identity, it is the emphasis on God's word, God's work, and God's being as promise which centers everything that can be said about the human response to a promising God on the understanding of faith.[7] This emphasis on God's promise elucidates how Luther's quest for a gracious God reaches its goal. The efficacy of the means of grace can only be understood by apprehending God's promise in faith, which is the basis, means and goal of the sacramental communication of grace. Word and sacrament therefore have their unifying foundation in God's promise. The new understanding of God's justice as the justice by which God makes sinners just rests on the efficacy of the promise as the means of the communication of grace.

The central distinction and relationship between law and gospel only become clear if we distinguish the logic of promise from the logic of prescription.[8] While the law follows the pattern "if (. . .), then (. . .)" in the form of the commandment "you shall (. . .)," "so that (. . .)," a promise has

---

7. The "classic" on Luther's theology of promise is Bayer, *PROMISSIO. Geschichte der reformatorischen Wende in Luthers Theologie*. The most interesting perspectives for the interpretation of Luther's theology are opened up when the emphasis on the theology of giving is brought into contact with Luther's theology of the Word. Cf. Saarinen, "Theology of Giving as a Comprehensive Lutheran Theology"; Ringleben, *Gott im Wort. Luthers Theologie von der Sprache her*. An inspiring example of this combination can be found in Walter, *Being Promised: Theology, Gift, and Practice*.

8. Cf. Schwöbel, "Law and Gospel."

the logical pattern "because (...), therefore (...)"[9] The decisive difference is that while the law binds the outcome to antecedent conditions in the past, the promise opens up a future, which also changes the way the past is determined by the future. While the law is focused on an obligation laid upon the second person, the addressee of the commandment, the promise expresses a commitment that can only be expressed in the first person: "Because I shall do (...), therefore you will receive (...)" A promise therefore involves the being of the first person in the act of promising, the time during which the promise is upheld, and the fulfillment of the promise in the future in such a way that the future fulfillment qualifies each of the moments of the promise. In this way the promise also qualifies the being of the promiser and, consequently, the being of the addressee of the promise: "Because I shall be (...), you will be (...)" The being of both promiser and addressee of the promise can only be grasped as a relational being, constituted by the communicative act of the promise and all that it entails. Understood in the category of promise, this being is in its core a personal being—people are people because they can promise and can receive promises—that is always directed towards establishing a communion in which being is correlated to the becoming that is involved in the actualization of the promise.[10] The reciprocity of this relational being is dependent on its non-circular asymmetry. In this sense the logic of promising entails the logic of giving, the unconditionality of the promise as pure gift that does not presuppose anything other than the being of the promiser as the capacity to enter into a free, yet reciprocal relationship.

It is here that we cannot proceed by simply exploiting the logic of promising without making its theological presuppositions explicit. Luther has done that in a most radical way in the explication of the name of God in Ex 3:14 "I AM WHO I AM." This self-identification of God explains the radical difference between the being of God and the being of all creatures, and so draws all human beings from attending to creatures to attending to God. According to Luther, no creature can say "I am," or "I will be," but only "I am decaying": "Wesen non habet creatura, quod non wancke et semper maneat." Therefore God's self-identification means: "'Ero': per fidem puram here in me, alia nihil sunt."[11] Luther reads Ex 3:14 as God promising God-

---

9. This is most clearly developed as the organizing center of what Christianity is about in: Jenson, *Story and Promise: A Brief Theology of the Gospel about Jesus*, 8.

10. "Neque enim deus, ut dixi, aliter cum hominibus unquam egit aut agit quam verbo promissionis. Rursus, nec nos cum deo unquam agere aliter possumus quam fide in verbum promissionis eius." Luther, *De captivitate Babylonica ecclesiae praeludium*, WA 6, 516:30–32. Cf. LW 36, 42.

11. The full passage reads in Rörer's notes: "Per hoc verbum trahit omnes homines

self, so that this promise is God's essence in relation to which no creature has any essence. God's essence, we can say, is that God promises Godself unconditionally. By promising Godself, God is the ultimate goal and in this sense the primordial beginning, the only one who has essence. God as the "ground of being" is dependent on God being "the *telos* of being," and the being of every creature is in this way dependent on the God who is promise. Any created essence is dependent on this divine promise. There is no prior participation of created being in the ground of being, but only the participation communicated in God's promise. Therefore only trust in God's promise can know God on the basis of the witness to God's promise as it is communicated in word and sacraments. Luther therefore claims that God's self-identification is the First Commandment.[12]

This view of promise, which is so radically expressed in Luther's understanding of Ex 3 and which can be supported from many other instances in Luther's theology, has a number of implications. The God who is promise is the God of radical freedom so that *liberum arbitrium* can only be understood as a divine attribute. God is radical self-determination. According to Luther, God's self-determination is not the reflexive act of a solitary subject, but the conversation of the Father, Son, and Spirit.[13] This self-determination includes the active ability to be determined by what is not God, i.e. by God's creatures, which must therefore be understood as communicative beings, called into being in order to hear the address of the creator, and respond to the creator. However, by identifying God's being in this way to God's human creatures, God must also be understood as radical self-communication so that in this self-communication God identifies himself as the only one who is to be trusted unconditionally.[14] The self-communication of God has the

---

ex eo, quod non est deus, quando dicit 'Ego sum' vel 'ero'. Nulla creatura dicere potest 'ego sum' vel 'ero', sed 'ich fhar darhin'. Wesen non habet creatura, quod non wancke et semper maneat. Ibi oculos nostros traxit ex omnibus creaturis (...) 'Ero': per fidem puram here in me, alia nihil sunt." Luther, *Reihenpredigten über das 2. Buch Mose*, WA 16, 41–54; WA 16, 49:1–4, 12.

12. Ibid., WA 16, 49:7–8: "'ego sum deus, in quo inherendum et in nulla creatura alia.' Ibi est 1. praeceptum."

13. "Querunt quidam, quid egerit deus ante creationem rerum. Respondet Moses et Joannes 'loquutus est', ehr hat gepredigt: verbum fuit in principio, secum locutus et se impsum et in seipso, sibi ipsi seipsum expressit et indicavit, ergo tantum est verbum quantus est deus." Luther, *Luthers Predigten gesammelt von Joh. Poliander*, WA 9, 329: 28–31. Cf. Ringleben, *Gott im Wort*, 70–90. Cf. also Schwöbel, "God as conversation. Reflections on a theological ontology of communicative relations."

14. This view of God's promise is at the heart of the two halves "of the whole sum of things Christian, since on it both knowledge of oneself and the knowledge and glory of God quite vitally depend" in Luther, *On the Bondage of the Will*. (1) "It therefore behooves us to be very certain about the distinction between God's power and our own,

form of God's self-presentation in Christ. In Christ God promises all grace, justice, peace, and freedom by appropriating all the virtues of God's word to the soul of the believer.[15] The unconditionality of God's promise—to be more precise: that there is no other condition for God's promise than God, and so no other condition for trust in God than God's self-presentation—is most clearly expressed in the formula of God's threefold divine self-giving in the conclusion of the explication of the Creed in the *Large Catechism*:

> In these three articles God himself has revealed and opened to us the most profound depths of his fatherly heart, his sheer unutterable love. He created us for the very purpose, to redeem and sanctify us. Moreover, having bestowed upon us everything in heaven and on earth, he has given us his Son and his Holy Spirit, through whom he brings us to himself. As we explained before, we could never come to recognize the Father's favour and grace were it not for the Lord Christ, who is a mirror of the Father's heart. Apart from him we see nothing but an angry and terrible Judge. But neither could we know anything of Christ had it not been revealed by the Holy Spirit.[16]

The promissory character connects creation, redemption, and sanctification. That God's human creatures can know and trust God's promise is an integral part of the promise, which God fulfills by the work of the Holy Spirit, who discloses Christ to us as "the mirror of the fatherly heart" and so God's being as "sheer unutterable love." God's promise and God's love belong inextricably together. Just like God's promise is unconditionally creative, God's love is creative love. However, just like the fulfillment of a promise cannot be a fulfillment only for the promiser and not for the addressee of the promise,

---

God's work and our own, if we want to live a godly life." (LW 33, 35; WA 18, 614:15–18) (2) "The other half of the Christian *summa* is concerned with knowing whether God foreknows anything contingently, and whether we do everything of necessity." (Ibid., LW 33, 36; WA 18, 614:22–23) If God is radically understood as promise, i.e. as the only one who can say "I will be what I will be" it follows both that there is a certain distinction between God's power and our own, and that God's foreknowledge necessarily includes everything that he promises. If we understand God's foreknowledge as the foreknowledge of the God who will be what he will be, then it implies God's omnipotence, omnipresence, immutability (as faithfulness to his promise) and eternity as necessary corollaries of the God who is promise.

15. Cf. Luther, *Von der Freiheit eines Christenmenschen*, WA 7, 24:12–13: "Sihe da, glaub in Christum, yn wilchem ich dir zusag alle gnad, gerechtickeyt, frid und freyheyt, glaubstu, so hastu, glaubstu nit, so hastu nit", and WA 7, 24:22–25: "Nu syn diße und alle gottes wort heylig, warhafftig, gerecht, fridsam und aller guete voll, darrumb wer yhn mit rechtem glauben anhangt, des seele wirt mit yhm voreynigt, ßo gantz und gar, das alle tugent des worts auch eygen werden der seelen." Cf. LW 31, 348–349.

16. Luther, *Large Catechism*, The Apostles Creed, sect. 64–65, 149.

it is the very character of love that the one who loves intends the fulfillment of the one who is loved and is not content with a fulfillment that is not also the fulfillment of the one who is loved. Just like God's self-determination includes the ability to be determined by what is not God, so God's love vindicates its creative character by becoming reconciling love, reconciling God's rebellious human creatures to God, and perfecting love, in being faithful to God's original creative love, the original promise against all resistance and contradiction from God's human creature. The asymmetrical yet reciprocal character of God as promise also shapes the understanding of God's love.

This understanding of God's promise and of God as promise can be summarized by speaking, first of all, of God's *promise as gift*, radically understood as God's Trinitarian self-giving which enables God's human creatures to know the "fatherly heart" of God through the Holy Spirit in Christ. Secondly, we must speak of God's *promise as address*, calling for the response of God's human creatures and so defining their existence as responsible existence before God. Thirdly, we also have to understand God's *promise as enablement* to cooperate with the promises of God by knowing God and doing God's will.

A promising God of love is also a vulnerable God in the sense that God's gift may be ignored by accepting other offers, God's address may be questioned by listening to other promises, and the cooperation with God for the benefit of creation may be replaced by envy and competition leading to murder (Gen 4).[17] Holding fast to the original promise is only possible for a God of promise who accepts this vulnerability, bears the pain of the broken relationship and restores it by promising a renewal that strictly follows the logic of promise by not being defined by the evil of the past but by the overcoming of all evil in the future that has its only ground in God's essence as the power of the future. Dealing with Cain's murder becomes the first instance when the promise to Adam, contained in the curse of the serpent (Gen 3:15), is put to the test. According to Luther's interpretation, it is as though Adam and his people have been carried and preserved in the arms of God because such a promise, since it is the truth of God, would even save those in hell, if they believe it and await its fulfillment.[18] The promise of the

17. Cf. Luther, *Commentarius in Epistolam ad Galatas. Praefatio*, WA 40.I, 34:1–6: "Vexavit hanc petram Satan in paradiso, quando primis parentibus persuasit, ut propria sapientia et virtute Deo similes fierent, relicta fide in Deum qui vitam dederat et duraturam promiserat. Mox propter eandem ille mendax et homicida, sui similis semper futurus, impulit fratrem in fratricidium. (. . .)" Cf. LW 27, 145.

18. Luther, *De Captivitate Babylonica ecclesiae praeludium*, WA 6, 514:28–29 and 33–34: "In hoc promissionis verbo Adam cum suis tanquam in gremio dei portatus est et fide illius servatus... Nam talis promissio, cum sit veritas dei, etiam in inferno servat credentes et expectantes eam." Cf. LW 36, 39.

promising God who says "I will be what I will be," is always the first in a succession of promises given and must be understood in such a radical way that neither evil nor death can ultimately impede or exclude from its fulfillment.

What does all this mean for the understanding of Lutheran identity? If it is true that "Lutheran" should be understood as a way of reading the message of Christianity as promise, and if the different religions have their distinctive identities in the gods they worship, then "Lutheran identity" consists in witnessing to the promising God, the only one who promises that he will be what he will be and therefore defines the being and meaning of everything by this promise. This involves the radical critique of all other promises claiming our ultimate trust. Furthermore, it involves the criticism of all forms of Christian faith and practice, within and without the Lutheran churches, where the relationship to God is bound to antecedent conditions in the past instead of the promised future. Lutheran identity is therefore an eccentric identity in the sense in which Luther could claim that our theology is certain because it places us outside ourselves: I do not need to find foundations for my faith in my conscience, my physical person or effort, but in the divine promise and truth, which cannot fail.[19]

TRUSTING ANIMALS AND CREATURES OF PROMISE

For Luther promise and trust are inextricably linked, and this relationship shapes his theology throughout its development. So we read in the *Lectures on Genesis*:

> Promise and faith belong together naturally and inseparably. For what is the use of making any promise if there is no one to believe it? On the other hand, what would be the advantage of faith if there should be no promise? Hence promise and faith are related terms (. . .)[20]

The constitutive relationship between promise and faith[21] can be seen as grounded in the relational existence of human beings. Human beings are trusting animals. Because as creatures they are not able find absolute and infallible orientation in themselves, they are bound to give shape and meaning to their life by rooting it in a foundational relationship, which provides

---

19. Luther, *In epistolam S. Pauli ad Galatas Commentarius*, WA 40.I, 589:8–10: "Ideo nostra theologia est certa, quia ponit nos extra nos: non debeo niti in conscientia mea, sensuali persona, opere, sed in promissione divina, veritate, quae non potest fallere." Cf. LW 26, 387.

20. Luther, *Lectures on Genesis*, LW 1, 266 (on Gen 12:4); WA 42, 451:36–38.

21. Cf. the excellent overview by Schäufele, "'*Fiducia*' bei Martin Luther."

reliable orientation for all dimensions of life. The *locus classicus* of this is the explication of the First Commandment in the *Large Catechism*:

> To have a God is nothing else than to trust and believe him with your whole heart. As I have often said, the trust and faith of the heart alone make both God and idol (...) For these two belong together, faith and God. That to which the heart clings and entrusts itself is, I say, really your God.[22]

As trusting animals human beings are also capable of being deceived by putting their trust in and hanging their hearts on finite entities. Because of that, human beings are potentially idolatrous beings, since their heart is dependent on finding a foundation outside itself, in a relationship that is constituted *for* humans and not *by* humans. The promise of the true God must therefore contend with other promises, notably those of Satan, which, as Luther writes in the *Lectures on Genesis*, are "pleasurable and readily received."[23] They do not seem "altogether impossible" as reason perceives the Promise of God. Why should that be the case? For Luther, the seductive character of Satan's promises and of the promises of the idols consists in the fact that they create the illusion that we might fulfill the promises on the basis of what we ourselves are able to do: "(...) reason is delighted by the lie, by its flattery and the glory of its virtues; it enjoys hearing that by its own works it is able to earn salvation, fulfill the Law, and obtain righteousness."[24] The dependence on the promiser becomes reliance on one's own powers. The promise of God is turned into a commandment, which human reason can fulfill on the basis of its own resources. In this way, reason can be deceptive because it flatters the human sense of power and self-reliance. Faith in God is turned into faith in our own capacities.

In contrast to "setting ourselves up as God,"[25] Luther emphasizes that faith consists in "a change and renewal of the entire nature so that the ears, the eyes, and the very heart hear, see, and feel something altogether different from what everyone else perceives."[26] Comparing this change to the heating of water Luther states that "faith, the work of the Holy Spirit, fashions a different mind and different attitudes, and makes an altogether new human being."[27] This is not an unproblematic thesis. What distinguishes

---

22. Luther, *Large Catechism*, 365.
23. Luther, *Lectures on Genesis*, LW 1, 266; WA 42, 452:5.
24. Ibid., LW 1, 267; WA 42, 452:39–41.
25. Luther, *Large Catechism*, 367.
26. Luther, *Lectures on Genesis*, LW 1, 266; WA 42, 452:14–16.
27. Ibid., LW 1, 267; WA 42, 452:19–21.

the perspective of faith from the "ordinary" human perspective? Moreover, does this imply that what "the eyes of faith" see is so different from what everyone else sees that real communicative change becomes impossible?

We can try to clarify this radical understanding of trust by highlighting four dimensions, which characterize faith as radical trust in Luther's understanding:

(1) For Luther faith is passively constituted for human beings and is therefore contrasted with everything human beings can achieve on the basis of their own powers. The logic of the constitution of faith and the logic of grace as unconditional gift follow the same pattern. The promise of God includes the acceptance of the promise in radical trust. Luther expresses this in the language of the illumination of the Holy Spirit. In the operation of the Holy Spirit every Trinitarian work of God is perfected. The purpose of creation is realized in the sanctification of the believer in faith, classically expressed in the explication of the Third Article of the Creed in the *Small Catechism*:

> I believe that by my own reason or strength I cannot believe in Jesus Christ, my Lord, or come to him. But the Holy Spirit has called me through the Gospel, enlightened me with his gifts, and sanctified and preserved me in true faith, just as he calls, gathers, enlightens, and sanctifies the whole Christian church on earth and preserves it in union with Christ in the one true church.[28]

The constitution of faith is made possible by the communication of the promise in the external word of preaching and the sacraments. This is the effect, and, as Luther says in a number of places, the purpose of the Incarnation in which the creative Logos communicated through the created means of communication. This relationship between the external word and the internal constitution of faith is crucial for an understanding of the Reformation and prevents both elevating the external word to the status of a divine authority (which would result in fundamentalism) and making the internal testimony of the Holy Spirit independent of the communication by means of external signs (which would lead to spiritualist subjectivism). The internal life of the human person is centered on the affections of the heart and these can only be changed from without and not from within. "Affectus affectu vincitur," an affection can only be overcome by another affection, is the briefest form in which Melanchthon casts this insight in the *Loci communes* of 1521.[29] However, the result of the illumination of the

---

28. Luther, *Small Catechism*, 345.
29. Melanchthon, *Loci Communes 1521: Lateinisch-deutsch*, 36 (II.44).

Holy Spirit, confirming the truth of the promise in our heart, is certainty of the truth of the promise which rests on the unshakeable truthfulness of the promising God. "Quid enim incertitudine miserius?" As Luther asks Erasmus in *De servo arbitrio*, what is more miserable than incertitude?[30] Because it is passively constituted for the believer, this certainty, which is the foundation of ultimate trust, is not at the disposal of the believer, nor of anyone else. One cannot argue oneself, or anyone else, into this certainty, which enables existential trust. This certainty must remain unamenable to any kind of intervention, since for the believer it is without alternative and in that sense certain. The recognition of its contingent, passive constitution for the believer is the material ground of the freedom of religion.

(2) Trusting *in* implies believing *that*. In the traditional formulae: *fides qua creditur* implies *fides quae creditur*. A good example is, again, Luther's explication of the First Commandment in the *Large Catechism*. First Luther transforms the form of the commandment "You shall have no other gods" into the promise of God: "I am the one who will satisfy you and help you out of every need."[31] Then he develops this in statements explaining the content of this promise in such a way that it becomes clear that: "It is God alone (...) from whom we receive all that is good and by whom we are delivered from all evil." Luther combines that with an etymology, which traces the word "God" back to the word "good" and defines God as "an eternal fountain which overflows with sheer goodness and pours forth all that is good in name and in fact."[32] Luther emphasizes that God's giving of all that is good and God's rescuing from every evil ("no other consolation or comfort than in him") is both comprehensive and occurs through the creatures as "the hands, channels and means through which God bestows all his blessings."[33] If we consider the quantifying expressions "all," "everything," or "nothing," the universal scope of what has to be said about the one who is trusted immediately becomes clear. The one who is to be trusted in such a comprehensive and exclusive way is no other than the one who is confessed in the Creed as the creator, reconciler, and consummator of everything there is. To trust God with all our heart is to believe that God is all that the Creed states about the triune God. What the Creed states are the necessary and jointly sufficient conditions for trusting in this ultimate sense. However, if one looks at Luther's explication of the articles of the Creed, one can see that the universal creedal statements are reformulated in a personal and

30. Luther, *De servo arbitrio*, WA 18, 604:33.
31. Luther, *Large Catechism*, 365.
32. Ibid., 368.
33. Ibid., 368.

self-involving way. To believe in God, the Father, the almighty, maker of heaven and earth, is to believe that God has "created me and all that exists." Believing in Jesus Christ, God's son, our Lord, is to believe that "he has redeemed me, a lost and condemned creature (. . .)" Belief in the Holy Spirit is to believe that it is God who constitutes my personal faith and the whole church as a community of faith in which I am directed by the forgiveness of all things and by the resurrection of the body to eternal life. The whole existence of the believer, of the community of believers and of everything that is not God is in this way enveloped in the realization of the promise that God is. While the certainty of faith is unamenable to human intervention and not at the disposal of human beings, not even of the believers themselves, the propositions in which the content of faith is explicated are publicly debatable and publicly contestable.

(3) The passive constitution of faith by granting certainty concerning the truth of God's promise is, at the same time, the enablement of an active life of faith, grounded in receiving all that God has given us. The logic of the Christian faith does not therefore follow the Kantian logic of "ought implies can," but rather follows the logic of God's promise as Trinitarian self-giving: "because I am and I have given to you (. . .) you will do with love and delight." As the *Large Catechism* pointedly phrases this enabling transformation:

> Through this knowledge (i.e. "what we must expect and receive from God," the content of the Creed) we come to love and delight in all the commandments of God because we see that God gives himself completely with all his gifts and his power, to help us keep the Ten Commandments: the Father gives us all creation, Christ all his works, the Holy Spirit all his gifts."[34]

By trusting in God unconditionally, we are turned from trusting animals into creatures of promise.

(4) Because ultimate trust is passively constituted and consists in hanging one's heart on God alone, and because the certainty of faith has no other ground and content than the promising God, in itself it never becomes an unshakeable foundation of human life as a secure epistemic foundation or as a set of moral absolutes, apart from in relation to God's promise. Luther has emphasized that because the trust of faith rests exclusively on God's promise, the certainty of faith has to contend with *Anfechtung*, it is exposed to temptation and shaken in the trials of faith. Because of its constitution in God's promise, the trust of faith can only be shaken where this constitution is called into question, so that God must be the author of *Anfechtung* even

---

34. Luther, *Large Catechism*, 420.

where God appears in the mask of the devil. *Anfechtung*, the experience of the trials and tribulations of faith, has three contexts: a) the apparent incomprehensibility of God's actions in the world when we are confronted with suffering, evil, and death; b) the experience of the grace of Christ and love of God being called into question as God's grace and mercy for me; c) the experience of the certainty of salvation being shattered as trust in God's election. It is in these experiences that the hiddenness of God overshadows God's promise so that they produce images of a wrathful and angry God. Luther's only remedy against these experiences of *Anfechtung* is to hold fast to God's promise by focusing on the *Christus tentatus* and to be reminded that our "holding fast" has no other grounds than God's faithfulness. Even as creatures of promise our trust remains trust, taking leave of ourselves to hold fast not to our faith but to God's promise. *Anfechtung* keeps our faith in touch with reality where we trust in God, enlightened by the light of grace that clarifies the riddles of the light of nature, but still expect the ultimate illumination by the light of God's glory. We remain creatures of promise until the perfect disclosure of the fulfillment of God's promise in the Kingdom of God. Anchoring ourselves in this promise destroys the images we paint when we cannot understand ourselves as the creatures of God's promise.

The relevance of these aspects of Luther's theology, which shape the contours of Reformation theology and form the backbone of Lutheran ideas about community organization in church and society, becomes clear when we reflect on the significance of trust for our communal life. Many of the problems of our society have been analyzed as crises of trust in the economy, in forms of government, in social institutions, and in the structures of communication on which we rely. It is easy to see, especially with regard to economic crises, that many problems begin with false promises and misplaced trust, resulting in broken promises and disappointed trust. The expansion of the economic market logic of supply and demand beyond the economy to all areas of life has exacerbated the risk of abuse of trust. Treating promises of salvation and spiritual welfare as marketable commodities should not be entirely unfamiliar to students of the Reformation. When people experience a crisis of trust, it is all too easy to call for new forms of accountability and transparency which effectively replace trust with control and so engender a hermeneutics of suspicion in the place of trust—with disastrous consequences for the fabric of social relationships and the character of social interaction.[35]

Luther's trenchant critique of idolatry as misplaced trust in the name of trust in the true God has lost nothing of its relevance in a situation where

---

35. Cf. O'Neill, *A Question of Trust*.

we witness the worship of that most fickle deity of late modern capitalism, "the market," which has been invested with personal attributes and affections, and seems to suffer from violent mood swings, although we already know from the study of social history that this deity eats its children. However, far from supporting an attitude of mistrusting trust, Luther's insights help us to invest our trust wisely, to become aware of what we can promise one another as the creatures of God's promise, who are in need of liberation from entanglement in the effects of our trusting false promises, and can only be amazed by grace that God maintains God's promise where we fail to trust.

LUTHERAN CONTRIBUTIONS TO LIFE IN A MULTICULTURAL SOCIETY

It would be a mistake to think that the question of Lutheran identity in a multicultural society can be interpreted as a desire to preserve a Lutheran identity in a multicultural setting. Multicultural societies already have enough problems of identity politics without Lutherans joining the fray. The Lutheran identity can most effectively be preserved by reflecting on what Lutherans can contribute critically, self-critically and constructively to life in a multicultural society. Since the Reformation is one of the factors at the root of the religious pluralism that characterizes many multicultural settings, Lutheranism has a responsibility to engage with its historical effects and after-effects. This can be done most effectively by employing the insights of Luther's theology as resources to attempt to diagnose some of the problems of multicultural communities and reflect on possible ways for their solution. The challenge can be seen in the fact that what Luther described as the modes of Christian faith and life must be understood as being not only true for Lutherans and all Christians, but for all human beings who are created in the image of God, reconciled in Christ and called to communion with the triune God in the Holy Spirit. In the Christian faith, because it has been convinced by the truth of God's promise, the purpose of God's creation for humanity ("He created us for the very purpose, to redeem and sanctify us") is realized by the self-giving of the triune God.

One of the central areas where this seems relevant is, as we have already indicated, the understanding of identity itself. For Luther human identity is rooted in the relationship of God to particular people, which has the form of the promise of enduring identity in all the changing situations of life, even beyond death. This is most clearly expressed in baptism, which establishes our identity beyond every human contradiction and sin in the promise of God, which gives us freely all that can be given.³⁶ Where we act in contradiction to this promise in thoughts, words and deeds, this promise is confirmed and reestablished in the words of absolution in Holy Communion in which, according to Luther, Christ promises nothing less than himself.³⁷ The tradition of the Gospel is the memory of a promised future.

For the question of identity this implies that the identity of human beings is not established by their differences from other people. It is ultimately rooted in their relationship to God. This relativizes all other claims to identity based on other identity definitions. For the Lutheran Reformation it was absolutely central that who we are, and what we are in relation to others and in relation to God, is not established by what we do. The doctrine of justification explicitly challenges the common anthropological claim that humans are what they do so that they can be defined by the sum of their works. Rather, human beings are who they are and what they are in virtue of what God gives and promises to them. The promise of God distinguishes between who we are because of God's promise and what we are as a consequence of our actions and brackets what we are by God's unconditional grace. This is the fundamental recognition of each particular human person as a promise and gift of God. In all our relationships with one another this constitution of human beings in relation to God must be recognized as a given promise. It is here that the Lutheran understanding of identity shows many points of contact with the critique of an account of justice, which is exclusively focused on defining justice in terms of distributive justice as the granting of individual freedom without recognizing that the starting-point for justice must be the recognition of people in social relationships.³⁸

---

36. Luther, *Der Grosse Katechismus*, WA 30.I, 217:15–19: "Daruemb hat ein yglicher Christen sein lebenlang gnug zulernen und zu uben an der Tauffe, denn er hat ymmerdar zuschaffen, das er festiglich gleube was sie zusagt und bringet: uberwindung des Teuffels und tods, vergebung der sunde, Gottes gnade, den gantzen Christum und Heiligen geist mit seinen gaben." Cf. Luther, *Large Catechism*, 441–442.

37. Luther, *De Captivitate Babylonica ecclesiae praeludium*, WA 6, 514:17–26: "Est itaque Missa secundum substantiam suam proprie nihil aliud quam verba Christi praedicta 'Accipite et manducate &c.' ac si dicat 'Ecce o homo peccator et damnatus, ex mera gratuitaque charitate, qua diligo te, sic volente misericordiarum patre, his verbis promitto tibi, ante omne meritum et votum tuum, remissionem omnium peccatorum tuorum et vitam aeternam, et ut certissimus de hac mea promissione irrevocabili sis, corpus meum tradam et sanguinem fundam, morte ipsa hanc promissionem confirmaturus et utrunque tibi in signum et memoriale eiusdem promissionis relicturus. Quod cum frequentaveris, mei memor sis, hanc meam in te charitatem et largitatem praedices et laudes, et gratias agas." Cf. LW 36, 40.

38. Cf. Honneth, *The I in We*; Honneth, *Freedom's Right. The Social Foundations of Democratic Life*.

The assurance that identity can neither be constituted by human action nor deconstructed through human action is good news for multicultural societies which are torn by conflicts over the recognition of the identity of their different communities and members. This is particularly important in a religiously pluralist situation. The concrete way in which different, religiously grounded identities can be recognized is by recognizing the certainties on which they are based. Recognizing freedom of religion implies recognizing the religious certainties of others as formative and normative for their understanding of themselves and the world. Because they know that their trust in God is passively constituted by their certainty of faith in God's promise, Christians can respect and recognize the religious certainties of others. We can trust others on the basis of the recognition of what they trust in. Rather than encountering others with an attitude of suspicion, we encounter them in the hope that ultimately we can trust them on the basis of what they trust in. Trusting is not at our disposal and remains outside our control. Nevertheless, it does make a difference whether we encounter others with an attitude primarily of mistrust or distrust or with the expectation that we might trust them. Recognition that is based on respect for the religious convictions of others can take many forms: from respect and tolerance, to forms of the acknowledgement of our interconnection with others, and our responsibility for our common life and thus for one another, to forms of active cooperation.

Multicultural and religiously pluralist societies are often burdened with the memories of past conflicts, of suffering and oppression in the intertwined histories of different communities. In such a situation it can be very difficult to identify a common ground of agreed norms and shared values, which are regarded as foundations for the common life of multicultural societies. If we are inspired by the Lutheran vision of the gospel of Christ as a promise of God and of Christian faith as ultimate trust in a promising God, our perspective for seeking commonalities will change. Our view will not be focused on the past, which so often is a past of divisions, conflicts and battles for dominance; rather it will be focused on the future in trying to identify common aims, for which each of the different cultures of a multicultural society will adduce different grounds from its respective traditions, and for which the diverse religious communities of a religiously pluralist situation will refer to different foundations. Common aims will not only be visions of such a future in which the common good of society will be realized, but also of a future which includes the others sharing in it. Furthermore, it is the promise of a shared future, which enables the reconciliation that seemed unattainable as long as it was based on the conflicting histories of the past. Only a common hope makes a reconciliation of memories possible. Formulating common aims requires an intercultural and interreligious dialogue between the different communities, and an intrareligious and intracultural dialogue on how these aims can be supported from the different traditions.

The achievement of common aims on the basis of the different grounds provided by religious communities will depend on the acceptance of common rules, which have to be followed in working for a shared future. Common rules presuppose and can help to nurture a culture of differentiated trust where rules, supported as they may be from different grounds of different communities, help us to "calibrate" trust with respect to the areas where the rules apply. For the Christian communities this presupposes consideration on how ultimate trust in God, grounded in the promise that God is, helps us to develop a realistic view of what kind and what extent of trust should be invested in the different dimensions of trust. The Lutheran insistence that believers remain justified sinners helps to keep our own promise-making and trusting in the realm of what is possible for God's fallible and fallen creatures who by the message of reconciliation are called to be pilgrims on the way to the perfected communion of the triune God with God's reconciled creation.

The common denominator of the new perspective for life in a multicultural society, which is made possible by the Lutheran interpretation of the Christian message, has its focal point in a change of the order of conditionality. It is not the "if (. . .) then" structure of "wordly" wisdom that shapes this understanding of promissory conditionality, but the "because (. . .) therefore" structure of God's promise and human faith. The distinctive contribution that Lutherans can make to the life of a multicultural society seems to be the *art of drawing distinctions* which is at the heart of Luther's theology, and which helps us to apply the new structure of conditionality to the concrete problems of life in a multicultural society. The crucial elements are the distinctions and relations between: God's power and our power, God's work and human work,[39] person and work,[40] gospel and law, and between the "two kingdoms."[41] They all revolve around the change in the structure of conditionality, which is at the heart of Luther's interpretation of the relationship between promise and trust. If they can handle these distinctions diligently and constructively, Lutherans can make a promising contribution to a multicultural society.

---

39. Luther, *De servo arbitrio*, WA 18, 614: 15–16. Cf. LW 33, 35.

40. Luther, *Die Zirkulardisputation de veste nuptiali*, WA 39.I, 283:9–12.

41. Cf. Härle, "Luthers Zwei-Regimenten-Lehre als Lehre vom Handeln Gottes"; Herms, "Leben in der Welt."

BIBLIOGRAPHY

Bayer, Oswald. *PROMISSIO. Geschichte der reformatorischen Wende in Luthers Theologie*. 2nd rev. ed. Darmstadt: Wissenschaftliche Buchgesellschaft, 1989.

Härle, Wilfried. "Luthers Zwei-Regimenten-Lehre als Lehre vom Handeln Gottes." *MJTh* 1 (1987) 12–32.

Herms, Eilert. "Leben in der Welt." In *Luther Handbuch*, edited by Albrecht Beutel, 2nd ed., 423–35. Tübingen: Mohr Siebeck, 2010.

Honneth, Axel. *Freedom's Right: The Social Foundations of Democratic Life*. Malden, MA: Polity, 2014.

———. *The I in We*. Malden, MA: Polity, 2012.

Jenson, Robert W. *Story and Promise: A Brief Theology of the Gospel about Jesus*. Philadelphia: Fortress, 1973.

Luther, Martin. *Commentarius in Epistolam ad Galatas. Praefatio* (1535). WA 40, Erste Abteilung. Weimar: Hermann Böhlaus Nachfolger, 1911.

———. *De Captivitate Babylonica ecclesiae praeludium* (1520). WA 6. Weimar: Hermann Böhlau, 1888. LW 36. Philadelphia: Fortress Press, 1959.

———. *Der Grosse Katechismus* (1529). WA 30, Erste Abteilung. Weimar: Hermann Böhlaus Nachfolger, 1910.

———. *De servo arbitrio* (1525). WA 18. Weimar: Hermann Böhlaus Nachfolger, 1908.

———. *Die Zirkulardisputation de veste nuptiali*. WA 39. Erste Abteilung. Weimar. Hermann Böhlaus Nachfolger, 1926.

———. *In epistolam S. Pauli ad Galatas Commentarius* (1535). WA 40, Erste Abteilung. Weimar: Hermann Böhlaus Nachfolger, 1911; WA 40, Zweite Abteilung. Weimar: Hermann Böhlaus Nachfolger, 1914; LW 26. St Louis: Concordia Press, 1963; LW 27. St Louis: Concordia Press, 1964.

———. *Large Catechism*. In *The Book of Concord*, edited by Theodore G. Tappert. Philadelphia: Fortress Press, 1959.

———. *Lectures on Genesis*. LW 1. St. Louis: Concordia, 1958; WA 42. Weimar: Hermann Böhlaus Nachfolger, 1911.

———. *Luthers Predigten gesammelt von Joh. Poliander* (1519–1521). WA 9. Weimar: Hermann Böhlaus Nachfolger, 1893.

———. *On the Bondage of the Will* (1525). LW 33. Philadelphia: Fortress Press, 1972.

———. *Reihenpredigten über das 2. Buch Mose* (1524–1527). WA 16. Weimar: Hermann Böhlaus Nachfolger, 1899.

———. *Small Catechism*. In *The Book of Concord*, edited by Theodore G. Tappert. Philadelphia: Fortress Press, 1959.

———. *Von der Freiheit eines Christenmenschen* (1520). WA 7. Weimar: Hermann Böhlaus Nachfolger, 1897.

Melanchthon, Philipp. *Loci Communes 1521: Lateinisch-deutsch*. 2nd ed. Gütersloh: Gütersloher Verlagshaus, 1997.

Nussbaum, Martha C. *Creating Capabilities: The Human Development Approach*. Cambridge, MA: Harvard University Press, 2011.

O'Neill, Onora. *A Question of Trust*. The BBC Reith Lectures 2002. Cambridge: Cambridge University Press, 2002.

Putnam, Robert D. "*E Pluribus Unum*: Diversity and Community in the Twenty-first Century." The 2006 Johan Skytte Prize Lecture. *Scandinavian Political Studies* 30/2 (2006) 137–77.

Ringleben, Joachim. *Gott im Wort. Luthers Theologie von der Sprache her.* HUT 27. Tübingen: Mohr Siebeck, 2010.
Saarinen, Risto. "Theology of Giving as a Comprehensive Lutheran Theology." In *Transformations in Luther's Theology: Historical and Contemporary Reflections,* edited by Christine Helmer and Bo Kristian Holm, 141–59. Leipzig: EVA, 2011.
Schäufele, Wolf-Dietrich. "*'Fiducia'* bei Martin Luther." In *Gottvertrauen. Die ökumenische Diskussion um die fiducia,* QD 250, edited by Ingolf U. Dalferth and Simon Peng-Keller, 163–81. Freiburg: Herder, 2012.
Schwöbel, Christoph. *Christlicher Glaube im Pluralismus. Studien zu einer Theologie der Kultur.* Tübingen: Mohr Siebeck, 2003.
———. "God as conversation. Reflections on a theological ontology of communicative relations." In *Theology and Conversation: Towards a Relational Theology,* BEThL 172, edited by Jacques Haers and Peter de Mey, 43–67. Leuven: Peeters, 2003.
———. "The justice of God and justice in the world." In *Van God gesproken: over religieuze taal en relationele theologie,* edited by Theo Boer et al., 217–32. Zoetermeer: Boekencentrum B.V., 2011.
———. "Law and Gospel." *RPP* 7 (2010) 357–60.
———. "Talking over the Fence. From Toleration to Dialogue." In *NZSTh* 45 (2003) 115–30.
Sen, Amartya. *The Idea of Justice.* Cambridge MA: Harvard University Press, 2009.
———. *Identity and Violence: The Illusion of Destiny.* London: Penguin, 2007.
Walter, Gregory. *Being Promised: Theology, Gift, and Practice.* Grand Rapids IL: Eerdmans, 2013.

3

The Experience of Justification

CHRISTINE HELMER

The late American liberal theologian, Gordon Kaufman, once said something to me that struck my religious sensibilities. "Experience and God," he said, "is a category mistake." Kaufman came to his claim by his particular reading of Kant's *Critique of Pure Reason*. Kant, according to Kaufman, argued that the ideal of God was a symbol with no corresponding reality.[1] It can be debated whether Kaufmann's interpretation of Kant is correct. According to Kant scholar Allen Wood, Kant actually held on to the existence of God as the ground of all possibility, namely a "subjectively necessary hypothesis (A 581–2/B 609–10)" in the first *Critique* and in the second *Critique of Practical Reason*, a "morality [that] is compatible with a hopeful agnosticism about God's existence, even though something stronger than this would be preferable."[2] Yet while God's existence is debated by Kant scholars,

---

1. Kaufman offers the following autobiographical account in Kaufman, *In the beginning . . . Creativity*, 109–110: "During my year in Colorado Springs I read for the first time (with very little understanding) a book I would read many times over: Kant's *Critique of Pure Reason*. . . . I seem to be 'tone deaf' with respect to so-called religious experience. When others speak of their 'experience of God' or of 'God's presence,' or the profound experience of 'the holy' or of 'sacredness,' I simply do not know what they are talking about . . . I have long since concluded that talk about *experience* of God involves what philosophers call a 'category mistake,' and should not, therefore, be engaged in. (My gradually developing understanding of the symbol 'God' as a human imaginative construction [to be sketched in what follows] explains how and why I came to this conclusion.)"

2. Wood is citing Kant here. Wood, "Rational theology, moral faith, and religion," 398, 405.

the concept of experience is uncontroversial. Experience has to do with real objects in space and time, not supersensible realities.

The discussion of Kant on the experience of God is not just meant for the inner circle of Kantians. The issue is also of significance in Lutheran theology. Kant was intellectually and spiritually shaped by Lutheran Pietism. Even though his parental home and educational formation in Pietism "gave rise to his having a life-long antipathy to this movement," as Pamela Sue Anderson and Jordan Bell write, Kant is important because he took core Lutheran commitments into modern philosophical reconfiguration.[3] Kant's theory of religion, in short, has a decisively Lutheran flavor. Kant is moreover noteworthy because of the way in which his thought was appropriated by Lutheran theologians at the turn of the twentieth century for articulating new approaches to Luther's thought that would prove influential for the remaining century. Twentieth-century Lutheran theology, in brief, was forged in a Kantian, specifically neo-Kantian mold.

I begin my foray into the topic of justification from this Kantian stepping-stone. The chapter has two parts. The first is a historical diagnosis of why contemporary Lutheran theology has lost the notion of experience in relation to justification. The Luther scholar I investigate is Karl Holl (1866–1926), who is credited with inspiring the new historical turn to Luther, the *Lutherrenaissance*, in the 1910s and 20s. Holl's interest is the religious experience that provoked what was called the reformation breakthrough. In constructing a concept of religion that would be adequate to describe the shift in Luther's experience of God, Holl used terms that he held in tension with each other. But eventually, the tension loosened and the terms were pulled apart. The second part of the chapter describes how contemporary Lutheran theologians Oswald Bayer and George Lindbeck pay attention to word and language and in the process lose Holl's dynamic probing of Luther's experience. The third part of the chapter offers some suggestions for reclaiming experience as central to justification. This constructive move may result in some shifts in understanding what experience (and even justification) means. I begin by transposing Kaufman's claim into a Lutheran register: "Experience and justification is a category mistake."

KANT AND EXPERIENCE

The comment of "category mistake" provides a clue as to what might be wrong with the conjunction between experience and justification. The term "category" invokes Kant's categories of the understanding, or, the conceptual structures of the mind that "work up" the sensible manifold in distinct

3. Anderson and Bell, *Kant and Theology*, 3.

ways so as to result in the experience of objects in the world.[4] The categories of the understanding, as Kant defined them, have to do with the way that all human beings perceive reality as it appears to them through sense perception. The experience of reality is the way that the categories shape the content of sense perception in order to relay what is sensed as perceptible and distinct objects. A category mistake, according to Kant, is the application of a category of the understanding to what cannot appear to sensation. God, self, and world, are not objects that appear in the same way as the table, dog, and another person. The assignment of categories, such as shape, color, size, to God, self, and world is a category mistake, hence the category of experience, reality, and sense perception cannot be applied to these metaphysical entities. Experience and God is a category mistake.

Yet any Lutheran who has read the 1545 *Preface to the Latin Edition of his Writings* must come to the fork in the road: either Luther is making a category mistake or Kant is wrong. Either Luther's account of the dramatic transition from hating "the righteous God who punishes sinners" to "truly the gate to paradise"[5] is an erroneous application of the categories of the understanding to supersensible reality or Kant's definition of experience is severely truncated. Either religious experience, with its glimpses into the fantastic, or the sober world of rationalized sense perception. It is this ambivalent legacy—Luther's claim that experience, particularly of *Anfechtung*, is required in order to truly become a theologian[6] and Kant's prescription that the categories of the understanding cannot provide knowledge of divinity through sense experience—that haunts the Lutheran theological tradition.

HOLL AND PARADOX

The historical question as to how the Lutheran tradition could be informed by such an intriguing tension can be investigated by going back to the early twentieth-century *Lutherrenaissance*.[7] This movement, credited to Holl, viewed Luther not as a systematic theologian, as the previous generation

---

4. For an excellent introduction to Kant's philosophy see the recent volume, Anderson and Bell, *Kant and Theology*.

5. Luther, *Preface to the Latin Edition of his Writings*, LW 34, 336–337.

6. The famous assertion, "Sola experientia facit theologum" is found in Luther, *Tischreden*, WA TR 1, 16, 13. He also writes: "Vivendo, immo moriendo et damnando fit theologus, non intelligendo, legendo aut speculando." Luther, *Operationes in Psalmos*, WA 5, 163:28–29.

7. For an edited volume that looks at distinctive case studies of the *Lutherrenaissance* celebrated around the 400th centennial of Luther's Reformation, and then current 500th centennial, see Helmer and Holm, *Lutherrenaissance: Past and Present*.

of Luther scholars had done, but as a religious virtuoso whose dramatic and novel experience of God would inaugurate modernity. The religious experience that led Luther to his critical attitude vis-à-vis both pope and emperor caught the scholarly, ecclesial, and even popular imagination of the early twentieth century. Investigation of the historical-biographical subject would demand another set of scholarly tools. How could Luther's spiritual, psychological, and intellectual makeup be described in order to demonstrate a significant shift in religious outlook? A new concept of religion was required that could probe the different levels of Luther's religious consciousness. The re-birth of Luther studies in historical perspective coincided with the emerging field of modern religious studies.

Karl Holl is regarded as the significant Luther scholar of the Lutherrenaissance. Not only did he identify Luther's doctrine of justification as the conceptualization of a novel religious experience, but he sought to categorize Luther's breakthrough as a *religious* occurrence. Luther's biography was to be described by applying a concept of religion that could measure change and innovation. Thus Holl set the historical-biographical parameters for Luther scholarship in the twentieth century by working out a concept of religious experience that informed the doctrine of justification.

Bo Kristian Holm points out in a forthcoming article that Holl's religious and theological innovations hold together elements in tension with each other.[8] While Holm focuses his article on the tension between gift and sociality, my interest has to do with the dual perspective that informs Holl's account of Luther's religious experience. Holl distinguishes between two sides to the experience of justification, a divine and a human perspective. The two sides are radically different from each other.[9] The human has no access to what God knows. From its perspective, the human merely has knowledge of the divine will as unconditional demand. Holl describes Luther's consciousness of the divine will:

> As over against his own 'rational' striving, Luther perceives the emergence in himself of another, unconditional will, which he is bound to distinguish from his own and yet cannot avoid recognizing as right. Thus the concept of God, and specifically of a personal God, is, for Luther directly connected with the sense of obligation.[10]

---

8. Holm, "Resources and Dead Ends of the German Lutherrenaissance: Karl Holl and the Problems of Gift, Sociality, and Anti-Eduamonism."

9. Ibid.

10. Holl, *What Did Luther Understand by Religion?*, 49.

The human will recognizes the divine will as entirely different from the human will. God reveals the divine will in the unconditional command of the First Commandment. Holl identifies the first commandment as the quintessence of the divine will. "For the First Commandment sums up all duty to God (. . .)" This is the "obligation to God" as "the most basic of all duties."[11] Or as Holl describes the same phenomenon from religious rather than biblical-theological perspective, religion consists of a confrontation at a "higher order of reality which God desires to establish beyond the level of mere creation."[12] Religion orients the will to the unconditioned—obedience to the First Commandment.

Yet what the human does not, and cannot know, is whether his striving can ever fulfill the divine demand. Holl describes the tremendous stress that ensues once the human is confronted with the divine will. The self experiences a conflict between two desires. One desire of the will seeks its own end. This "desiring will," as Holl describes, is "a self-will that seeks to assert itself in the surrounding world and evaluate everything with which it comes in contact in terms of personal advantage."[13] This is the will's desire for its own happiness. Yet the self experiences another desire in its encounter with the "Holy," a designation Holl explicitly uses for the appearance of God in this context of the two desires of the will. "It dawns upon us that we always instinctively want something different from our prescribed duty, something other than what we are commanded to will, for to will ourselves and the will to serve God are irreconcilable opposites."[14] The experience of the Holy's unconditional demand calls the unity of the self into question. The self knows that it cannot fulfill the divine demand, and therefore cannot unite the human will with the divine will. The self is torn between the opposites of self-seeking will and the will that longs to fulfill the unconditional command of total obedience to God. At this stage in its religious awareness, the self experiences a rupture in the face of the divine. "Luther did not want to base religion on the desire for benefits or on any will originating in us, but rather on the impress that is given by God, which lays hold of us and shatters us in our feeling of selfhood."[15]

The self is split in two between two opposing desires. Yet in discerning the competition between self-seeking happiness and the divine command, the self acknowledges the truth that the unconditional demand must be

11. Ibid., 79.
12. Ibid., 67.
13. Ibid., 69.
14. Ibid., 70.
15. Ibid., 66.

fulfilled. The human desires to fulfill the divine command and thereby reach a unity between human and divine will. Yet the human recognizes that it is incapable of realizing a union with the divine will because of its competing self-interest. Holl invokes guilt as the content of human self-knowledge in the face of the unconditional command. What the human knows is "that before God one is absolutely guilty, that one's whole person is completely reprehensible in the sight of God."[16]

God has another perspective. While the human recognizes its incapacity to conquer its self-seeking desires, God too has a desire. God desires "personal fellowship with human beings," a desire that, as Holl describes, "finds fulfillment" "in the human "recognition and affirmation of God's gifts (. . .) the honor that God asks above all else."[17] While the human on its own is incapable of achieving this "communion with God,"[18] the divine will desires to conquer the self-seeking will in order that it would honor God. God acts in order to justify the sinner, which for Holl means to create a unity between human and divine will. God's love accomplishes this unity, a love that is active in dispensing God's gift of righteousness, and "by imparting himself (. . .) makes them [sinners] righteous."[19]

If God knows that the divine love actively imparts the gifts that God is, what does the human experience and know? At this juncture, Holl invokes the concept of the *resignatio ad infernum* (the resignation to hell) that he discovers in the early Luther of the *Lectures on Romans* from 1517. Holl uses the resignation idea to explain that the human experience of justification consists precisely in the person's surrender to the divine will to the point that the person can accept being condemned to hell if this condemnation accords with the divine will. "[Luther] holds that the genuinely pious individual would be willing to renounce heaven and be damned in hell if this should be God's will. (. . .) Never has this doctrine been preached more forcefully."[20] This willed self-sacrifice is activated in the confrontation with the holy God, who "desires this supreme goal so emphatically and with such determination that in his wrath he annihilates everything that arises to oppose it."[21] The divine wrath is the cause of *Anfechtung*, the terror associated with the "acute sense of sin," the "sense of guilt as pure agony," in the face of the Holy God.[22] Holl brings the concept of *Anfechtung* to bear

16. Ibid., 73.
17. Ibid., 87.
18. Ibid., 42.
19. Ibid., 56.
20. Ibid., 65–66.
21. Ibid., 67.
22. Ibid., 74.

on Luther's experience of the terrified conscience, but with a particular concentration on the divine wrath that is experienced in the moment of "absolute self-condemnation."[23] The human acknowledges his guilt in the face of God. By "enduring" the divine wrath, the sinner acknowledges God's righteousness, and condemns himself. "[T]he wrath of God must be bravely not defiantly endured, but in such a way that God's judgment of condemnation—and, consequently, God himself—is recognized as completely just."[24] Obedience to the First Commandment is unconditionally required, even if it entails the annihilation of the self. In this moment of self-condemnation, the self cannot press forward to any resolution in an experience of grace. Rather, the self endures judgment as God's "cure" for the self-seeking will.[25]

Holl's account of the experience of justification is no less than terrifying. Yet his theological genius consists precisely in holding together a basic tension between two perspectives, at the cost of the human experience of grace. The moment of self-condemnation is a paradox. At the moment of resignation, when all is lost, the human in effect fulfills the moral duty to love God above all else, and thereby fulfills the First Commandment. Yet this fulfillment is only available from divine perspective. God knows that the divine love is self-giving, willing that the sinner might live. And thus God gives the gift of righteousness that, in effect, unites the divine with human will. This is the quintessence of forgiveness: "for one cannot live before him [God]" "unless one's sins are forgiven."[26] While the human will never experience or know that his sins are forgiven, the human can hope that his self-condemnation, his self-annihilation in effect, is not the final word from God's perspective. God's will for the sinner's life "implies the hope of forgiveness," while this implication of hope in no way diminishes or removes the "full severity of the previous judgment."[27]

Holl's concept of religion, which tracks the process of justification in Luther's biography, ends in a paradox. On the one hand, the human experience of the self in the act of self-condemnation is a paradox. The self's act of self-condemnation paradoxically spells its self-annihilation. On the other hand, the self "recognize[s] the love of God that seeks us precisely in the relentless integrity with which God holds us under judgment."[28] The self "peer[s] through the gloom and fury of the divine wrath into the loving

---

23. Ibid.
24. Ibid., 79.
25. Ibid., 81.
26. Ibid., 80.
27. Ibid., 80–81.
28. Ibid., 81.

will of God."[29] While the sight and experience of divine love is blocked by the moment of self-condemnation, the human presses forward to the hope that "judgment upon us is not the last word."[30] In full recognition of divine wrath, the self dares to believe "the teaching of the gospel, that God is interested in the sinner."[31] The surrender to the divine righteousness is paradoxically "not, after all, the 'real' God."[32]

Paradox is the innovation that Holl introduces into twentieth-century Luther scholarship. The human is constituted as new creation by God's justifying activity, yet remains tied to the old Adam. God reveals the divine love under its opposite, *sub contrario*. The two paradoxes—the new self "under" its annihilation, God's love "under" wrath—are held together by the tension Holl maintains through the double theological perspective. The human cannot know but can hope in God's love through the paradox of personal self-annihilation. God knows that the divine love is more central to the divine will than wrath. With this double view, Holl insists that the human never presses through to the experience of divine love. There is no resolution to the tension. Religion is not about experiencing blessedness. Religion has to do with the shattering of the creaturely morality. Through the shattering, the self is elevated to the higher reality of the divine will.[33] Yet the encounter with the Holy precipitates only the shattering, the tension between the paradoxes of self and God is not resolved in the blessedness of union.

What is at stake in Holl's prohibition? The background is Kant: the idea of paradox underlines Kant's interdiction. The experience of the self in its annihilation is a paradox. The experience of God in the judgment of self-condemnation is a paradox. As paradoxical, both experiences cannot be experienced as events in time and space. Holl explains the paradox in the religious terms of a shattering of time and space, a pressing forward to a higher reality that, paradoxically, is never experienced. The paradoxes instantiate Kant's restriction of experience to sense perception. The self's encounter with God is only "experienced" in the paradoxical term of a shattering of the self that is correlated with the divine wrath as paradoxical revelation of the divine love. Paradox infuses religious "experience" that transcends sense perception by refusing to apply the category of selfhood

29. Ibid., 80.
30. Ibid., 82.
31. Ibid., 81.
32. Ibid., 82.
33. "This sensation always means that we become aware of a higher reality that tears us loose from our ordinary existence and world-view. The Holy obtrudes upon us as something far above common experience, something that seeks to draw us up to itself and yet at once sets up limits if we rashly approach too closely." Ibid., 67.

in relation to divine causality. Paradox points to an "experience beyond experience" that, ironically, is never experienced. Holl succeeds in marrying Luther to Kant in the construction of a concept of religion that informs Luther's experience of justification. Needless to say, this idea of experience has heroic overtones, characterizing the quest for the Germanic Luther at the turn of the twentieth century. The notion of experience invoked by paradox is only applicable to a strong Christian, who can will his condemnation.

Although Holl restricts the candidates for the specific experience of justification, the effect of his interpretation introduces Kant's interdiction against experience of God into twentieth-century Lutheran scholarship. Holl takes this prohibition into account by constructing a concept of religious experience that is infused with paradoxes. These paradoxes represent key points in Luther's theology: a mystical idea of the self and a God who is available in worldly reality *sub contrario*. Holl keeps the human and divine perspectives in tension with each other through paradoxes that open up religious experience in relation to Kant's critical claims about experience beyond sense perception. God cannot be experienced, yet according to Holl's application of Luther's theology to resolve Kant's difficulty, the paradoxes can be experienced. Unfortunately, Holl's precarious resolution will lose its balance. By the end of the twentieth century, the experience of justification will be subverted by the word.

BAYER AND *PROMISSIO*

While the beginning of the twentieth century heralded possibilities for a discussion concerning the distinct idea of experience associated with Luther's reformation breakthrough, the end of the twentieth century addressed experience from a different perspective. The experience of justification in Lutheran theology came to be channeled through the category of "word" in such a way as to restrict the notion of experience. In the second part of the chapter I discuss two contemporary Lutheran theologians, on either side of the Atlantic, in order to demonstrate how experience in relation to justification is restricted by the "linguistic turn" in theology. My aim is to show how Lutheran theology oriented to the word continues to hold onto two perspectives—divine and human—that Holl kept in tension, but without the tension. When theology advocates the external word, the *verbum externum*, as the way in which justification occurs, paradox is lost. The experience of justification is restricted to the hearing of the word.

Holl's lasting impact on Luther scholarship of the twentieth century consists of his marrying Kant's dictum—experience and God is a category mistake—to Luther's paradox of the experience of God under divinity's opposite (*sub contrario*). The enduring question for Luther scholars would be: If justification could not be experienced in Kant's sense of experience as the categorization of the content of sense perception, then what kind of experience could it be?

Oswald Bayer, a contemporary German Luther scholar, proposed a new way of understanding Luther's reformation breakthrough. Justification is the experience of a particular word of God that declares forgiveness in present tense, first to second person direct speech.[34] "Ego te absolvo," God speaks "to you" in the word of the *promissio*, "I forgive you all your sins." The *promissio*—the identity of promise and fulfillment—is the content of Luther's new understanding of justification according to Bayer. The *promissio* is a "speech act," a performative utterance that creates the reality it actually communicates. The word of forgiveness is the experience of justification.

Bayer's contribution to contemporary Lutheran theology is his insistence on the characteristics of the word God speaks. The word of forgiveness is an extension of the way God announces divine identity in relation to hearers of the word. God announces who God is in the First Commandment: "I am the Lord your God."[35] The self-identification is set in the present tense as well as in the first to second person speech. These two characteristics identify God's word as a tangible, bodily word, a concrete word that contextualizes the external word in a liturgical setting.[36] When Bayer treats the word of forgiveness, he explains that this word extends God's self-disclosure to include the activity of forgiving sins. God alone has the capacity to forgive. The liturgy performs God's word by exhibiting its characteristics. In the speech-act of "ego te absolvo," the word declares the reality of the forgiveness of sins "to you" and "now." The experience of justification is a present tense hearing of the word directed "to you."

Bayer orients justification to the liturgical word by appropriating Holl's two distinct perspectives, divine and human. Yet in Bayer's conceptuality, God's present tense and personal word are constantly in view. The human perspective is interrupted at the moment at which the external word is actually spoken. The external word remains God's prerogative; it can never

34. On Bayer's most recent rehearsal of his identification of the *promissio* as breakthrough in Luther's theological development and as liturgical center of Luther's reformation theology, see: Bayer, *Martin Luther's Theology: A Contemporary Interpretation*, 55–58.

35. The idea of God's self-introduction in the First Commandment is a recurrent theme in Bayer's theology. See for example: Bayer, *Gott als Autor: Zu einer poietologischen Theologie*, 97.

36. Bayer insists on the "bodily word" as way in which God speaks. This term appears in the title of one of his books: Bayer, *Leibliches Wort: Reformation und Neuzeit im Konflikt*.

become incorporated into human subjectivity in such a way as to exchange the divine for the human word. Furthermore, the experience of the gospel can never be embodied as a permanent state. The personal self must have constant recourse to the divine word because humans do not ever really get the message. While God is always active, the human is always hearer, never speaker of this word.

The distinction Bayer sets up between divine word and human hearing underscores sole divine agency in justification, but it loses the tension that had made Holl's position dynamic. The human perspective, interrupted by the gospel, is determined by the divine perspective. The human relies on God's word of gospel—and the preceding word of law—to disclose human reality. God's perspective encompasses the human perspective: the liturgically communicated word of promise is really God's word that creates the new human reality of justification. Bayer insists on the divine perspective—the word of forgiveness—that constitutes the church's new reality: "Everything that makes the church the church is contained in the 'Word': the *preaching* of the gospel, its visible and tangible form in the *sacrament*, and the *Holy Spirit* by the gospel, whose office is to sanctify."[37] The church's word is identical with God's word, provided that it communicates forgiveness in Christ. Thus Holl's tension is replaced by the identity between God's word and liturgical word, the word determining the human perspective. Where Holl's Luther is characterized by dynamic tension, Bayer's Luther has the certainty of the God's external word of forgiveness.

What has happened to experience? With the loss of a tension between two perspectives and the identification of God's *verbum externum* with the church's proclamation of forgiveness, the experience of justification is hidden to all the senses except hearing. The human recipient of the word is the hearer of the gospel. Hearing is privileged as the sense that reliably perceives God's true word. Bayer's theology restricts a semantics of experience to liturgical specificity: the liturgically spoken word concentrates a precise experience of gospel in present tense hearing. Ongoing reliance on the external word is made theologically necessary; the human is prohibited from embodying the gospel because subjective appropriation would compromise the externality of divine truth. With the reliance on the divine word that creates the human perspective, the paradox that Holl had situated at the heart of the human experience of justification is erased. The human hears its new reality declared from divine perspective, while God's forgiving activity is present, although not paradoxically, in the word. The contemporary "experience of justification" is not an experience of paradox at the intersection

---

37. Bayer, *Martin Luther's Theology*, 257 (italics in original).

of a tension between human and divine perspectives. It is restricted to a determination from divine perspective that is disclosed upon hearing the liturgical word.

LINDBECK AND CHRISTIAN DISCOURSE

Bayer's interpretation of Luther crystallizes the contemporary Lutheran theological restriction of experience to hearing. But it was the American Lutheran theologian George A. Lindbeck who theorized this restriction. Lindbeck's well-known book, *The Nature of Doctrine*,[38] represents three groups in modern theology's understanding of doctrine. Lindbeck situates the "experiential expressivist" group in direct opposition to his own preferred "cultural linguist" group. (A third group that thinks that doctrinal propositions make claims about objective realities is not given much attention.) He represents the origins of experiential expressivism in nineteenth-century German theology, specifically Schleiermacher,[39] who posit, he says, a pre-conceptual and pre-linguistic experiential foundation as the religious basis on which language is layered as a secondary, and therefore accidental accretion.[40] Experience, on this reading, is "generic" because it is not conceptually embedded or linguistically articulated. It is foundationally religious, because it is characterized in terms of a religious dimension of consciousness that is inaccessible to thinking or willing. Religious consciousness serves as its non-linguistically articulated foundation of a subsequent layer of linguistic formulation. At this secondary level, the generic element is distinguished into distinct religious traditions by linguistic differentiation. Religious particularity is a function of language, not its experiential foundation.

What is at stake in positing an antithesis between language and experience that is deemed foundationally prior to religious particularity? Lindbeck has a particular understanding of religious discourse in view that has primacy in shaping a particular religious worldview. Experience poses a threat to religion because, on Lindbeck's reading, it is generic and universal, not particular and linguistically determined. As such experience as expressed in language can have the truth value associated with "symbolic efficacy." Lindbeck writes,

> In an experiential-expressivist approach, in contrast, "truth" is a function of symbolic efficacy. Religions are most likely to be

---

38. Lindbeck, *The Nature of Doctrine: Religion and Theology in a Postliberal Age*.

39. Lindbeck singles Schleiermacher out at the origins of "Continental developments" of "liberal theologies." Ibid., 16.

40. Lindbeck identifies features of "experiential-expressivism." Ibid., 16–17, 21–23, 31–32.

compared, if at all, in terms of how effectively they articulate or represent and communicate that inner experience of the divine (or, perhaps, of the "unconditioned") which is held to be common to them all. All religions are by definition capable of functioning truly in this nondiscursive, symbolic sense, but they can vary in their potential or actual degree of truth (i.e., efficacy).[41]

Symbolic efficacy, however, is not enough for comparing religious worldviews. Rather, symbols compromise on truth because they express foundational sameness in different ways. Efficacy of expression is the criterion applied to comparative work, and this is not sufficient to distinguish between "incommensurable notions of truth, of experience, and of categorical adequacy, and therefore also of what it would mean for something to be most important (i.e., 'God')."[42] Religious experience, on Lindbeck's reading, compromises the particular truth value assigned to articulations in language. If truth is a function of language, then it is diminished when associated with a generic experience that is only expressed in language as an accidental feature of religion. The danger experience presents to religion is its truth.

EXPERIENCE AND WORD

What happened to a Lutheran theological concept of experience in the twentieth century? Two soundings, one at the beginning, the other at the end of this century, disclose a perceptible shift. Holl introduced Luther scholarship to the possibility of constructing a concept of religious experience in order to view the process by which Luther arrived at a new idea of justification. Holl borrowed from the conceptual resources available to him: Kant's restriction of experience to sense perception and the neo-Kantian aim to make room for religious experience by moving beyond Kant. The way Holl accomplished his goal was to take Luther's theology of paradox as powerful tool in working out experience beyond sense perception, while embedding it in the tension between divine and human perspectives.

By the end of the twentieth century, the tension was relaxed in terms of the human reliance on the divine perspective for its determination. Paradox was erased from the divine perspective and an identity established between God's word of the gospel and the liturgical word of forgiveness. Paradox was eliminated from the human perspective and the certainty of forgiveness secured by the external word. Once the external word of the gospel was

---

41. Ibid., 47.
42. Ibid., 49.

identified as the particular word that creates the new reality of forgiveness, the sense of hearing was isolated as sole way by which the word could be experienced. Other dimensions of experience then became the object of polemic in a battle for truth. Religious experience is generic and unarticulated, and antithetical to linguistically articulated doctrinal truth.

Ultimately Kant's position on experience and God won out in the Lutheran tradition. Experience and justification is a category mistake.

RELIGIOUS EXPERIENCE BEYOND KANT?

How can Lutheran theology move beyond Kant? This question is imperative in the contemporary situation of mainline Lutheranism that is characterized by the "empty church."[43] Creative, even dangerous thinking is required. Lutheran theologians must dare to criticize the Kantian legacy of experiential restriction and investigate new resources to explore possibilities for experience. One avenue is to turn to the modern discipline of religious studies to see if empirical inquiries into the phenomenon of religion can provide descriptive categories for probing dimensions of religious experience. This avenue is not an obvious one. Proponents of the modern study of religion in (at least) contemporary North America tend to define the field in hostile relation to the discipline of theology.[44] As the following examples show, some proposals are more productive for theology than others.

Talal Asad, a contemporary theorist of religion, has recently suggested that the focus of the study of religion should be the five bodily senses.[45] Religion shapes the way in which the body senses, tastes, touches, so that a study of the senses can be referred to interests and forces at stake in their production.[46] Asad proposes this move to the full sensorium in view of a criticism that he and many other scholars of religion share about the domination of a Protestant notion of faith or belief that has illegitimately

---

43. On the phenomenon of the "empty church" see the new book by American theologian Shannon Craigo-Snell. See Craigo-Snell *The Empty Church: Theater, Theology, and Bodily Hope*.

44. For details on the (hostile) relation between religious studies and theology see Helmer, "Theology and the study of religion: a relationship."

45. Asad, "Thinking about religion, belief and politics."

46. Asad writes, "To explore how religion, belief, and politics are linked to one another, we need to enquire not only into institutional landscapes but also ask a number of questions about the body, its senses, and its attitudes. For this, we need ethnographies of the human body—its attitudes toward pain, physical damage, decay and health, as well as toward bodily integrity, growth and enjoyment, and the conditions that isolate persons and things from or connect them strongly with others. What architecture of the senses—hearing, seeing, smelling, touching and tasting—do particular embodiments and sensibilities depend on?" Ibid., 51.

determined the definition of religion. Religion is not to be identified with faith, as this term imposes a Western Protestant theological bias in religion. Rather the subject of religion must be defined in ways that are freed from a Protestant Christian theological determination and open to historical and ethnographic investigation. The five senses in Asad's proposal is suited to this study because they are the immediate sites on the body that register the environmental production without compromising it by cognitive or ideational activity of the self. The study of the body's senses eliminates religion's alleged task of interpreting its behaviors in terms of faith or belief, thereby freeing the study of the body from the vestiges of theological meaning imposed on it by a Western conceptuality.[47] Religion as the study of the senses tis connected directly to politics as its explanation.

While Asad reduces religion to politics, Tanya Luhrmann, an anthropologist and psychologist of religion ventures in a more expansive direction. In her award-winning book, *When God Talks Back*, Luhrmann describes the many different ways in which American evangelical Christians experience God.[48] She shows how evangelicals cultivate their imaginations and mental faculties in order to perceive God more clearly and how they understand experience in the immediacy of a relationship with God. The theoretical aspect of her work is to argue that the phenomenon of "hearing God" is a function of mind. Experience of the supernatural is not to be dismissed as irrational in a secular world, but to be taken on its own terms. Luhrmann's contribution also rests with her descriptive insight into American evangelicals who "reach for a personal experience of God" in many ways. The most dramatic include "tongues; supernatural healing, where a pastor calls down the Holy Spirit to cure a painful back being slain in the spirit, when the Holy Spirit moves down a room like a force and knocks someone over: and prophecy, when someone utters truths about the future that have come from a supernatural source."[49] The supernatural and its encounters with people are the subject matter of religious study. Yet these encounters presuppose preparation that orients the mind to be able to perceive God. Experience of God requires practice.

Another avenue for exploring ways in which religious experience is cultivated is undertaken by scholars of Catholicism. Devotional practices,

---

47. Again Asad, "I suggest, therefore, that instead of approaching such behavior in terms of belief... one might enquire into how the bodily senses are cultivated or how they take shape in a world that cannot be humanly controlled, and hence in what politics these formations make possible or difficult." Ibid., 54.

48. Luhrmann, *When God Talks Back: Understanding the American Evangelical Relationship With God*.

49. Ibid., 14.

rituals, pilgrimages, and apparitions are here the objects of empirical study. The Catholic imaginary is expansive; experience is described in different bodily and relational registers as people cultivate relationships with Mary and the saints and as they expect manifestations of the supernatural in the ordinary.[50] For example, a recent study by Belgian scholar of religion, Tine Van Osselaer, describes the unique effects that Mary had on particular working class men in Belgium in the 1930s.[51] At the time, Catholic literature advocated for a masculine Christianity, yet the men describing their experiences told of the encounter's unique effects in their bodies, such as tears and weeping. Tears have long been signs associated with women whose spiritualities bring them into close proximity to the Holy Spirit, even to the point of being regarded by others as insane and out of control. What Van Osselaer's study of masculine weeping in the presence of the Virgin shows is that, even in contexts in which gendered behavior is encouraged, unexpected emotional and physical responses register the holy's interruption into ordinary lives. Experiences of the supernatural are sometimes uncanny, and usually displayed on bodies.

The modern study of religion runs the range from reductionism to attentive description. Theology can learn from both. Lutheran theologians can compare their own experiential restrictions to deconstructive moves predominant in the study of religion. For example, Asad takes the "the body" as a theoretical category, the site at which external forces construct and produce it. The body is passive. "Matter" is shaped by political causes that construct its identity, and shape its responses. How does the Lutheran fascination with hearing compare with Asad's theory that bodily sensation registers active external forces?

Lutheran theologians can also appreciate descriptive studies of religion in order to expand their repertoire of ways in which people experience divinity. God reveals the divine word in a myriad of ways, in singing and communal ritual practice, in ecstatic glossalia and "falling out." Furthermore, these studies challenge the Lutheran theological preoccupation with the interruptive character of the divine word. Lutherans have much to learn from accounts of religious practice that demonstrate the mindful cultivation of physical and mental dispositions. Religion may be ecstatic and momentary, but it is also habitual repetition and intentional immersion into

---

50. The work of American religious historian Robert A. Orsi stands at the forefront of describing the rich facets of the Catholic "imaginary" without reductionism. See Orsi, *Between Heaven and Earth: Religious Worlds People Make and the Scholars Who Study Them*.

51. Van Osselaer, "Sensitive but Sane: Male Visionaries and their Emotional Display in Interwar Belgium."

imaginaries. Religion is about liturgy. And it is about spiritual exercises that orient body and mind to seek and maintain relationships with supernatural beings. Spirituality, like other aspects of physical and intellectual development, requires patience, attention, and guidance by a master. It is as much learning and doing, as it is receiving.

TOWARDS A LUTHERAN THEOLOGY OF EXPERIENCE

What can theologian offer scholars of religion who ask questions about the causes of religious experience or the mechanisms by which experience gives rise to literary production[52]? At this point we can resort to the classic methods, task, and content of theology. The theologian's métier is to describe and explain religion by applying categories it has developed in order to get at deeper dimensions of human experience. Theology has as its subject matter the soul, its orientation to God, and the human capacity to relate to fellow humans in its worldly environment in ways oriented by the divine. Whether descriptive or prescriptive, the theological construction of experience represents a significant aspect of its work.

I conclude by mentioning possibilities for Lutheran theologians to conceive justification in view of a more capacious understanding of religious experience.

(1) Luther's vocabulary of justification, as Swedish linguist Birgit Stolt has argued, is replete with an incredible range of emotional notes. Through careful linguistic analysis, Stolt shows Luther's doctrine of justification is not couched in the sterile dogmatic vocabulary of a cognitive appreciation for the distinction between law and gospel, but that the word of justification elicits a joy that "jumps and skips."[53] The affect that characterizes justification is joy, and the emotion is expressed in physical postures of dancing and leaping "for joy." Luther's terminological palette of emotions is descriptive of a distinct experience of the good news of freedom that Christ addresses. Yes, Luther's experiential theology has its moments of *Anfechtung*, melancholy, anxiety, and depression, but the emotional markers of the transformed self, open to new relations between self, others, and God, offers terminological possibilities for getting at the experience of justification.

---

52. On the topic of doctrine as production that is based on experience with the divine, see ch. 4 ("Language and Reality: A Theological Epistemology with a Little Help from Schleiermacher") of Helmer, *Theology and the End of Doctrine*.

53. This is the title of one heading in ch. 9 of her most recent book ("Die 'hüpfende und springende Freude'"): see Stolt, *"Laßt uns fröhlich springen!" Gefühlswelt und Gefühlsnavigierung in Luthers Reformationsarbeit: Eine cognitive Emotionalitätsanalyse auf philologischer Basis*.

(2) Experimentation with new theological vocabularies can help recover experiential dimensions to justification. The language of gift, for example, as Bo Kristian Holm and Risto Saarinen have explored and theorized, has the potential to orient believers to a new perspective on justification opened by this analogy to a phenomenon of life. Gift-giving is a human activity. By applying this concept to Luther, Holm and Saarinen have teased out aspects to justification hidden by the common terms used to unpack the doctrine. Holm works out the new angle of reciprocity in justification[54] while Saarinen sees knowledge and teaching from the gift perspective.[55] If justification has to do with the reception of God's gift of forgiveness, then knowledge about justification can be communicated as part of its gift. Teaching prepares believers as part of the experience.

Risto Saarinen has recently launched another project situating theological ideas in new semantic contexts.[56] His present focus is on the term "recognition" as overarching rubric for interpersonal relations. Recognition has deep psychological resonances. Recognition is perhaps the most fundamental psycho-spiritual need that establishes the foundation for coherent personality. Research into ways in which recognition can be nurtured both psychological and spiritually will have implications for understanding the experience of justification as a distinctive recognition of the human person by God, opening up the self to healthy psychological development. If the experience of justification is to take into account the "new creation" in Christ (cf. 2 Cor 5:17), then the embodied soul must be described using resources that disciplines such as psychology have at their disposal. Justification has to do with the experience of a new self-understanding unleashed by Christ's spirit who frees the self from confining worldly determination.

(3) The term religious experience connotes an ephemeral and transient episode. Lutheran theology emphasizes this meaning. The Lutheran person is passive at the moment of justification. She suffers the "word-event," and must continue to rely on its episodic declaration. One reason for this connotation has to do with an underlying anthropology that rejects a notion of development and change. Luther's hostility to Aristotle had to do with his rejection of the idea of habit that forms the self. Luther connected this developmental anthropology to the self's desire for self-glorification through works. An attempt to describe human development in terms of

---

54. See Holm, "Resources and Dead Ends of the German Lutherrenaissance."

55. See Saarinen, "Luther und humanistische Philosophie," 83.

56. See the website for this project, "Reason and Religious Recognition", online at http://blogs.helsinki.fi/reasonandreligiousrecognition/ (accessed 26/06/ 2014).

habit formation seems to preclude the central claim of justification's God-centered agency.

This resistance to a model of developmental anthropology, however, skews much of the evidence in the theological tradition that religious experiences are for the most part concentrated on long periods of preparation and anticipation. The preparation for a mystical encounter requires decades of practice, reflection, prayer, and discipline. Ascetic practices and habitual participation in religious ritual shape the self to anticipate a unique moment of divine presence. At the same time, these practices spiritually mitigate against a logic that would make God's free gift of relationship an effect of human causation. Religious literature focuses on lengthy guidance towards a possible experience. Compelling accounts are written by mystics who have spent decades in lengthy reflection after the fact. The African American theologian and mystic Howard Thurman describes the play between preparation and the episodic encounter:

> For a long time I thought that the saints, the mystics, the individuals deeply concerned about religion regarded spiritual exercises as prerequisites for the inflooding of the living God. These prerequisites seemed to be regarded as the disciplines, the faithful carrying out of which would bring the Presence of God actively into awareness. And yet I have often found that the sense of the Presence of God may not always be experienced in prayer and in meditation. (. . .) Then there are other times when one has the sense of being invaded by the Spirit of God even though one is not involved in any of the disciplines.[57]

Can Lutheran theology emphasize the episodic quality of divine grace, while also providing resources for a developmental spirituality? Techniques of mystical contemplation open the senses to experiences at different levels of spiritual meaning. In the disciplined practices of spiritual exercises, different aspects of the self—the intellect, bodily perception, and the imagination—are fashioned to perceive and know God. Can Lutheran theology integrate the resources of spiritual development with the commitment to God's justifying action?

In short: a Lutheran theology of justification must work out a more complex dialectic between faith and experience that makes room for the religious development of the self in relation to God, self and others, and the world's reality. It must also move beyond a restricted semantics of justification to experiential dimensions of the self, such as emotions, physical postures, relationship with the divine. The aim is a robust semantics of

---

57. Thurman, *Meditations of the Heart*, 38.

experience, inflected with the idiosyncrasies that Lutheran theology brings to the concept of religious experience (such as paradox and tension), while remaining stubbornly committed to justification as the work God does for us, to us, and in us. The experience of justification is a relationship with God.

BIBLIOGRAPHY

Anderson, Pamela Sue and Jordan Bell, *Kant and Theology*. London: T. & T. Clark, 2010.
Asad, Talal. "Thinking about religion, belief and politics." In *The Cambridge Companion to Religious Studies*, edited by Robert A. Orsi, 36–57. New York: Cambridge University Press, 2012.
Bayer, Oswald. *Gott als Autor: Zu einer poietologischen Theologie*. Tübingen: Mohr Siebeck, 1999.
———. *Leibliches Wort: Reformation und Neuzeit im Konflikt*. Tübingen: Mohr Siebeck, 1992.
———. *Martin Luther's Theology: A Contemporary Interpretation*. Grand Rapids, MI: Eerdmans, 2008.
Craigo-Snell, Shannon. *The Empty Church: Theater, Theology, and Bodily Hope*. New York: Oxford University Press, 2014.
Helmer, Christine. *Theology and the End of Doctrine*. Louisville, KY: Westminster, 2014.
———. "Theology and the study of religion: a relationship." In *The Cambridge Companion to Religious Studies*, edited by Robert A. Orsi, 230–54. New York: Cambridge University Press, 2012.
Helmer, Christine and Bo Kristian Holm, editors, *Lutherrenaissance: Past and Present*. (Forschungen zur Kirchen- und Dogmengeschichte). Göttingen: Vandenhoeck & Ruprecht, forthcoming.
Holl, Karl. *What Did Luther Understand by Religion?*, edited by James Luther Adams and Walter F. Bense. Philadelphia: Fortress Press, 1977.
Holm, Bo Kristian. "Resources and Dead Ends of the German Lutherrenaissance: Karl Holl and the Problems of Gift, Sociality, and Anti-Eduamonism." In *Lutherrenaissance: Past and Present*, edited by Christine Helmer and Bo Kristian Holm. (Forschungen zur Kirchen- und Dogmengeschichte). Göttingen: Vandenhoeck & Ruprecht, forthcoming.
Kant, Immanuel. *Critique of Judgment*. Oxford: Oxford University Press, 2008.
———. *Critique of Practical Reason*. Cambridge: Cambridge University Press, 1998.
———. *Critique of Pure Reason*. Cambridge: Cambridge University Press, 1998.
Kaufman, Gordon D. *In the beginning . . . Creativity*. Minneapolis: Fortress Press, 2004.
Lindbeck, George A. *The Nature of Doctrine: Religion and Theology in a Postliberal Age*. Louisville, KY: Westminster, 1984. [This book has been re-issued by Westminster Press in a 25th Anniversary Edition in 2009. In this chapter I refer to the 1984 edition.]
Luhrmann, T. M. *When God Talks Back: Understanding the American Evangelical Relationship With God*. New York: Vintage, 2012.
Luther, Martin. *Lectures on Romans* (1515–1516). LW 25. St Louis: Concordia, 1972.
———. *Operationes in Psalmos* (1519–1521). WA 5. Weimar: Hermann Böhlau, 1892.

———. *Preface to the Latin Edition of his Writings* (1545). LW 34. Philadelphia: Fortress, 1960.

———. *Tischreden* (1531). WA TR 1. Weimar: Hermann Böhlaus Nachfolger, 2000.

Orsi, Robert A. *Between Heaven and Earth: Religious Worlds People Make and the Scholars Who Study Them*. Princeton, NJ: Princeton University Press, 2005.

Saarinen, Risto. "Luther und humanistische Philosophie." *Lutherjahrbuch* 80 (2013).

Stolt, Birgit. *"Laßt uns fröhlich springen!" Gefühlswelt und Gefühlsnavigierung in Luthers Reformationsarbeit: Eine cognitive Emotionalitätsanalyse auf philologischer Basis*. (Studium Litterarum 21). Berlin: Weidler Buchverlag, 2012.

Thurman, Howard. *Meditations of the Heart*. Boston: Beacon, 1953.

Van Osselaer, Tine. "Sensitive but Sane: Male Visionaries and their Emotional Display in Interwar Belgium," *BMGN—Low Countries Historical Review* 127, no. 1 (2012) 127–49.

Wood, Allen W. "Rational theology, moral faith, and religion." In *The Cambridge Companion to Kant*, edited by Paul Guyer, 394–416. Cambridge Companions Series. Cambridge: Cambridge University Press, 1992.

4

Atonement in Theology and a Post-Einsteinian Notion of Time

ANTJE JACKELÉN

There are a number of obstacles for a consistent presentation of the doctrine of atonement today. How can the suffering and self-sacrifice of the One be salvific in our global context? Does the atoning activity of God in Christ presuppose total passivity on the human side? Is not atonement terminology remote from the realities of human life in contemporary Western societies? In this chapter I argue that post-Einsteinian notions of time may contribute to theological attempts to cope with some of these obstacles. Albert Einstein's theories of relativity mean that the previous Newtonian concept of time is inadequate. A reception of these revisions of the understanding of time within physics should have important consequences in theological reflection. The post-Einsteinian perspective is combined with complementarity, relationality, and dialectics, which will make it easier to handle some of the problems within atonement theory.

SKETCHING THE DIFFERENCES BETWEEN THE PRE- AND THE POST-EINSTEINIAN CONCEPTS OF TIME

For two and a half centuries the Newtonian concept of time remained undisputed. Isaac Newton stated that absolute time flows equally without regard to anything external, whereas relative time is some external measure of duration by means of motion.[1] This means that nature is in time,

---

1. Newton, *Mathematical Principles of Natural Philosophy*, 9.

as it were. Time can be understood as a container for all there is, or as a tape measure keeping track of the speed of change. This "classical" thought suggests an image of space and time as the permanent stage for the cosmic drama: visible to everyone and in perfect symmetry, plank beside plank, allowing for an objective determination of every position of the actors. No matter how much the plays differ in character, the stage remains basically untouched by what happens on it. God is the guarantor of its solidity. The task of the physicist is merely to explain the action of the drama. Due to its practical applicability to the scales of ordinary life, this model remained unquestioned till the turn of the twentieth century. Its shortcomings became obvious only when physicists started to deal with the very small, the very large and the very fast.

Einstein's theories of relativity showed that the difference between the stage and the play is an artificial one. The thought of nature being in time was replaced by its opposite: time is in nature. Metaphorically speaking, space and time are as much a part of the drama as are the actors. Scientific research must therefore accomplish more than a description of the performing actors. It must be able to describe the actors, the drama, the stage, and the audience, as well as their interaction.[2] The special theory of relativity disempowered the concept of a universally valid "now." It replaced the one absolute time with proper times dependent on motion (Eigenzeiten), which can be determined and compared to each other. Not only do the different proper times relate to one another; even space and time are closely linked. As a result of the general theory of relativity, time continued to lose its sovereignty. Einstein had succeeded in linking time, space, matter, and energy, including gravity. Newton's absolute, true and mathematical time turned out to be curved space-time.

Quantum theory was even more iconoclastic in its treatment of time: its ability to be measured disappeared in the fog of the uncertainty relation. Mathematical indeterminacy and nonlocality suggest that we can never have complete information and thus never have complete control over the reality in which we participate—unless there are hidden parameters, yet to be discovered, that would reestablish the complete determinacy of nature.

Remaining in the theater image, the difference between pre- and post-Einsteinian can be summed up as follows. Newtonian time is just as barren and lifeless as an empty theater stage. Einstein exchanged the hard stage floorboards for a trampoline in constant motion. On top of that, Werner Heisenberg doused the trampoline with dry ice and installed a strobe light: lightning-like illumination shows snapshots of a nebulous drama. This

---

2. Jackelén, *Time & Eternity*, 173.

scenario contradicts the idea of a cosmology with an infinitely uniform flow of time. It is far more compatible with the image of a dance, marked by qualities like non-linearity, relationality, multiplicity, non-predictable determinism, and openness.

THE PREVALENCE OF A PRE-EINSTEINIAN VIEW IN THEOLOGY

Although the theories of relativity have been around for a century, their theological reception has been rather sparse. On the one hand this is not surprising, since, according to our perception, Newtonian concepts work well on an every-day scale. Why then bother about advanced physics? On the other hand, since theologians—for example in theology of creation and eschatology—deal with issues that presuppose ideas about cosmology, space, and time, it is problematic if their thinking is out of sync with the best scientific knowledge available. How then can theology afford not to engage with modern physics? The almost unbroken, rarely-acknowledged prevalence of pre-Einsteinian notions of time affects the understanding of biblical texts as well as theological reflection. The following two examples illustrate this.

When it comes to biblical texts, the interpretation of the well-known passage Ecclesiastes 3:1–15 provides a good example of the significance of different understandings of time. "For everything there is a season, and a time for every matter under heaven: a time to (. . .), and a time to (. . .)" and so on, in fourteen dialectical pairs. If this is merely about chronological-linear time, we will end up with the rather dull and fatalistic image of an infinite conveyor belt bringing to us birthing and dying, weeping and dancing, war and peace in a predetermined order. In fact, this is exactly what numerous Bible commentaries do: they indulge in determinism, emphasize the fateful character of time, and the uselessness of human activity.[3] A very different interpretation emerges, however, if the frame of reference is post-Einsteinian. Such an interpretation will operate with proper or internal times, multi-temporality, openness, and relationality. Eternity is not necessarily the antithesis of (human) time; it can easily be construed as God's "proper time," which is related to the other times but not identical with them. In light of a post-Einsteinian interpretation, it is the gift of mystery of life that God has laid God's own (form of) time, namely eternity, into everything. We can speak of human discernment in regard to time—a time for every matter under heaven—as well as of the dependence of the time of the world on God's proper time: God "has made everything suitable for its

---

3. Ibid., 227.

time; moreover, he has put a sense of past and future into their minds, yet they cannot find out what God has done from the beginning to the end" (Eccl 3:11). A relational understanding of time also helps with Ecclesiastes 3:15, which has been called a *crux interpretum* because of its difficulty: "That which is, already has been; that which is to be, already is; and God seeks out what has gone by." The relativizing of present and future, the possibility of still being able to do something with that which has already hardened into a necessity, is a consequence of the overarching dynamic nature of the many proper times. "Everything has its proper time, and everything has its internal dynamic" would then be a more adequate paraphrase of the words from Ecclesiastes than German hymn writer Paul Gerhardt's "Alles Ding währt seine Zeit, Gottes Lieb in Ewigkeit" (Everything has its time, but God's love is eternal).[4] Widening the frame of reference from an exclusive linear and deterministic understanding to include the dynamics of proper times will be of significance for a theology of the atonement.

Bible scholar and theologian Oscar Cullmann's work is another example illustrating the limitations that an exclusively pre-Einsteinian understanding of time puts on theology. Cullmann's seminal book *Christ and Time* provides an example of what I perceive as an unconscious option for Newtonian physics in theological reflection.[5] He argues that the New Testament does not distinguish qualitatively between time and eternity and therefore only knows linear time. For Cullmann, "salvation is bound to a *continuous time process* (. . .) Revelation and salvation take place along the course of an ascending timeline."[6] He calls time "the scene of redemptive history" and claims that "all points of this redemptive line are related to the one historical fact at the mid-point,"[7] namely the death and resurrection of Jesus. God is in control over the entire timeline in its endless extension.[8]

Cullmann leaves no room for proper times or a multiplicity of times. Instead, his concept mirrors the Newtonian stage model. Neither does his model account properly for the multilayered dynamics of the biblical concepts of time and eternity.[9] Instead, his ascending timeline looks more like an interpretation of the Newtonian model of absolute time spiced with a pinch of Enlightenment progress thought. Its difficulties to account for the

---

4. Ibid., 228.
5. Cullmann, *Christ and Time*.
6. Ibid., 32.
7. Ibid., 32–33.
8. Ibid., 72.
9. Jackelén, *Time & Eternity*, 64–81.

eschatological tension between *already* and *not yet* as well as for a dynamic relation between God, time, and eternity are obvious.

Cullmann's approach did not remain without critique. Old Testament scholar James Barr argued, based on "biblical words for time," that a specific biblical concept of time cannot be developed in a Cullmannian way because "the lexical stock of neither Hebrew nor New Testament Greek is laid out in a plan or pattern which corresponds with the distinctiveness of biblical thought."[10] In terms of linguistics, neither the Old Testament nor the New Testament permits the postulate of biblical uniqueness. Due to the lack of explicit statements about time and eternity in the Bible, which does not really permit the development of a philosophical-theological concept of time, Barr resists attempts to extrapolate such a concept of time. At the very least, the syntactical context must also be constantly kept in mind. An understanding of time can be built only on the narratives and not on the terminology of the Bible. There is no concept of time without narrated time.[11]

WHAT POST-EINSTEINIAN NOTIONS OF TIME CAN DO FOR THEOLOGY

The adoption of post-Einsteinian notions of time is certainly not a panacea for the shortcomings of theology. Neither is it a quick-fix to increase the timeliness of current language of the atonement. However, some conclusions can be drawn as to what is encouraged and what is discouraged. In fact, in light of the post-Einsteinian some things are prohibited while others are commanded.

The adoption of post-Einsteinian notions of time *prohibits* some features not unusual in the theology that has formed many contemporary Western theologians:

- A one-sided view of time as a chronological time line eating its way like a machine into the yet uncharted realms of a Newtonian universe.
- The setting-up of binaries undergirded by normative judgments that favor time over space and linear over cyclical time.

Consequently, accounts have to be abandoned that associate Christianity with time and paganism with space, so that the predominance of time gives rise to prophecy and monotheistic faith, whereas space is linked with tragedy, mysticism, polytheism, and nationalism.[12] The triumphalistic

---

10. Barr, *Biblical Words for Time*, 160.
11. Jackelén, *Time & Eternity*, 11–59.
12. Tillich, "The Struggle Between Time and Space," 30–39. For a critical appraisal, see Westhelle, *The Scandalous God*, 146–48.

undertone in these accounts is quite pertinent. Likewise, it is unhelpful to elevate linear time as associated with history, eschatology, Yahweh, the one, masculine God of Israel, and to look down upon cyclical time as relating to mythology, apocalypticism, fertility goddesses and the syncretism of the nations, as several well-known Old Testament scholars did.[13]

However, these assumptions did not remain unchallenged. Leo G. Perdue stated in his critique of the American biblical theology movement and of the "German school" that, influenced by the Enlightenment, Old Testament scholarship was in the grips of historical categories. He sees this expressed in, for example, Gerhard von Rad's questionable assumption of the superiority of the historical over the mythical. According to Perdue, the postulation that Israel was unique because it had the idea of a God revealed in history, while other cultures were bound to nature and myth by their concepts of God, proved to be a dead end. The anchoring of revelation in theological uniqueness and the presumption that the historical is superior to the mythical is untenable in two ways: First, non-Israelite cultures also believed in divine action in history; and, second, the Israelites also held the notion that God was in nature.[14]

Nevertheless, the language of setting up the one against the rest, Israel against the pagans, history against myth, apocalypticism, fertility goddesses, syncretism, and the like, appears to have been quite attractive. It may well be that the Newtonian image of the permanent stage for the cosmic drama encouraged a rhetoric of contrasting. If the task is to explain the interaction of two actors—as complex as that might be—without having to pay any attention to the nebulous drama performed on Einstein's moving floorboards in Heisenberg's strobe light illumination, it may indeed be tempting to focus on contrast rather than complex relationships. There is after all a pedagogical lure in contrasting the one with the other: time with eternity, linear with cyclical, male with female, white with black, Israel with pagan, Jesus with Jewish . . .

Contrasting is a much-loved—and often useful—pedagogical device. Focus on contrasts makes it easy to catalogue, memorize, and evaluate different positions. Contrasting has all the attraction and advantages of methodological reductionism. When it comes to the complexities of history, however, the method of contrasting turns out to be a high-cost device. It creates pedagogical clarity at the cost of hiding or even negating crucial facts, nuances, and relationships. Contrasting Israel with the rest of

---

13. Examples of such theologians would be Gerhard von Rad, Sigmund Mowinckel, and Martin Noth. Cf. Jackelén, *Time & Eternity*, 65–72.

14. Perdue, *The Collapse of History*, 39–40. Cf. even Albrektson, *History and the Gods*, 11–13, 120–22.

the world, and denying the Jewishness of Jesus by contrasting him with the (dark) background of the old covenant proved to be a slippery slope towards negation of quite obvious facts. The consequences in terms of antisemitism were utterly serious.

Post-Einsteinian notions of time provide an impetus to resist the gradual move of a merely methodological contrasting towards normative judgments, bolstered by a methodological reductionism that has slid into becoming ontological. They encourage theologians to move their focus from a pedagogy of contrasting to a pedagogy of relationality.

We will now look at what a post-Einsteinian notion of time *commands*. In this endeavor it is easy to cross the thin line between "literal" and metaphorical uses of physics. For the sake of new perspectives on familiar issues, it is a risk worth taking. Although there is no straight line running from curved space-time and indeterminacy to theological doctrines, some directions can be charted.

One may say that the invalidation of the universal *now* killed the "absolutes." This left us with a set of "relatives." Exactness and precision did not disappear in that move, however. We are told that reality is relational, rather than relativistic. Reality is about comparatives more than superlatives. This insight has consequences for theology.

Theology has often been occupied with finding and defining the correct superlatives: greatest, strongest, mightiest, Almighty! Superlatives are about the top of hierarchies and about exclamation marks. Comparatives are about relations in multiple directions and about question marks. They are about the "in-between" rather than the beginning and the end of a line. Introducing the comparative opens the way for conversations that create new relations: greater than what, stronger than what?

Focus on the comparative is right for us, in time and space. For about four decades, we have been seeing a decline of the ontology of superlatives in favor of the relationality of comparatives in philosophical as well as theological discourses. I would say that the comparative is even more crucial in theology than in philosophy. Where philosophical hermeneutics can be said to be occupied with "the fusion of the horizons" of understanding (Gadamer), theological hermeneutics claims that there always remains a horizon that can never disappear in any fusion of horizons. The ultimate beyond, transcendence, cannot be merged into immanence. This means: theological hermeneutics will always insist on the significance of the comparative. Neither positive nor superlative alone will do. Rather than about "much" (positive) or "most" (superlative), truth is about the "more" (comparative), understood in terms of the relationship of something to something that is "other."

Post-Einsteinian notions of time are relevant in several areas of theology. Let me give some short examples. The theory of evolution has impacted modern theologies of creation. However, the standard expression of the evolution concept remains utterly tied to Newtonian, univocally forward-flowing time, which, of course, is a concern not only for theology. In a more distinctly theological sense, post-Einsteinian notions of time have an impact on how we understand apocalypticism and eschatology, as well as the relationship between those two. The notion of eternal life will not look the same when considered within the framework of Newtonian time or post-Einsteinian time. The same will go for the understanding of "the resurrection of the body," as the church confesses in the Apostles' Creed. Even the broad debate on divine action in the world has been able to harvest some fruits that have grown in the post-Einsteinian world.

It is not the case that a post-Einsteinian understanding has the power of rendering theological issues as such obsolete. Rather, it adds or highlights dimensions that have been invisible or neglected and reveals others as outdated. For the sake of this article, I will focus on the understanding of the atonement, asking whether and how current debates may benefit from moving beyond a Newtonian understanding of time.

WHERE MIGHT POST-EINSTEINIAN NOTIONS OF TIME HELP US IN UNDERSTANDING ATONEMENT?

In academic as well as in pastoral theology a number of obstacles for a consistent presentation of the atonement in a contemporary global context have been identified. Five of them will be exemplified here.

First, the issue of violence. The death of Jesus was a violent death. It is a challenge to standards of love and justice to preach that the love of God is expressed in the brutal death of the beloved son. Feminist and postcolonial theology has pointed this out far more clearly than the European theology that has been dominant for a long time. If God wants or needs the violent death of Jesus, doesn't that turn God into a child abuser of cosmic dimensions?[15] How can the suffering and self-sacrifice of the One be salvific "in our global context, where sacrifice on the part of millions serves a privileged few"?[16] With the emphasis on the salvific character of suffering, it is only a small step towards the glorification of human suffering. Where human suffering is legitimized with reference to the suffering of Christ (and with scriptural support such as 1 Peter 2:19–21), human beings are dehumanized, as the following example shows:

15. Nakashima Brock and Parker, *Proverbs of Ashes*, 157.
16. Jones and Lakeland, *Constructive Theology*, 171.

"I haven't talked to anyone about this for a while," she began, the smile fading, and sadness deepening in her eyes. "But I'm worried for my kids now. The problem is my husband. He beats me sometimes. Mostly he is a good man. But sometimes he becomes very angry and he hits me. He knocks me down. One time he broke my arm and I had to go to the hospital. But I didn't tell them how my arm got broken."

(. . .) She took a deep breath and went on. "I went to my priest twenty years ago. I've been trying to follow his advice. The priest said I should rejoice in my sufferings because they bring me closer to Jesus. He said, 'Jesus suffered because he loved us'. He said, 'If you love Jesus, accept the beatings and bear them gladly, as Jesus bore the cross.' I've tried, but I'm not sure anymore. My husband is turning on the kids now. Tell me, is what the priest told me true?"[17]

Second, the issue of human nature. Atonement naturally has a focus on both the one(s) who atone(s) and the one(s) who is (are) in need of atonement. When God's need of atonement becomes the center of attention, as for example in the Anselmian theory of satisfaction, the issue of violence emerges as a problem. When the needs of humanity take the front seat, the issue of the depravity of human nature arises. How can we speak of the radical need of atonement without the complete denial of the human potential to do good and oppose evil? How do we address issues of human activity and passivity in atonement theory? Does the atoning activity of God in Christ presuppose total passivity on the human side and thus in the end promote an ethics of quietism?

This issue depends on the understanding of original sin and interpretations of Genesis 3. The questions raised relate to evolutionary biology to a higher degree than to physics.[18]

Third, the issue of substitution. This issue addresses a consequence of the two prior issues: Christ substituting for a depraved humankind, carrying the sins of the world on the cross. Both the passivity and the collectivism implied by such understanding of the atonement are at odds with a modern understanding of what a human being is, particularly in the Western world. Substitution gets into conflict with the experience of human individuality and autonomy.[19]

---

17. Nakashima Brock and Parker, *Proverbs of Ashes*, 20–21.

18. Cf. Grantén, *Utanför paradiset*, 67–98.

19. Cf. the early work of Dorothee Sölle (e g *Christ the Representative*) as an attempt to overcome this problem.

Fourth, the issue of scope. Current formulations of a doctrine of atonement often fail to keep salvation through the death of Christ and the resurrection of Christ together. The cross remains separated from the empty tomb. Good Friday supersedes Easter morning. Should the doctrine of the atonement not take into account the full scope of the Christ event? Furthermore, it should take seriously the sin of individuals but not be restricted to the individual scope. A doctrine of the atonement should be able to harbor individual, communal as well as systemic sin, and it should reach beyond patriarchal systems. A hitherto not much explored issue of scope is the fruitfulness of models of atonement in interreligious communication.

Fifth, the issue of language. Atonement terminology in dogmatics as well as in liturgy has come to be very remote from the realities of human life in contemporary Western societies. Language such as sacrifice, satisfaction, the slaughtered lamb, blood that cleanses, is dependent on phenomena and images that have become largely unfamiliar.

Quite a number of these difficulties have been addressed in various ways by contemporary theologians, many of them within the Lutheran tradition.[20] Focus in this chapter is on what post-Einsteinian notions of time may be able to contribute to theological attempts to cope with some of these obstacles.

THE HERMENEUTICS OF RELATIONALITY

It is striking how well Newton's mathematical system fits his theological system. The clarity of absoluteness and determinism calls for a God who is one—Newton detested the doctrine of the trinity—and whose foremost attribute is power, understood as omnipotence and omnipresence. For the inventor of calculus (especially in the form Newton did) it makes perfect sense to conceptualize God above all as the determiner of the initial conditions. Only well-defined starting conditions guarantee a well-defined solution of a differential equation. God's omnipotence and the elegance of calculus make up a perfect couple. Intuitively, the one, uniformly flowing time of Newton provides a safer match with divine omnipresence than Einsteinian curved space-time. It seems to be more than mere coincidence that already Gottfried Wilhelm Leibniz in the early eighteenth century, when arguing against the absoluteness of space and time and for their relativity, also differed regarding God's most prominent quality. For Leibniz, God's

---

20. For example Thompson, *Crossing the Divide* (proposing the model of friendship as an alternative to "the joyous exchange"); and Westhelle, *The Scandalous God* (reading the cross in an epistemological key). For a broader overview see also Trelstad, *Cross Examinations*.

foremost attribute is not power but wisdom.²¹ In God's works, a harmony, a pre-established beauty, can be discerned.²²

Without drawing the parallels too far, these considerations suggest that it might be worth the attempt to look at the Anselmian theory of satisfaction through the lens of a Newtonian universe. We see well-defined actors on a solid stage, performing in a linear drama where the distribution of power and honor drives the plot of the story. When I imagine the same in the Einstein-Heisenberg theater, I sense a possibility to retell that story from the perspective of wisdom rather than power. The dominance of the power-and-honor discourse would be, if not replaced, complemented by the energy of a wisdom-and-beauty theme.²³

With the theories of relativity and quantum uncertainty, twentieth century physics has strengthened the case of complementarity and dialectics. Multiplicity of times and mathematical undecidability demand explanations that make use of complementary and dialectical thought-models. Complexity and relationality win over simplicity and absoluteness. The same can apply to contemporary thinking about atonement. One-dimensional static theories of satisfaction have lost ground, whereas complementary, dialectical, dynamic and relational models keep gaining more attention. We find ourselves in a favorable position to speak of God acting in the atonement as God hidden *sub contrario*—God's proper work hidden under God's strange or alien work—without having to fear an irreparable crack in the image of God. To move the emphasis from the power of God to the suffering of God alone, will not be enough. It certainly is a decisive and necessary step to acknowledge that "God lets Godself be driven out of the world onto the cross" and to affirm that "only the suffering God can help."²⁴ But remaining at the cross falls short of empowering people to fight oppression and evil. The dialectical thought-model needs to provide a language that can accommodate both the love of God and the wrath of God so that we can speak of a God who is not abusive, yet powerfully loving and passionately caring for justice.

The hermeneutics of relationality, boosted by modern physics, throws a critical light on Western anthropology and its tendency to tip over into individualism and anthropocentrism. Overcoming these limits in scope will

---

21. Alexander, *The Leibniz-Clarke Correspondence*, 18, 64, 80.

22. Ibid., 18.

23. This theme has been explored by Celia Deane-Drummond (*Christ and Evolution*, 159–192), albeit within the framework of evolution (rather than that of post-Einsteinian physics) and in dialogue with the esthetic theology of Hans Urs von Balthasar and Sergii Bulgakov's notion of shadow sophia.

24. Bonhoeffer, *Who Is Christ for Us?*, 74 (DBW 8:534–35, Letter from Tegel Prison, 1944).

strengthen the following themes in atonement discourse: the importance of embodiment, communal dimensions, the significance of atonement and reconciliation for the rest of nature, and the cosmic aspects of the work of Christ. These considerations as well as the dialectical mode of thought will also be helpful in addressing the question of substitution. In light of this relationality, it seems more congenial than before to highlight the fact that the "the symbol of the cross performs a double gesture and requires a double reading."[25] It is "comforting, empowering, and hope-filled, while simultaneously horrifying, threatening, suffocating, contradictory, and offensive."[26] Feminist and postcolonial approaches to atonement and salvation have found the space opened by such dialectics both helpful and necessary, as exemplified by the following statement: "The cross becomes a resource for opening up the interstitial spaces for the postcolonial and feminist semiotic of the divine through our radical recognition of the abject not merely as Other but as part of our selves."[27]

With dialectics, relationality, and comparative rather than superlative as catalysts, it will be easier to handle aspects of atonement that otherwise could stand out as mutually exclusive. For example: Was Jesus's death part of a divine plan? Or was it a consequence of an oppressive political system, and/or of Jesus's naming the law that kills and practicing the healing that restores?[28] How can we account for the dialectic of disaster and love of a God dying and a savior becoming sin for us? How can we say that Jesus died once and for all (Hebr 9:26) and yet is suffering and dying today before our eyes (Matt 25:31–46)? It is precisely the post-Einsteinian understanding of time that makes it possible to accommodate both the uniqueness (the "hapax" in linear chronology) and the thought that "the cross is part of the larger mystery of pain-to-life, of that struggle for the new creation evocative of the rhythm of pregnancy, delivery, and birth (. . .)"[29] (circularity). This would be consonant with the new interpretation of Ecclesiastes 3:1–15 in light of a post-Einsteinian notion of time, as outlined above.

An understanding of time that does not stop at the Newtonian empty stage will include structures and relations, being and becoming. It has an openness that encourages interpretations that go beyond physics, yet are consonant with it. Proper times (Eigenzeiten), *chronos* and *kairos*, linear and cyclical time, proleptic time, future and advent, eschatology of the *already*

---

25. Joh, *Heart of the Cross*, 104.
26. Ibid.
27. Ibid., 105.
28. Westhelle, *The Scandalous God*, 85.
29. Johnson, *She Who Is*, 159.

and the *not-yet*—there is a synergy between physical concepts and theological interpretations that must perceive linear chronology as constantly disturbed by the breaking-in of that which is other, also known as the realm of God and as the *eschaton*. No particular history can legitimately pretend to be universal history.[30]

Eschatology will then have to be understood as a ferment working in and throughout history rather than as the attempted account of a more or less imminent grand finale of history. Or maybe as a *kairos*-detector: allowing us to see moments of nexus between time and its other, between immanent and transcendent, and thus framing answers to the question. What may we hope for, today, and when time is out even for the very last calendar ever to be opened. And as to eternity, rather than as unlimited continuation of a time line, it will have to be seen as a "dimension" of existence.

These shifts will be beneficial for an atonement language that can communicate widely, in various settings. It may be functional even in interreligious settings. Elaborating the consequences of such shifts will open possibilities of revisiting the centers of doctrine while being conscious of the dynamics that arise from the spatial and temporal margins. It is striking that much of theological reasoning about the atoning work of Christ has been performed in a seemingly timeless manner. Emphasis on divine transcendence, human sinfulness, and Christ as the Center, was supposed to result in theological doctrine that was free from the projections of a certain time and the ideals of a specific period. In hindsight, it becomes clear that such timelessness was rather illusionary. In this regard, contextual theologies, especially from the perceived margins, have been helpful. As a Sri Lankan theologian has put it: an authentic Asian theology emerges only when Christianity is baptized in the "Jordan of Asian religion" and the "Calvary of Asian poverty."[31] In the framework of Newtonian space and time, such a statement is merely metaphorical, or else it would make no sense, since there is no direct relationship between the phenomena implied. In the post-Einsteinian framework, the "merely metaphorical" can be enriched, for example by the model of the light cone. The speed of light permits causality between two events only when the events lie within the particular area that light, with its finite speed, can reach at a certain time. Graphically, this area corresponds to a cone that, if the speed of light were infinite, would be opened maximally. Events that lie within a light cone are considered to be situated time-like to one another. Those outside the light cone are situated space-like to one another. Those that have a space-like

---

30. Cf. Westhelle, *The Scandalous God*, 148–51.
31. Aloysius Pieris, as quoted in Jones and Lakeland, *Constructive Theology*, 182.

position cannot interact with each other. Now, there may be a difference between looking at the Jordan of Asian religion and the Calvary of Asian poverty in these two ways. On the one hand, imagining the baptism in the Jordan of Asian religion and the Calvary of Asian poverty as events sitting on a time line at considerable distance from the baptism and crucifixion of Jesus leaves us with a more or less abstract metaphor. On the other hand, conceiving of all four events as situated in a light cone flipped open into eschatological dimensions gives them a time-like position that allows for causal interactions as opposed to a space-like position. In the first case, the Asian context remains secondary to the original one. In the second case, both contexts are contained in the same sphere of relationality, in a world of crisscrossing light cones.

Moreover, the distinction between time-like and space-like may offer ways of conceiving concepts of judgment and justification: Outside the cone, no interaction, no being drawn into God's household of grace; within the light cone, the possibility of transformation through relationship and interaction. Eschatological fulfillment would correspond the complete opening of the light cone, "so that God may be all in all" (1 Cor 15:28).[32]

Taking into account post-Einsteinian notions of time will compel Lutheran theology to work on the language of atonement not only within the framework of sin and grace, but also within the framework of nature and grace. Maybe the curved space-time of physics has a theological parallel in the image of the perichoretic Holy Trinity embracing creation towards its consummation—but to say that is clearly to have crossed the line between the literal and the metaphorical.

BIBLIOGRAPHY

Albrektson, Bertil. *History and the Gods: An Essay on the Idea of Historical Events as Divine Manifestations in the Ancient Near East and in Israel*. Coniectanea biblica. Old Testament Series 1. Lund: CWK Gleerup, 1967.

Alexander, H. G., editor. *The Leibniz-Clarke Correspondence: Together with Extracts from Newton's Principa and Opticks*. Manchester: Manchester University Press, 1956.

Barr, James. *Biblical Words for Time*. Studies in Biblical Theology 33. London: SCM, 1962.

Bonhoeffer, Dietrich. *Who Is Christ for Us?* Edited by Craig L. Nessan and Renate Wind. Minneapolis: Fortress, 2002.

Cullmann, Oscar. *Christ and Time: The Primitive Christian Conception of Time and History*. 1946. Philadelphia: Westminster, 1964.

---

32. For a discussion of eschatology in the context of relativistic physics see Jackelén, "A Relativistic Eschatology," 955–73.

Deane-Drummond, Celia. *Christ and Evolution: Wonder and Wisdom.* London: SCM, 2009.
Grantén, Eva-Lotta. *Utanför paradiset. Arvsyndsläran i nutida luthersk teologi och etik.* Stockholm: Verbum, 2013.
Jackelén, Antje. "A Relativistic Eschatology: Time, Eternity, and Eschatology in Light of the Physics of Relativity." *Zygon: Journal of Religion and Science,* 41/4 (2006) 955–73.
———. *Time & Eternity. The Question of Time in Church, Science, and Theology.* Conshohocken: Templeton, 2005.
Joh, Wonhee Anne. *Heart of the Cross. A Postcolonial Christology.* Louisville, London: Westminster John Knox, 2006.
Johnson, Elizabeth A. *She Who Is. The Mystery of God in Feminist Theological Discourse.* 1992. New York: Crossroad, 2001.
Jones, Serene, and Paul Lakeland, editors. *Constructive Theology. A Contemporary Approach to Classical Themes.* Minneapolis: Fortress, 2005.
Nakashima Brock, Rita, and Rebecca Ann Parker. *Proverbs of Ashes. Violence, Redemptive Suffering and the Search for What Saves Us.* Boston: Beacon, 2001.
Newton, Isaac. *Mathematical Principles of Natural Philosophy.* London, 1729.
Perdue, Leo G. *The Collapse of History: Reconstructing Old Testament Theology.* Overtures to Biblical Theology. Minneapolis: Fortress, 1994.
Sölle, Dorothee. *Christ the Representative: An Essay in Theology After the 'Death of God'.* London: SCM, 1967.
Thompson, Deanna A. *Crossing the Divide. Luther, Feminism, and the Cross.* Minneapolis: Fortress, 2004.
Tillich, Paul. "The Struggle Between Time and Space." In *Theology of Culture*, edited by Robert C. Kimball. New York: Oxford University Press, 1959.
Trelstad, Marit, editor. *Cross Examinations. Readings on the Meaning of the Cross Today.* Minneapolis: Augsburg Fortress, 2006.
Westhelle, Vítor. *The Scandalous God. The Use and Abuse of the Cross.* Minneapolis: Fortress, 2006.

5

Healing as an Image for the Atonement

A Lutheran Consideration

CHERYL M. PETERSON

In Western theology, the doctrine of the atonement has been dominated by forensic language and the image of the courtroom. Forensic language has been particularly important to a Lutheran understanding of justification: where, by grace through faith, sinners are "declared righteous" on account of Christ. Such language has been criticized, however, for not doing justice to a fuller New Testament understanding of salvation which includes the forgiveness of sins, healing, reconciliation, restoration, and wholeness, and which is experienced communally as well as individually. By so strongly emphasizing forensic imagery in both the doctrine of justification and the atonement, Lutheranism is in danger of ignoring both the personal (and social) nature of forgiveness and reconciliation, and a relational view of God and salvation, both of which have become more prominent in contemporary theology.

In this chapter, I propose that we consider healing as an image for the atonement that can better address the human predicament in more relational and transformational ways than forensic imagery alone, and one that has the potential to speak to both the west and the global south. After briefly surveying the contextuality of atonement theories in the past and present, I briefly examine the use of this image in the theology of Augustine and John Wesley. I consider this image in light of possible Lutheran objections, to determine if and how it also may be embraced by Lutheran theologians today.

ATONEMENT THEORIES IN CONTEXT

Atonement theories have always been contextual, and contemporary atonement theories must take context into account. Whether consciously, or not, the great theologians of the past reflected the questions and concerns of their own ages in constructing their ideas about the atonement. F.W. Dillistone and Paul Fiddes have illustrated how in various ages and contexts, particular understandings of the human predicament have given rise to particular atonement images or motifs.[1] For example, in the New Testament, atonement was often imaged in ways that would address the people's understanding of sin and evil. The motif of "cleansing" addressed people's view of sin as impurity, and the motif of "victory" addressed people's fear of demons and hostile powers. The images of recapitulation and divinization arose when Christianity came into contact with Hellenistic philosophy, which was concerned with the deep division between a world of purity, truth, and immortality on the one hand, and an earthly world of natural ills, delusion, and morality, on the other.

In medieval society, atonement images addressed the cultural concern for order. In *Cur Deus Homo?* Anselm argued it was impossible for God to leave the world in a state of disorder caused by human sin. For him, the atonement restores order and justice to universe, thus "satisfying" God. Similarly, Luther's view of justification as "freedom from the law" and Calvin's idea of Christ's death as vicarious substitution must be considered from the perspective of their historical and cultural context, where the question of God's law and righteousness held center stage. In the nineteenth century, an era dominated by Enlightenment thinking, concern for morality, the autonomy of the individual and interpersonal relationships effected more subjective understandings of the atonement and a different nuance to sacrificial language. More recently, in the context of their own economic oppression, liberation theologians in Latin America and elsewhere have brought back the motif of atonement as victory and deliverance over oppressive systems of injustice.

However, as Douglas John Hall points out, "not only does the history of atonement theology demonstrate the inherently contextual character of the Christian message, but it also demonstrates an antithetical proposition, namely the propensity of powerful theological dogmas to persist beyond the

---

1. Dillistone, *The Christian Understanding of Atonement*; Dillistone, "Atonement," 50–53; and Fiddes, *Past and Present Salvation*, esp. ch. 1.

point of their timeliness."[2] This can be seen in the case of the legal imagery in both forensic justification and the penal substitutionary theory of the atonement. Although this theory has been most strongly associated with John Calvin and his heirs, particularly Charles Hodge, Luther has been interpreted as holding this view as well. For example, in his systematic theology, Ted Peters equates Luther's "happy exchange" motif with the penal substitutionary atonement theory, whereby Christ assumes the penalty for humanity's sin and in exchange bestows upon sinners his righteousness and new life.[3] By continuing to interpret the death of Jesus—and its benefits for us—primarily in juridical categories, are Lutherans in danger of theologically remaining in the sixteenth century, interpreting the human predicament in terms of law, personal guilt, unrighteousness, etc.? Are these categories and images still able to speak in the same way to people today, who live in a very different context? Or does what once sounded like good news for those in the sixteenth century today mostly fall on deaf ears?

HEALING AS AN ATONEMENT IMAGE FOR TODAY'S CONTEXT

Indeed, less and less scholars are content with juridical terminology for understanding both the doctrine of the atonement and justification. James Tull proposes instead the language of reconciliation, arguing that:

> The advantage which the word 'reconciliation' has over 'justification' is that it lifts our relationship to God from the level of the law-court to that of personal association. It more easily allows us to think of our relationship to God in terms of his fatherhood and our sonship, of love rather than law, of fellowship rather than legal acquittal.[4]

The language of reconciliation and personal participation seems better suited to address our contemporary understanding of the human predicament.[5]

---

2. Hall, *Professing the Faith*, 404.

3. Peters, *God—The World's Future*, 225. He argues that the penal substitutionary theory is largely a further development of Anselm's notion of satisfaction. Peters does not believe that the sources support Gustaf Aulén in his famous attempt to claim Luther as an adherent of the "classic view," the dramatic "Christus Victor," rather than the Latin view. See Aulén, *Christus Victor*.

4. Tull, *The Atoning Gospel*, 52.

5. These include Dillistone, Fiddes, Hall, and David L. Wheeler, who argues that process theology provides the best vehicle for a "relational" theology of the atonement. See Wheeler, *A Relational View of the Atonement*.

Along with reconciliation, healing also has emerged in contemporary discussions of the atonement. Fiddes contends that healing is becoming a more prominent image for the atonement because it is able to address what he considers to be at the heart of the human predicament today: "an alienation which has its base in the fragmenting of the personality and in friction between social groups."[6] Douglas John Hall agrees, suggesting that although reconciliation is a conspicuous theme in the Christian tradition, liberal Christianity has helped us focus the shift from heaven to earth. We now recognize our need not only to be reconciled with God, but also with each other, individually and socially, as well as with other forms of life and the earth itself. This need is part of our quest for meaning. He posits that "What is being asked for both in relation to our alienation from other human beings and our alienation from nature is really conciliation *to our own creaturehood.*"[7]

We see the language of healing used analogously both in religious and non-religious discourse, in the west and global south, to address the need for reconciliation and wholeness in those who experience alienation from God, themselves, one another, and creation itself. In this regard, healing as an image includes but goes beyond reconciliation, because healing happens both within persons, as well as between them. The word "healing" in the Greek is σῴζω [sozo], which means to be made whole again (and is also the word used in the New Testament for salvation). Writing from a South African perspective, Ernst M. Conradie points to the need for the healing of memories in South Africa. He notes that it is perhaps here, "where the Christian message of forgiveness of sins, also when sin is understood as alienation between God and humanity, may be more relevant than what social activists inside and outside the church may have imagined."[8]

The Lutheran World Federation chose for its Tenth Assembly in 2003 the theme, "For the Healing of the World," with the purpose of exploring ways to be God's instrument for healing, justice, and reconciliation in the midst of brokenness in both church and society. While the theme encompassed concerns of health and health care, the assembly also addressed healing in a much broader sense, including healing from the walls of exclusion

---

6. Fiddes, *Past and Present Salvation*, 10. He does not limit the understanding of sin as alienation to the modern age but suggests that each age reflects on that alienation contextually. The contemporary discussion of the human condition is influenced by insights from sociology and psychology; we become alienated from ourselves, others and the whole of reality in our anxiety over the competing tensions of our existence (freedom/finiteness, possibilities/actualities).

7. Hall, *Professing the Faith*, 505.

8. Conradie, "Healing in Soteriological Perspective," 18.

and discrimination between peoples, often related to huge economic disparities in the world; healing from the wounds of violence and injustice, both interpersonal and institutional; and healing from the ways we pollute and abuse the earth and other life-forms. "Healing restores the right relationship with God, with other persons, communities, and with the rest of creation. It has dimensions that are spiritual, physical, psychological, and social, and in these ways, is 'salvific.'"[9]

While a number of theologians acknowledge both the relationship between healing and salvation, and the possibility of healing as an image for the atonement, only a few have developed these ideas in any theological depth. Bruce Reichenbach, building from the conceptual connection the Bible and traditional healers make between sickness and sin, has proposed healing as a motif that can address the whole human predicament. He draws on the Suffering Servant figure in Isaiah 53 as a way to understand the death of Jesus as restorative, healing act. The Servant/Physician is sent by God to take on the root of our disease, our rejection of God and pride, assuming its virulence to the point of death: the poison of our sin is "so strong that it brings death, but at the same time not so strong that death can permanently hold the Physician in its grasp." Thus, it is not God who demands the death of the servant, but our sin; God's part is in having been merciful by sending the Servant.[10]

African theologian Cécé Kolié makes a similar point in her discussion of the cross as a symbol of healing. She writes, "With the Crucified One, suffering becomes a remedy for disease, and death a happy issue."[11] She also makes this interesting point, which could easily be applied to Jesus' death as well as to his healing ministry: "to do the work of a healer is to give a part of one's own humanity to those in need of the same." She explains with a quote from Daniel Friedman: "The upshot of the gift of self is in fusion with the patient. The healer, however, fuses, merges with the 'ill-ness,' so to speak, and the therapeutic enterprise of the healer is necessarily pathogenic for himself, otherwise the therapeutic relationship of fusion cannot take place."[12]

---

9. Lutheran World Federation, *Study Book*, "For the Healing of the World," 17.

10. Reichenbach, "By his Stripes we are Healed," 559. See also Reichenbach, "Healing View," 117–42.

11. Kolié, "Jesus as Healer?," 144.

12. Friedman, *Les guerisseurs*, 1, quoted in Kolié, "Jesus as Healer?," 131.

HEALING AS AN ATONEMENT IMAGE IN THE WESTERN THEOLOGICAL TRADITION

Healing has not been a prominent image for the atonement in Western theology. The atonement theories that have dominated Western theology have been the Latin view (satisfaction, and its close cousin, the penal substitutionary theory), the subjective view (moral example), and the classic patristic view (*Christus Victor*). A common way of distinguishing and evaluating atonement theories is whether they have a primarily objective or subjective focus. In other words, does Christ's death on the cross change something in God or the fabric of the universe (which then, benefits the sinner)? For example, in objective theories such as the satisfaction or penal substitutionary theory, the cross respectively takes God's wrath or restores God's honor. In subjective theories, such as the one attributed to Abelard, Christ's death changes something in the sinner (rather than God or the universe); the sinner so moved by the example of Christ's sacrifice that she becomes more loving herself, bringing reconciliation between her and God. Such distinctions frequently assume that a so-called "objective" understanding of the atonement could not have a subjective component to it, and vice versa. Aulén clearly recognized this as a false alternative and has set up his threefold typology as a way to get out of it. Although he insists he is only doing a historical survey and not an apologetic, he is clearly steering his readers toward the "classic" type, since it avoids the problems inherent in the Latin and "subjective" theories. But this is hardly a satisfactory solution, since in effect, we are only left with *one* image or motif to truly consider, that of the dramatic "Christus Victor."

Healing is also an atonement image that, like the "classic" theory, has the ability to bring together objective and subjective aspects of the atonement, by locating it in the relationship between the doctor (Christ) and patient (sinner). Although healing is a major theme in the synoptic gospels, the focus is on healing as an activity of Jesus' earthly ministry. Nowhere does Jesus refer to his death on the cross as "healing," although he does refer to himself as a physician of souls in Matt 9:11–13; Mark 2:13–17; Luke 5:27–32.[13] When the Pharisees ask why he eats with tax collectors and sinners, Jesus replies, "Those who are well have no need of a physician, but

---

13. It should be noted that many Pentecostal and charismatic traditions teach the "doctrine of divine healing in the atonement." In other words, God has already provided the means for divine healing through the cross of Christ; believers are urged to claim the victory available in the atonement through prayer and faith to bring healing to those who are sick (in body or spirit). A consideration of this teaching lies beyond the scope of this chapter. For a discussion and evaluation of this teaching (and alternative views of divine healing), see Hejzlar, *Two Paradigms for Divine Healing*.

those who are sick. Go and learn what this means, 'I desire mercy, not sacrifice.' For I have come to call not the righteous, but sinners." Although the sacrificial image has received the most attention in 1 Peter,[14] one also finds the healing language of Isaiah 53 to describe Jesus as the suffering servant: "He himself bore our sins in his body on the cross, so that, free from sins, we might live for righteousness; by his wounds you have been healed. For you were going astray like sheep, but now you have returned to the shepherd and guardian of your souls" (1 Pet 2:24).

Although the predominant atonement theory of the patristic era was the ransom theory, healing emerged as an image for the atonement in the second and third centuries in the midst of the intense struggle between the cult of Asclepius, the pagan 'Savior and Healer,' and the worship of Christ, whose earthly ministry had been depicted by the synoptic writers as that of a physician of body and soul.[15] With the rise of a number of other healing cults in the fourth century, the concept of Christ the Physician became more conventionalized. It is against this background that Augustine drew on the image of "Christus Medicus" to articulate the meaning of salvation.[16]

In *De Trinitate*, Augustine combines the concept of "Christ as Healer" with the servant motif echoed by Paul in the famous hymn in Philippians 2:5–8. Christ the Physician is able to heal because of his mediatorial role, in which he both shares our infirmities in the form of a servant and heals them in the form of God. Augustine writes, "Again, there is the point that man's pride, which is the greatest obstacle to his cleaving to God, could be confuted and cured by such humility on the part of God. Man also learns how far he has withdrawn from God, which is useful for him as a remedial pain, when he returns through a mediator like this, who comes to aid men as God with his divinity and to share with them as man in their infirmity."[17] Christ heals humanity from its pride by the medicine of his own humanity.[18]

---

14. "You know that you were ransomed from the futile ways inherited from your ancestors, not with perishable things like silver or gold, but with the precious blood of Christ, like that of a lamb without defect or blemish"(1 Pet 1:18–19).

15. Arbesmann, "The Concept of 'Christus Medicus' in St. Augustine," 3.

16. See Arbesmann, "Christ the *Medicus humilis* in Saint Augustine," 623–29; and Arbesmann, "The Concept of 'Christus Medicus' in St. Augustine." Augustine uses many different motifs, including justification, ransom, victory, sacrifice, as well as that of healing/curing; however, his use of healing has long been overlooked as a possible resource for atonement theology. Cf. Hill, *The Works of Saint Augustine: A Translation for the 21st Century*. Part I: Books, vol. 5: *The Trinity*, chapter 13, esp. 353–62.

17. Augustine, *The Trinity* XIII.22, in Hill, *The Works of Saint Augustine*, Part I: Books, vol. 5, 361.

18 According to Arbesmann, "Augustine depicts Christ in the role of the Divine Physician, who by the medicine of his humility, heals man from the festering wound of

In his sermons, Augustine also describes sin as a sickness that blocks us from seeing God. He goes on to describe Christ as the healthy doctor who carries our infirmity on the cross (Christ being described as both doctor and cure) and drank the bitter cup for us; therefore, we are admonished to believe and be healed (and encouraged to drink our own cup as well).[19] Although Christ the Physician freely receives all patients for treatment, the remedy, made from his own blood, is only appropriated by those who "come to the doctor, clung to Christ, listened to him, followed him and been converted,"[20] who, in other words, trust the doctor and follow his orders, or, in theological terms, have faith and live that faith out in good works.

Although Abelard is best known for his critique of Anselm and his promotion of a "moral exemplar" view of the atonement, Fiddes credits Abelard for stating that "sin is a matter of the rebellion of our hearts against God, not some impersonal debt to be paid off outside us, but rather a broken relationship to be healed within us. Salvation must be a healing of our wills which are resisting God here and now in the present."[21] In his commentary on Romans, Abelard appeals to the image of Christ as a Physician who offers us the medicine of redemptive grace that we were on our own powerless to receive.[22] In a similar manner, John Wesley used therapeutic imagery to describe the transformation that happens in the process of sanctification that follows the sinner's justification: Jesus Christ is the Great Physician of souls who heals our souls diseased by sin and who restores our human nature back to God's original design.[23] He writes, "For the love of the world in all its branches, the love of God is the sovereign remedy."[24]

We can see how the image of healing is able to bring together objective and subjective aspects of the atonement. The healing comes from God through Christ's death on the cross, where Christ as the Divine Physician takes on the infirmities of his "patients" even unto death—the doctor whose desire to heal is so great that he gives up his life for the patient. Even Abelard states that "If God didn't offer sinners the grace they needed in order to

---

pride, which had caused humanity's fall, thus accomplishing redemption and inviting man to imitate him in this virtue. Arbesmann, "The Concept of 'Christus Medicus,' in St. Augustine", 11.

19. Augustine, "Sermon 88," in Hill, *The Works of Saint Augustine*, Part III: Sermons, vol. 3, 418–38.

20. Ibid., 352.

21. Fiddes, *Past and Present Salvation*, 152.

22. See Williams, "Sin, Grace, and Redemption in Abelard," 258–78.

23. See for example, "The One Thing Needful (1734)," 34–38, and "Original Sin (1759)," 326–34, in Outler and Heitzenrater, *John Wesley's Sermons: An Anthology*.

24. Outler and Heitzenrater, *John Wesley's Sermons: An Anthology*, 333.

accept his saving grace, it isn't their fault that they aren't saved." As Thomas Williams notes,

> In such a case, Abelard says, God would be like a doctor who brings in the medicine that would cure a desperately ill patient who is too weak to sit up on his own and take the pill. If the doctor doesn't help the patient sit up and take the medicine, it is hardly the patient's fault that he isn't cured, and the doctor deserves no praise for bringing in the medicine if he does not take the necessary steps to ensure that it effects a cure [*Comm. Rom.* 240].[25]

In other words, the saving death of Christ does more than move the sinner's heart in love and humility; his death becomes our sacrament, offering real medicine for our souls. In this way, healing is something that continues to be appropriated anew whenever one receives that medicine: through receiving the Eucharist, receiving absolution, hearing the Word proclaimed. While healing comes from the doctor's medicine (or surgery), it is appropriated by the patient through faith. Healing happens to the sinner and is experienced in one's very being; it is not something which happens elsewhere and "reckoned to us."

A LUTHERAN ENGAGEMENT WITH THE IMAGE OF HEALING FOR THE ATONEMENT

Before considering atonement as healing from a Lutheran perspective, it is important to distinguish between atonement and justification. The word "atonement" (literally, "at-one-ment") was coined in 1526 by William Tyndale to translate the Latin term *"reconcilio"* and has been used ever since to refer to the salvific consequences of Christ's death on the cross, most typically through reference to "atonement theories."[26] Although many have tried to attribute one atonement theory or another to Martin Luther (most famously, Gustaf Aulén's *Christus Victor*), Kenneth Hagen has shown the difficulty of this undertaking. Further, he argues that Luther has no theory of atonement, but rather, that "atonement" serves as "an important interpretative tool" for many "genuine articles" in Luther's theology, including the "happy exchange," reconciliation, expiation, cross, redemption, justification, sacrament and example, and salvation.[27] While it is true that Luther

---

25. Williams, "Sin, Grace, and Redemption in Abelard, 271.
26. "Atonement," in McGrath, *The Blackwell Encyclopedia of Modern Christian Thought*, 20.
27. Hagen, "Luther on Atonement: Reconfigured," 251–76.

draws on a variety of New Testament images to interpret Jesus' death on the cross, including the image of victorious champion,[28] the preponderance of images in his writings associated with the substitutionary theory, such as payment, punishment, satisfaction, leads Ted Peters to argue that "the notion of satisfactionary atonement underlies his doctrine of justification by faith (just as it does for Calvin)."[29]

If theories of atonement explain the salvific consequences of the death of Christ on the cross, the doctrine of justification articulates how those consequences benefit the sinner. In other words, atonement theories speculate on the meaning of the cross for salvation (how does the death of Christ save?); the doctrine of justification presumes that the death of Christ atones for sin and articulates how those saving consequences are applied to the sinner (by grace, through faith). Juridical categories have predominated in the Lutheran doctrine of justification, just as in the case of atonement theology. The objectivity of both the atoning death of Christ and the justification of the sinner are important to emphasize for Lutheran theologians. God's act on the cross in Jesus Christ is an event that happens "*extra nos*," outside of us, which is then applied to the sinner, bringing God's favor and reconciliation, rather than something given to the sinner which changes her and thus justifies her in God's sight. Whatever transformation or change happens as a result of justification (regeneration and sanctification) happens as a result of justification; it does not precede or cause it.

Healing has not been a prominent motif in Lutheran discussions of the doctrine of justification. The medical terminology can lead a view of grace as a "medicine," a substance that becomes part of us, changing us from within, "infused grace" that enabled the believer to grow in righteousness and thus be justified. Such a view (which has its roots in Augustine) is rejected by Luther, as Regin Prenter has shown.[30] However, Luther himself uses the healing image and the corresponding doctor/patient relationship in a striking passage from his commentary on Paul's Letter to the Romans[31] in a way that avoids this danger and offers a way forward for Lutherans who wish to employ this image in discussions of justification, and perhaps by extension, the atonement.

In his commentary on Romans, Luther writes that justification "is similar to the case of the sick man who believes the doctor who promises

28. For example, in the Large Catechism, Luther describes Christ as snatching us "poor creatures from the jaws of the devil." Kolb and Wengert, *The Book of Concord: The Confessions of the Evangelical Lutheran Church*, 434, §27–30.

29. Peters, *God—The World's Future*, 225.

30. See Prenter, *Spiritus Creator*.

31. Luther, *Lectures on Romans*, LW 25, 260–326. See also LW 25, 336.

him a sure recovery and in this meantime obeys the doctor's orders in the hope of the promised recovery and abstains from those things which have been forbidden him, so that he may in no way hinder the promised return to health or increase his sickness until the doctor can fulfill his promise to him."[32]

The sick man's trust in the doctor's promise is the basis for his restoration to health, not what he does, and yet he is not idle in the meantime: he follows the doctor's orders so as not to hinder the fulfillment of this promise.[33] Luther asks, then, if this sick man is well. He answers, "The fact is that he is both sick and well. He is sick in fact, but he is well because of the sure promise of the doctor, whom he trusts who has reckoned him as already cure, because he is sure that he will cure him;[34] for he has already begun to cure him and no longer reckons to him a sickness until death."[35] Luther does not describe his restoration as an increase in health, but as the paradoxical, yet simultaneous, existence of both illness and health. While the complete cure comes only in "eternal life,"[36] in the meantime, the sinner has God's promise that God will "continue to deliver him from sin until He has completely cured him."[37] Such ones are sick in fact but "healthy in hope"[38]—a hope grounded on the promise of the Physician, rather than the empirical increase of health within their bodies—but also "in the fact that they are beginning to be healthy, that is, they are 'being healed.'"[39]

With Luther's explanation in mind, Lutherans can affirm healing as a metaphor for the doctrine of justification, and by extension, the atonement. Lutherans affirm the objective reality of Christ's death (and resurrection) healing the estranged relationship between God and humanity, whereby we are reckoned as "healed." Objectively, the cure for sin is found in the event

---

32. Ibid., LW 25, 260.

33. Luther adds that the sick man will not get healthy either if he decides that he likes his disease and does not want to be cured, or if he fails to recognize his illness and therefore rejects the promised cure. This, Luther says, "is the kind of operation that wants to be justified and made well its own works. Ibid., LW 25, 260.

34. Regin Prenter writes that Luther's emphasis here is on the certainty of the physician's promise of a complete recovery, not on the daily progress of healing. Prenter, *Spiritus Creator*, 77.

35. Luther, *Lectures on Romans*, LW 25, 260. The basis for this is not—as Cécé Kolié has proposed—because of a fusion between the physician and patient, but it would be interesting to combine her idea with Luther's bridal imagery of the "happy exchange" for justification in "The Freedom of a Christian."

36. Ibid., LW 25, 260.

37. Ibid., LW 25, 260.

38. Ibid., LW 25, 260, 336.

39. Ibid., LW 25, 336.

of the cross and resurrection; subjectively it becomes the believer's through trust/faith in the physician. The believer lives in hope of the final cure, and yet, as Luther says, this hope can bring a kind of existential healing in the present, being "healthy in hope."

Augustine, Abelard, and Wesley go farther with this image, as we saw; for them, the atoning death of Jesus not only heals the sinner from the guilt of sin, but also from the power of sin in one's life. The atonement enables the sinner to be healed from sin of pride and spiritual blindness (Augustine) or our rebellious wills (Abelard) and be restored to the image of God (Wesley). I am interested in whether Lutherans also can speak of justification and atonement as "healing" in this sense. Are we simply declared well—or is there a sense in which Lutherans can affirm that we are "being made well" in the present—beyond living in hope for our ultimate "cure" in the eschaton?

Fiddes argues that if we wish to speak of atonement in relational terms, we need to recognize that "the healing of a relationship and personality cannot be accepted like a package, a ticket, or even a contract. It must be created anew through the meeting of persons."[40] The scholastic understanding of forensic justification as being "declared righteous" does not seem to do justice to the fuller picture of salvation in the New Testament. Indeed, Fiddes argues that this legal motif "loses the personal nature of forgiveness, and when transferred to God it evacuates love from his activity. The picture of a pardoned criminal fails to communicate the painful relational experience which lies at the heart of forgiving and being forgiven. The mere issue of a pardon cannot touch a person deeply; in life a prisoner can accept a pardon and go free, hating the authorities who gave it and the judge who sentenced him—or perhaps laughing at them."[41]

While Luther is clear that we remain sinners to the end, he affirms in the Romans commentary that God "continues to deliver [the sick man] from sin until He has completely cured him." If the relationship with the physician is on-going, in the sense that we continue to put our trust in him and place ourselves under his care,[42] do we receive something more than "hope" to get us through each day? I would say yes, if we can affirm that the "medicine" is not the infused grace of medieval Catholicism, but nothing other than the presence of the Holy Spirit itself. Lutheran theology teaches that in justification, the believer receives the gift of the Holy Spirit to keep us in faith, but also to battle the sin within us, allowing the fruits of the Spirit to grow in us, enabling us to better love God and neighbor. In his last sermon

---

40. Fiddes, *Past and Present Salvation*, 15.
41. Ibid., 15.
42. Luther, *Lectures on Romans*, LW 25, 336.

in Wittenberg on Romans 12:3 (January 17, 1546), Luther uses the image of healing in a striking way to describe the Christian life:

> If Christ, the Samaritan, had not come, we should all have had to die. He it is who binds our wounds, carries us into the church and it now healing us. So we are not under the Physician's care. The sin, it is true, is wholly forgiven, but it has not been wholly purged. If the Holy Spirit is not ruling men, they become corrupt again; but the Holy Spirit must cleanse wounds daily. Therefore, this life is a hospital; the sin has really been forgiven, but it has not yet been healed.[43]

The Lutheran Confessions teach that sanctification, while it must be distinguished from justification, necessarily follows it. Our relationship with God is healed completely by the objective act of the death and resurrection of Christ on the cross; we are justified by grace through faith on account of Christ. However, simultaneous with our justification is our regeneration (or the new birth), which brings the presence of the Holy Spirit into our hearts, not only enabling us to trust the Great Physician, but also healing our hearts so that we may weakly cooperate with God's will and (imperfectly!) love God and the neighbor, living in the promise of restored relationships in our daily life.

Lutherans can affirm healing as a motif for justification and atonement if healing is understood in this way, relationally through a "meeting of persons;" it is the relationship with the Great Physician itself that is healing, that brings new life (and the presence of the Holy Spirit) to the believer in order to transform not only his standing before God, but his relationship with God, other people, and indeed, all of creation. The basis for healing is given in the relationship with and the promise of the Great Physician. However, that promise includes more than a declaration; it does mean being made well, and being made well in all ways, and in all of our relationships.

CONCLUSION

In this chapter, I have proposed "healing" as an image or metaphor for the atonement that can speak powerfully to our context today, both to those in more dominant cultures as well as to those who are more marginalized, and one that can be embraced by Lutheran theology as a motif for justification as well as the atonement. The question remains, however, if, as I have tried to argue, Lutherans can affirm healing as an image for what Christ has done for us on the cross (justification and atonement)—and for what Christ is doing

---

43. Luther, "The Last Sermon in Wittenberg," LW 51, 373.

in us (sanctification), might we also expand that language to go beyond the individual's relationship with God and speak of God's work in the atonement in terms of healing relationships between persons, between groups/nations, and also of the earth itself? How does the healing that comes from the atonement address all levels of alienation that inflict the world (personal, social, and cosmic)? The 2003 LWF Study Document, "For the Healing of the World," proposes that the concept of "'healing' helps to bring out important dimensions of salvation and God's other actions that traditional language has tended to leave out—the whole bodily and spiritual reality of persons and their relationships in the world and with all of creation."[44]

Drawing on another of Luther's writings where he uses the language of healing in relation to justification (in the parable of the Good Samaritan), the LWF Study document notes that:

> In the parable's vivid bodily references, Luther saw the nature of God's saving activity in Christ: God becomes our neighbor. The wounded man is reborn through the gratuitous help of the Samaritan (Christ), who takes up his wounded and hopeless situation. The wounded man represents humanity in general, and Christians in particular."[45]

The document goes on to say that to be justified becomes almost synonymous with "to be healed," and further, for Luther, while we await the completion of this healing of all the wounded until God's kingdom comes in its fullness, we participate in God's healing work now on the basis of our own justification and healing. For "the healing that we receive can never become something we possess, a cure that we have achieved, a good that we own. It opens us up to others, connects with our social and natural environments." In short, "a life renewed by God is a life lived in responsible and caring relationships with other persons and the rest of creation."[46]

BIBLIOGRAPHY

Arbesmann, Rudolph. "Christ the *Medicus humilis* in Saint Augustine." In *Augustinus Magister* [Congress International Augustinien, Paris, 21–24, Septembre 1954], Communications, vol. II, 623–29. Paris: Estudes Augustiniennes, 1954.

———. "The Concept of 'Christus Medicus' in St. Augustine." *Traditio* 10 (1954) 1–28.

Aulén, Gustaf. *Christus Victor: A Historical Study of the Three Main Types of the Idea of the Atonement.* New York: Macmillian, 1966.

---

44. Lutheran World Federation, *Study Book,* "For the Healing of the World," 134.
45. Ibid.
46. Ibid., 135.

Conradie, Ernst M. "Healing in Soteriological Perspective." *Religion and Theology* 13/1 (2006) 3–22.

Dillistone, F.W. "Atonement." In *The Westminster Dictionary of Christian Theology*, edited by Alan Richardson and John Bowden, 50–53. Philadelphia: Westminster, 1983.

———. *The Christian Understanding of Atonement*. London: SCM, 1968.

Fiddes, Paul S. *Past and Present Salvation: The Christian Idea of Atonement*. Louisville, KY: Westminster John Knox, 1989.

Friedman, Daniel. *Les guerisseurs: Splendeurs et miseres du don*. Paris: Anne Marie Metaille, 1981.

Hagen, Kenneth. "Luther on Atonement: Reconfigured." *Concordia Theological Monthly* 61, no. 4 (Oct 1997) 251–76.

Hall, Douglas John. Hall, *Professing the Faith: Christian Theology in a North American Context*. Minneapolis, MN: Augsburg Fortress, 1993.

Hejzlar, Pavel. *Two Paradigms for Divine Healing: Fred F. Bosworth, Kenneth E. Hagin, Agnes Sanford, and Francis MacNutt in Dialogue*. Global Pentecostal and Charismatic Studies, vol. 4, edited by Andrew Davies and William Kay. Leiden: Brill, 2010.

Hill, Edmund. *The Works of Saint Augustine: A Translation for the 21st Century*. Part I: Books, vol. 5: *The Trinity*, edited by John E. Rotelle. Brooklyn, NY: New City, 1991.

———. *The Works of Saint Augustine: A Translation for the 21st Century*. Part III: Sermons, vol. 3, edited by John E. Rotelle. Brooklyn, NY: New City, 1991.

Kolb, Robert, and Timothy J. Wengert, editors. *The Book of Concord: The Confessions of the Evangelical Lutheran Church*. Minneapolis, MN: Fortress, 2000.

Kolié, Cécé. "Jesus as Healer?" In *Faces of Jesus in Africa*, edited by Robert J. Schreiter. Faith and Culture Series, 128–50. Maryknoll, NY: Orbis, 1991.

Luther, Martin. "The Last Sermon in Wittenberg" (1546). LW 51. Philadelphia: Fortress Press, 1959.

———. *Lectures on Romans* (1515–1516). LW 25. St Louis: Concordia Press, 1972.

Lutheran World Federation. *Study Book, "For the Healing of the World."* LWF Tenth Assembly, Winnipeg, Canada 21–31 July 2003. Geneva: The Lutheran World Federation, 2002.

McGrath, Alister, editor. *The Blackwell Encyclopedia of Modern Christian Thought*. Oxford: Blackwell Publishers, 1993.

Outler, Albert C., and Richard P. Heitzenrater. *John Wesley's Sermons: An Anthology*. Nashville: Abingdon, 1991.

Peters, Ted. *God—The World's Future: Systematic Theology for a New Era*. 2nd ed. Minneapolis, MN: Fortress, 2000.

Prenter, Regin. *Spiritus Creator*. Philadelphia: Muhlenberg, 1953.

Reichenbach, Bruce R. "By his Stripes we are Healed." *Journal of the Evangelical Theological Society* 41/4 (December 1998) 551–60.

———. "Healing View." In *The Nature of the Atonement: Four Views*, edited by James Beilby and Paul R. Eddy, 117–42. Downers Grove, IL: IVP, 2006.

Tull, James E. *The Atoning Gospel*. Macon, GA: Mercer University Press, 1982.

Wheeler, David L. *A Relational View of the Atonement: Prolegomenon to a Reconstruction of the Doctrine*. American University Studies, Series VII. Theology and Religion, vol. 54. New York: Peter Lang, 1989.

Williams, Thomas. "Sin, Grace, and Redemption in Abelard." In *The Cambridge Companion to Abelard,* edited by Jeffrey Brower and Kevin Guilfoy, 258–78. Cambridge: Cambridge University Press, 2004.

PART TWO

Lutheran Theology and Ethics in a Post-Christian Society

6

Law and Gospel in Lutheran Ethics

CARL-HENRIC GRENHOLM

The sharp distinction between law and gospel has been of great importance within Lutheran theology. As the Swedish theologian Einar Billing once maintained, the new element in Luther's thought is his understanding of the gospel. Luther did not remove the idea of the law from its central position, but he had a particular understanding of the gospel—in its sharp opposition to the law. According to Luther, the criterion of a good theologian is the capacity to understand this important difference between law and gospel.[1]

Luther gives a clear conception of this distinction between law and gospel in his *Greater Galatians Commentary*, where he also makes clear that it is related to the opposition between the two kingdoms. God is struggling against evil in two different ways. In the spiritual government he is using the gospel in order to promote salvation, the justification of faith (*iustitia fidei*). In the secular government he is using the law to promote social order, political justice (*iustitia politica*).[2]

In the Lutheran tradition, the doctrine of the two kingdoms has been one expression of the ambition to discriminate between law and gospel. This distinction has been interpreted in different ways by Lutheran theologians, but often it means that ethical reflection is based on the doctrine of creation, not on Christology or Eschatology. All human beings, as created by God are regarded to have a capacity for moral insight, independent of Christian

---

1. Billing, *Luthers lära om staten*, 89-90. See also Troeltsch, *The Social Teaching of the Christian Churches*, vol. II, 467-77.

2. Luther, *In epistolam S Pauli ad Galatas Commentarius*, WA 40.I, 40:16—41:26; WA 40.I, 392:19—393:29; WA 40.I, 46:19-30.

faith. The gospel and the conception of God's love in Christ are not regarded as giving any new substantial contribution to the content of ethics.

My purpose in this chapter is to give a critical analysis of this kind of Lutheran ethics, as developed by the German theologians Paul Althaus and Helmut Thielicke, and the Swedish ethicist Gustaf Wingren. My thesis is that the idea that moral insight is independent of the gospel and Christian faith is combined with a political ethic which is uncritical of the existing political power. Paul Althaus and Helmut Thielicke defend a theology of orders, which include a hierarchical ideal of justice and a sharp difference between individual ethics and social ethics. Gustaf Wingren does not accept this patriarchal theology of orders, but since his ethical position is based on creation alone, he does not succeed in elaborating a social ethical theory that provides resources for a critique of the prevailing social structures.

In this chapter I will argue that a more reasonable ethical theory in Lutheran tradition should be based not only on the doctrine of creation but also on Christology and Eschatology. This means that the sharp distinction between law and gospel should be challenged within a Lutheran ethical reflection in a post-Christian society. The doctrine of the two kingdoms should be abandoned in such a way that the conception of God's love and the idea of human equality, which are important in the gospel about Christ, are of also great relevance within political ethics. Thereby, Lutheran ethics could be an inspiration for social critique.

POLITICAL ETHICS IN LUTHERAN TRADITION

Political ethics in Lutheran tradition have often been related to the doctrine of God's two kingdoms. This doctrine, with its sharp distinction between law and gospel, has often been interpreted in such a way that it has legitimized existing social structures. According to the doctrine, the earthly authorities and political power should not be dependent on the church or any particular Christian ethic. The state should be governed by reason and natural law, which anyone can understand regardless of God's revelation in Christ. This means that the gospel does not inform the content of social ethics.

The distinction between the two kingdoms is closely related to three characteristic ideas in Luther's political ethics. First, it is based upon reason and natural law, as it is expressed in the Decalogue. The gospel does not give any contribution to the content of ethics. Secondly, Luther defends an ethical dualism according to which the content of political ethics is different from the Christian ideal of love, which is relevant only within private morality. Thirdly, his view of society is patriarchal, which means that it is our duty to obey superiors. Equality between humans before God has no relevance for the meaning of social justice.³

A clarifying analysis of political ethics in the Lutheran tradition is given by Ernst Troeltsch in his classical study *The Social Teaching of the Christian Churches*. He argues that the Lutheran ethic is of dual origin. On the one hand, there is an ideal of self-sacrificing love, but this is only relevant within individual ethics. On the other hand, natural law as summarized in the Decalogue is the norm that is guiding the state, the economic sphere, and the family. The law of nature is explained in an entirely conservative sense. It is interpreted in such a way that it glorifies power for its own sake and demands unconditional respect for authority as such.⁴

The social theory of Lutheranism is thus characterized by a patriarchal principle, according to which the authorities should care for the subordinate and those who are subordinate should respect the authority of those in power. In Lutheran ethics, increasing stress is laid on patriarchal virtues, such as care and responsibility for others, trust, and reverence. As Luther maintained both in his two Catechisms and in his *Treatise on Good Works*, the Fourth Commandment is the most important one in social ethics. The father who cares for his children and expects obedience from them is a model for those in political and economic authority.⁵

At the beginning of the twentieth Century, Lutheran ethics were given a distinct formation by some German theologians, who were most influenced by the Luther renaissance. They developed a theology of orders, according to which the state, the economy, the people, the family, and culture are orders, given by God in creation as frameworks for human life. God has a will for these orders of creation, but there is no Christian ethical model that differs from the morality of the people. This theology is developed in critique of modernist Protestantism, which was regarded as being too individualistic and too liberal.⁶

As Nils Ehrenström showed in his classical study of *Christian Faith and the Modern State*, the theology of orders is clearly related to the separation between the spiritual realm of the gospel and the temporal realm of the law. God works with human beings in two ways—as the Creator working in nature and history, and as the Redeemer who works in the spiritual sphere.

---

3. These three ideas are expressed quite clearly in Luther, *Von weltlicher Oberkeit, wie weit man ihr gehorsam schuldig sei*, WA 11, 251:1–31; WA 11, 253:17–32; WA 11, 254:27—255:21.

4. Troeltsch, *The Social Teaching of the Christian Churches*, vol. II, 523–27, 529–35.

5. Ibid., 540–44.

6. Ehrenström, *Christian Faith and the Modern State*, 99–107.

This means that the gospel is of no relevance for the formation of society. In society we should obey the secular authority and respect the existing order. Political ethics should emphasize the activity of the Creator in historically given orders of human life, above all in the nation and the state.[7]

There were three German theologians who were the most prominent advocates of this theology of orders, namely Friedrich Gogarten, Paul Althaus, and Emanuel Hirsch. They were all deeply influenced by Luther in their political ethics, and all of them supported National Socialism. Paul Althaus, who was professor of systematic theology in Erlangen, regarded the totalitarian state as an ideal and argued that the authority of the state was approved by God. In 1933 he looked upon Hitler and National Socialism as an expression of God's will. He based these political convictions upon his theology of orders, according to which the state, the people, the family, and the economy are orders, created by God to give stability to human life.[8]

A most clarifying exposition of this theology is given by Paul Althaus in his influential book *Theologie der Ordnungen*, first published in 1934. Here he writes that orders are frameworks for human life, which are necessary conditions for the historical life of humankind. They are given by God, but they also provide a task for humans. They are the means by which we can serve our fellow human beings and take responsibility for one another.[9]

The orders are given by God in creation and they are means for God's continuous creation at the present moment. At the same time, they are necessary in a world with sin and death, and they are often impressed by human sin. Even if they are given by God they are also God's law, which makes demands upon human beings. This law can be understood by all humans, but its most obvious expression is given in the Decalogue. Here it is made clear that God is the Lord of the orders, which means that they should not be given unconditional authority.[10]

According to Althaus, since orders appear in specific historical forms, they can always be criticized. They are formed by human beings, who as sinners do not always obey God's demands. Therefore, it is necessary to raise the critical question as to whether the orders in their historical shape fulfill the will of God. They should be evaluated from the perspective of God's law, as expressed in the Decalogue. This means that the gospel does not give any contribution to the content of social ethics. However, human reason is not

---

7. Ibid., 108–12.
8. Ericksen, *Theologians under Hitler*, 79–91, 98–109.
9. Althaus, *Theologie der Ordnungen*, 9.
10. Ibid., 13–18, 20–23.

enough to understand the content of the law. The Decalogue illustrates what is God's will, and is therefore a primary criterion in political ethics.[11]

The theology of orders should thus, according to Althaus, be combined with a critical evaluation of the state, the people, and the economic structure in their historical shape. These orders are namely not only created by God but also a part of human sin. An expression of this ambiguity of the orders is the relationship between the state and the people. Like Carl Schmitt, a leading legal theorist who supported National Socialism, Paul Althaus maintains that political life is characterized by an opposition between friend and enemy. Humankind is separated into different peoples, and every state is a means for its people. This separation means that we cannot serve our own people without fighting others.[12]

Contrary to the ambition to be critical, the theology of orders as it was developed by Paul Althaus was no basis for a critical evaluation of National Socialism. Quite the opposite, it gave strong support to the ideology of National Socialism, where the people were also given a particular role in history. This support was clearly expressed in the document which Paul Althaus together with Werner Elert and six other theologians signed in 1934. In this document, entitled "Der Ansbacher Ratschlag zur Barmen Theologischen Erklärung," they thank God that he has sent Adolf Hitler as a good leader of the German people. They write:

> In this knowledge we as believing Christians thank God that he has given to our *Volk* in its time of need the *Führer* as a 'pious and faithful sovereign', and that he wants to prepare for us in the National Social system of government 'good rule', a government with 'discipline and honor'. Accordingly, we know that we are responsible before God to assist the work of the *Führer* in our calling and in our station in life.[13]

GOD'S ORDERS AND GEOMETRICAL JUSTICE

The theology of orders maintains that ethical reflection is based upon the doctrine of creation and that the gospel does not give any substantial contribution to political ethics. This position is combined with a patriarchal principle, according to which the subordinate should obey the authorities. After World War II, most Lutheran theologians continued to defend this approach to ethics, which is related to the sharp distinction between law

---

11. Ibid., 29–36, 38–41.
12. Ibid., 48–51, 53–58.
13. Ericksen, *Theologians under Hitler*, 87.

and gospel. One of the German theologians in the middle of the twentieth century who were inspired by this theology of orders was Helmut Thielicke.

In his impressive work *Theologische Ethik* Thielicke argues that God has given us orders that are frameworks for human life. One of these orders—marriage—is given by God in creation. The others—state, economy, law, and culture—are given by God after the fall, in order to protect human beings from the evil that is a result of sin. This means that the orders are instruments used by God in a world impressed by human imperfection. The state—as well as economy, law, and culture—is related not only to creation but also to human sin, which means that it should never be given absolute authority.[14]

Helmut Thielicke emphasizes the sharp distinction between law and gospel. According to him, the capacity to understand this distinction is the criterion of a good theologian. On the one hand, we should not misunderstand law as a kind of gospel, since this would mean that we deny that justification before God is possible by grace alone. On the other hand, we should not misunderstand the gospel as a kind of law, in the sense that we believe that the gospel is a demand to live in the image of Christ, as a kind of particular contribution to ethics. We need to understand that God encounters human beings in two different ways.[15]

A consequence of this distinction is, according to Thielicke, that ethical reflection is not based upon Christology. He is criticizing the ideal of *imitatio Christi*, which means that we should try to follow Christ and regard his life as an ethical ideal. This is a way of making Christ into a law, and to abolish the distinction between law and gospel. According to Thielicke we should not accept a Christological political ethic, such as the one developed by Karl Barth. To believe that Christology can give a contribution to social ethics is to transform the gospel into law.[16]

In his political ethics Thielicke develops the doctrine of the two kingdoms instead. He argues that a primary idea in this doctrine is that social ethics should be based upon reason and human experience. In the secular realm there is no particular Christian ethic. Here Christians should cooperate with people without a Christian faith, and they have to argue in such a way that their reasons can be understood by all humans.[17]

---

14. Thielicke, *Theologische Ethik*, I. Band, 693–94, 701, 709. Thielicke, *Theologische Ethik*, II. Band, 2. Teil, 21–27, 135–38, 173–74.

15. Thielicke, *Theologische Ethik*, I. Band, 189–90, 203–4.

16. Ibid., 307–8. Thielicke, *Theologische Ethik*, II. Band, 2. Teil, 710–17.

17. Thielicke, *Theologische Ethik*, II. Band, 1. Teil, 371–83.

A main thesis in the doctrine of the two kingdoms is, according to Thielicke, that the secular realm should be governed by human reason and the law, not by the gospel. This means that this doctrine is closely related to the opposition between law and gospel. In the secular realm we cannot get any guidance from the gospel—instead we should rely upon reason and human considerations alone. If we in the political sphere try to derive guidance from the gospel, this would mean that we deny that human reason is given by God, and it would constitute an effort to transform the gospel into law.[18]

Therefore, the gospel should not be used as guidance in the political realm. Thielicke writes:

> Es würde eine Heteronomisierung der Vernuft und Zugleich ein Einstellung des Evangeliums zum Gesetz bedeuten, wenn das Evangelium zu einer Art Verfassung des Weltreiches und also auch des Politischen gemacht würde. Darum kann es keine Theokratie geben, sondern nur eine Ordnung, die nach dem Gesetz der von Gott verliehenen Vernunft und im Namen der Mündigkeit des Menschen gestaltet wird.[19]

Three ideas are important within the political ethics of Helmut Thielicke. First, he argues that the power of the state should be limited. In his view, the state is given by God after the fall, and its task is to protect human beings from the evil that is a result of human sin. Therefore, the state should use power and violence, in order to preserve human life. However, the authority of the state is not absolute, and we should avoid the risk of a totalitarian state. The state should be limited to a minimum, and its power should be shared with other institutions in society.[20]

This thesis of the minimum state means that Thielicke argues against the welfare state. If the state were to exceed its powers and take responsibility for the welfare of the citizens, it would be transformed into a pseudo-church with different tasks than protecting humans against evil. This would clearly be against the doctrine of the two kingdoms. It would also destroy the idea of human love for one's neighbor, as it is clarified in the parable of the Good Samaritan. What should be a personal and immediate love between individuals would then be transformed into planned and institutionalized care of fellow humans. This is a misunderstanding of the love commandment, and therefore the welfare state should be avoided.[21]

18. Thielicke, *Theologische Ethik*, II. Band, 2. Teil, 131–36.
19. Ibid., 131–32.
20. Ibid., 173–74, 216–20, 228–30, 302–6, 308–9, 314.
21. Ibid., 357–63.

Secondly, Thielicke argues that the state should be regarded as an authority (*Obrigkeit*)—even in a democratic society. This idea, that the state has a particular authority, is an important part of the doctrine of the two kingdoms. As an order, given by God after the fall, the state has the task of preserving human life against evil, and therefore it should be respected as an authority (*Obrigkeit*). This is not a defense of a totalitarian state, which according to Thielicke exceeds its powers by trying to develop a kind of welfare state. Instead, the idea of the state as an authority is a defense of the minimum state.[22]

However, the idea of the state as an authority (*Obrigkeit*) that should be obeyed by the citizens is possible to preserve in a democratic society. Even if Luther developed this idea in a feudal and patriarchal society, it is also applicable within modern democracy. Helmut Thielicke writes that democracy provides a new framework for the idea that the state is an authority (*die Obrigkeitsidee*), but it does not eliminate this idea.[23]

Thirdly, Thielicke has a conception of justice which is in accordance with a hierarchical view of society and the patriarchal principle. He argues that justice should take into consideration the equal worth of human beings and their similarities before God. At the same time justice should also consider the actual differences between human beings in society. Justice as *suum cuique* means, according to Thielicke, that everyone gets her due considering that all humans are different.[24]

Thielicke makes a distinction between "arithmetical justice" and "geometrical justice." Arithmetical justice means absolute equality, that is an equal distribution of goods. This kind of justice treats all humans equally and does not consider their individual differences. However, geometrical justice takes these differences regarding qualities and positions into consideration. Therefore, justice is not an equal distribution but a social arrangement where the differences between superiors and subordinates are respected. According to Thielicke we should promote this kind of geometrical justice within the state, the economy and the family.[25]

Thus, it is obvious that Helmut Thielicke defends a hierarchical view of society, according to which the state should be regarded as an authority and equality should not be promoted. This patriarchal ideal is justified by an ethical theory, which takes as its starting point a theology of orders. A sharp distinction is made between law and gospel, which means that

---

22. Ibid., 5–15, 20–29, 31–34, 68–77.
23. Ibid., 400–401, 452–53.
24. Thielicke, *Theologische Ethik*, III. Band, 330–38.
25. Ibid., 339–43.

ethical reflection is based on the doctrine of creation and not on Christology. Political ethics are a matter of reason and human considerations, and the gospel does not give any substantial contribution to ethics. This kind of Lutheran ethics does not provide resources for a critique of the prevailing social structures.

THE CREATION AND THE LAW

The theology of orders, which was developed by Paul Althaus and Helmut Thielicke, has been criticized by many theologians, even within the Lutheran tradition. One of those who did not accept this theology was the Swedish ethicist Gustaf Wingren. He regarded the theology of orders to be too conservative and too patriarchal. At the same time, he did defend the idea that ethical reflection is based on the doctrine of creation. God's creation is not finished but continuous, something going on at the present moment. It is related to an ethical demand, to take care of our fellow humans, but it cannot be articulated in any moral principles or static orders.

The thesis that the law is already given with the creation is developed by Gustaf Wingren in his important book *Skapelsen och lagen* (The Creation and the Law). Here he argues that creation means that my life is a gift and that it is always a relationship to God. In order to preserve human life we are always dependent of God's continuous creation. This creation is related to a radical ethical demand. In every relationship with another human being we are confronted with a demand to take care of her life. People in need are crying for help, and this demand to love our neighbor can be understood by all human beings, regardless of their belief in God.[26]

Gustaf Wingren is critical of the theology of orders. The idea that state, economy, family, and culture are orders of creation was related to an interpretation of creation that was too static. It did not take into consideration that God's creation is continuous, dynamic, and open to alteration. This theology was also too uncritical in its relationship with existing political and economic power. A more dynamic understanding of creation is open to a more critical attitude towards prevailing social structures and authorities.[27]

At the same time Wingren is also critical of the Christological ethics defended by Karl Barth, who argued that God's revelation in Christ is a necessity to acquire moral insight. This is a position that does not take into consideration that the law is given before the gospel and that every human being has the capacity to understand the ethical demand that is given by

---

26. Wingren, *Skapelsen och lagen*, 35–36, 39–40, 80–81.
27. Ibid., 54, 106.

life itself.[28] According to Wingren, Christology does not give any substantial contribution to the content of ethics. Christ can be understood to be a moral example, and we can be recommended to live in his image. But this means that we are recommended to do what we already know is good. Christ does not give us any new ethical demand that is different from what we know from creation.[29]

This means that Wingren makes a sharp distinction between law and gospel. If we want to understand Lutheran ethics, we need to understand that law and gospel are different in their nature and function in human life. The gospel is a message about justification by grace alone, thanks to the death and resurrection of Christ. It is a liberating address, which is proclaimed in the sermon. The law is given in creation and related to human life as such. It is a universal demand which is a part of every relationship between human beings.[30]

The opposition between law and gospel means that ethical reflection is based upon the doctrine of creation. There is an ethical demand to love our neighbor, which is given before Christ and independent of the gospel. Every human being can acquire moral insight and the gospel does not give any new contribution to the content of ethics. If we believe that Christology can contribute to ethics, the gospel is transformed from a radical message about liberation into a set of moral norms. At the same time the idea of creation is neglected and the universal character of ethics is obscured. The distinction between law and gospel should not be dissolved in this way.[31]

In his political ethics, Gustaf Wingren takes as his starting point the doctrine of the two kingdoms. According to him, this doctrine means that God acts with human beings in two different ways to obtain two different objectives. In the secular realm the Creator is acting through the law in order to protect human life and preserve peace. In the spiritual realm God is acting through the gospel in order to establish a kingdom where death is conquered and human sin does not prevent community between God and humans. The distinction between the two kingdoms is thus closely related to the opposition between law and gospel.[32]

Wingren argues that God is using the authorities in the secular realm in order to punish those who offend the law and harm their fellow humans.

28. Ibid., 21–24, 170–71.
29. Wingren, *Evangeliet och kyrkan*, 36–37, 190–91.
30. Wingren, *Etik och kristen tro*, 114–16.
31. Wingren, *Evangeliet och kyrkan*, 178–79. Wingren, *Växling och kontinuitet*, 174–175, 180.
32. Wingren, *Skapelsen och lagen*, 154–55. See also Wingren, *Luther frigiven*, 92–94.

In order to preserve social order and peace the authorities are allowed to use violence and coercion. This is God's way of protecting humans from evil in the secular realm. At the same time this is a danger, since power and violence can be misused. Therefore we should always be prepared to criticize existing authorities and social structures. However, we should know that God is ruling in the secular realm, even when the authorities are using their power in a way that is wrong.[33]

The doctrine of the two kingdoms has two implications for the political ethics of Gustaf Wingren. First, political ethics should not be related to the gospel and Christology. If Christians participate in the public debate by referring to Christology, their arguments cannot be accepted by all humans in a secular society. This is a kind of sectarianism that does not accept that God in his creation is using all human beings, regardless of their Christian faith. Instead, political ethics should be based upon creation and human reason should govern in political life. The gospel is a message about justification by grace alone and not a program for political actions.[34]

Secondly, Wingren makes a clear distinction between individual ethics and political ethics. In politics certain actions can be approved which are not acceptable in a relationship between individual persons. There is, according to Wingren, a difference between person and office. In office it is often necessary to use violence and coercion in order to protect humans, but in a personal relationship violence should never be acceptable. In individual ethics love can be sacrificial and may include a love of one's enemies, but this is not possible in political ethics. This is obviously a kind of ethical dualism.[35]

In Lutheran tradition the doctrine of the two kingdoms has often been related to a patriarchal principle, according to which the subordinate should obey the authorities and existing social structures should be accepted. This is not the case in the theology of Gustaf Wingren. On the contrary, he argues that this doctrine inspires a continuous critique of those in political power. They have the right to use violence and coercion, but in the secular realm we should always critically evaluate the way in which they exercise their responsibilities. Since God's creation is continuous, dynamic, and open to alterations we should also be prepared to critically examine existing political structures. In these ways Lutheran ethics should inspire social critique.[36]

33. Wingren, *Skapelsen och lagen*, 150–53, 157–58. Wingren, *Evangeliet och kyrkan*, 120–21.

34. Wingren, *Etik och kristen tro*, 132–34. Wingren, *Växling och kontinuitet*, 13–14, 65–66.

35. Wingren, *Skapelsen och lagen*, 151–52, 154–55, 158–59.

36. Ibid., 158. Wingren, *Växling och kontinuitet*, 41–42, 70–71.

However, Wingren does not give any guidance as regards such a critique of political authorities. He argues that there are no political ideals or moral principles within Christian social ethics. Instead Christians should live in the world together with other human beings, and in every new situation the individual should use her reason to try to find out what is the right thing to do. Above all, we should try to listen to the cry from persons in need. However, Wingren does not tell us what kind of society we should strive for. Sometimes he seems to accept the idea of human rights, but he does not elaborate any theory of justice.[37]

Thus, the political ethic of Gustaf Wingren is empty in its normative content. He is open to critique of the political authorities and the prevailing social structures, but he does not elaborate on any social ethical theory that provides resources for such a critique. The reason is the sharp distinction he draws between law and gospel, and his separation between God's two kingdoms. This means that we in political life should accept a lot of actions that are not permitted within individual ethics. Another consequence is that Christian faith does not make any substantial contributions to our reflection about what is good and fair in society. The law is given with creation, not with the gospel.

CHRISTOLOGY AND SOCIAL CRITIQUE

In this chapter, I have given a critical analysis of the interpretation of Lutheran ethics, as developed by the German theologians Paul Althaus and Helmut Thielicke, and the Swedish ethicist Gustaf Wingren. We have seen that all of them draw a sharp distinction between law and gospel, and that they make a clear discrimination between God's two kingdoms. These distinctions mean that ethical reflection is based on the doctrine of creation, not on Christology or Eschatology. All human beings, as created by God, have capacity to acquire moral insight, regardless of God's revelation in Christ. The gospel does not make any substantial contribution to the content of ethics.

My thesis is that this kind of Lutheran ethics is combined with a political ethic that is uncritical of the existing power. The British theologian Duncan Forrester has argued that there are three different ways of understanding the political responsibility of the church. One is a *legitimizing* position, which means that political theology supports the existing society and the authorities in power. This is a "Eusebian political theology," according to which there is perfect harmony between church and state, and the political authority is regarded to be God's representative on earth. This position

---

37. Wingren, *Credo*, 139–40. Wingren, *Växling och kontinuitet*, 133–34.

underlines the responsibility of those in power, but it is a theological justification of the status quo.[38]

The second is a *sectarian* position, which means that the church withdraws from society and develops an alternative Christian community. This is a "church political theology" which is associated with the name of Tertullian. Within the church, Christians live by their own moral standards which are quite different from those in the surrounding society. The sectarian position is represented today by Stanley Hauerwas who argues that the primary social task of the church is to be itself, and that the church is social ethics.[39]

The third is a *prophetic* position, which means that Christian ethics give perspectives for social critique and a vision for a more just society. This "prophetic theology" is related to the thought of Augustine and developed both by the Christian realism of Reinhold Niebuhr and Latin American liberation theology. This position demands a critical social analysis and a deep involvement in the complexities of political life.[40]

Without doubt Lutheran political ethics has often taken a legitimizing position. This is obviously the case with the theology of orders as it was developed by Paul Althaus. He accepted a patriarchal principle, according to which we should obey authority and respect the existing order, and he even supported National Socialism. It is also the case with Helmut Thielicke, who defends a hierarchical view of society, according to which the state should be regarded as an authority and equality should not be promoted. He justifies this patriarchal ideal by an ethical theory that is related to a theology of orders and a sharp distinction between law and gospel.

We have seen that even though Gustaf Wingren is critical of this patriarchal theology of orders, he does not succeed in developing a prophetic position. He does not elaborate on any ethical theory that provides resources for a critique of political authorities, and he does not provide any vision for an alternative and better society. The reason is the sharp distinction he draws between law and gospel, and his separation of God's two kingdoms. This means that the law is given with creation, and that the gospel does not make any contribution to political ethics.

My conclusion is that Lutheran ethics cannot be based upon creation and reason alone, if we wish to avoid a legitimizing position. A more reasonable ethical theory in Lutheran theology should also be based upon Christology and Eschatology. Ethical reflection is related to the doctrine of creation, which means that all humans have a capacity to acquire at least a

---

38. Forrester, *Theology and Politics*, 160–63.
39. Ibid., 163–68. Hauerwas, *A Community of Character*, 10, 113.
40. Forrester, *Theology and Politics*, 168–71.

partial moral insight through rational considerations. This means that the content of Christian ethics is not totally different from moral principles and values in other traditions. Thereby it is possible to avoid a sectarian position and to establish a dialogue between different traditions.

However, ethical reflection is also related to Christology and Eschatology, which means that we need the guidance of God's revelation in Christ to acquire a comprehensive moral insight. Ethical reflection is based upon both reason and revelation. We have moral insights that are based on reason, but Christology and Eschatology can provide new perspectives on morality. This means that Christian faith can give new perspectives on what constitutes a good human life and an ideal human community. Thereby it is possible to develop a prophetic position and critique of the society around us.[41]

Christology can contribute to ethical reflection in several ways. The message about God's love in Christ is related to an idea of equality, according to which all human beings have an equal worth before God regardless of their merits. This idea of equality should also be applied within political ethics. Furthermore, the gospel is related to an image of God's sacrificial love in Christ, which gives a new perspective on love between humans. This ideal of sacrificial love is relevant not only within individual ethics but also within political ethics. It is often combined with a sharp critique of the established authorities in society, as we can learn from the stories about Jesus Christ.[42]

Eschatology is also an obvious resource for a critique of existing social structures. Its primary focus is the image of an ideal human community in the future Kingdom of God. This is an ethical ideal, where the needs of the poor are satisfied, there is no oppression and all human beings are living in a community shaped by peace and justice. The relationships between humans are those characterized by Jesus in his Sermon on the Mount. This ideal can never be realized in this temporal society, but from this perspective every prevailing social structure is regarded as being imperfect. Thus Eschatology is an inspiration to continuous social critique.[43]

Christian ethics should thus be developed within a Trinitarian framework. As a consequence, the sharp distinction between law and gospel should be challenged within a Lutheran ethical reflection in a post-Christian society. This distinction can be accepted as a way of clarifying the doctrine of justification by grace alone. According to this doctrine, human beings

---

41. Grenholm, *Bortom humanismen. En studie i kristen etik*, 257–60.

42. On the role of Christology in politics, see Forrester, *Theology and Politics*, 117–27.

43. On the role of Eschatology in ethics, see Dussel, *Ethics and Community*, 13–16, 27–31, 47–54.

cannot deserve justification before God by acting in accordance with the law. The only thing required from humans is faith and trust in Christ. The gospel is a message about a justification that is possible regardless of the law.

However, the distinction between law and gospel should be abandoned as a starting point for ethical reflection if it means that the gospel about God's love by grace alone does not have any implications for the content of ethics. The consequence of this idea is an ethical theory that does not criticize social injustice and a hierarchical society. Self-sacrificial love is not regarded as relevant in political ethics and the equality between humans before God does not apply to the secular realm. Lutheran ethic will thus take a legitimizing position in its relationship to hierarchical societies and the existing authorities.

A Lutheran political ethic that promoted equality and took a critical position in relation to the existing society would need a different theological starting point. It would regard the Christian ideal of love to be relevant not only within individual ethics but also in politics. This would be a political ethic that accepts that all human beings can have an understanding of what love and justice means. At the same time it would be inspired by the gospel about God's grace and love in Christ. The gospel would give a deeper understanding of what love between humans should mean, and provide a perspective on the meaning of equality between humans.

It is important that ethical reflection in Lutheran tradition is not based upon the revelation in Christ alone. Models of Christian ethics that are entirely based on the gospel tend to become sectarian positions, which cannot develop a dialogue with people outside the Christian community. This is the case with the position of Stanley Hauerwas. However, ethical reflection in Lutheran tradition is also based upon creation. Thereby cooperation with persons in other traditions is possible in the public sphere. In order to develop a prophetic position it is necessary to admit that both human reason and the gospel can contribute to our ethical reflection.

If the opposition between law and gospel were challenged in this respect, it would be possible to develop a reasonable alternative to the hierarchical view of society in the Lutheran tradition. Lutheran political ethic would be an inspiration for social critique, if it took as its starting point not only creation but also Christology and Eschatology. The message about God's love in Christ would then be interpreted as a message about a radical love that challenges current relationships between humans. The image of the Kingdom of God would be regarded as a vision of solidarity, peace, and equality, and this vision would make apparent the deficiencies of the prevailing society.

To challenge the sharp distinction between law and gospel also implies questioning the doctrine of the two kingdoms. An important idea in Lutheran theology is that in the spiritual realm God acts through the Word and not through the law. Human deeds are not relevant in this realm, since we are justified by grace alone. However, it would be reasonable to admit that in the secular realm God is using not only the law and the sword. The gospel about God's love in Christ is relevant within this realm as well. It will inform us about the meaning of equality between human beings and the importance of sacrificial love. From this perspective, the justice we should strive for is not a patriarchal relationship between authorities and subordinates.

BIBLIOGRAPHY

Althaus, Paul. *Theologie der Ordnungen*. Zweite, erweiterte Auflage. Gütersloh: Bertelsmann, 1935.
Billing, Einar. *Luthers lära om staten*. Stockholm: Verbum, 1971.
Dussel, Enrique. *Ethics and Community*. Maryknoll, NY: Orbis, 1988.
Ehrenström, Nils. *Christian Faith and the Modern State*. London: SCM, 1937.
Ericksen, Robert P. *Theologians under Hitler. Gerhard Kittel, Paul Althaus and Emanuel Hirsch*. New Haven: Yale University Press, 1985.
Forrester, Duncan B. *Theology and Politics*. Oxford: Basil Blackwell, 1988.
Grenholm, Carl-Henric. *Bortom humanismen. En studie i kristen etik*. Stockholm: Verbum, 2003.
Hauerwas, Stanley. *A Community of Character: Toward a Constructive Christian Social Ethic*. Notre Dame: University of Notre Dame Press, 1981.
Luther, Martin. *In epistolam S Pauli ad Galatas Commentarius* (1535). WA 40, Erste Abteilung. Weimar: Hermann Böhlaus Nachfolger, 1911. WA 40, Zweite Abteilung. Weimar: Hermann Böhlaus Nachfolger, 1910.
———. *Von den guten Werken* (1520). WA 6. Weimar: Hermann Böhlau, 1888.
———. *Von weltlicher Oberkeit, wie weit man ihr gehorsam shuldig sei* (1523). WA 11. Weimar: Hermann Böhlaus Nachfolger, 1900.
Thielicke, Helmut. *Theologische Ethik*, I. Band. Tübingen: JCB Mohr (Paul Siebeck), 1951.
———. *Theologische Ethik*, II. Band, 1. Teil. Tübingen: JCB Mohr (Paul Siebeck), 1959.
———. *Theologische Ethik*, II. Band, 2. Teil. Tübingen: JCB Mohr (Paul Siebeck), 1966.
———. *Theologische Ethik*, III. Band. Tübingen: JCB Mohr (Paul Siebeck), 1964.
Troeltsch, Ernst. *The Social Teaching of the Christian Churches*. Vol. II. Louisville: Westminster John Knox, 1992.
Wingren, Gustaf. *Credo. Den kristna tros- och livsåskådningen*. Lund: LiberLäromedel, 1975.
———. *Evangeliet och kyrkan*. Lund: Gleerups, 1960.
———. *Luther frigiven. Tema med sex variationer*. Lund: Gleerups, 1970.
———. *Skapelsen och lagen*. Lund: Gleerups, 1958.
———. *Växling och kontinuitet. Teologiska kriterier*. Lund: CWK Gleerup, 1972.
———, editor. *Etik och kristen tro*. Lund: CWK Gleerup, 1971.

7

Outside Paradise

Renegotiating Original Sin in Contemporary Lutheran Theology

EVA-LOTTA GRANTÉN

What is a reasonable Lutheran understanding of Original Sin today? Is it possible to defend a doctrine of Original Sin in a society where a scientific world view is widely accepted? If so, how can this doctrine be developed and renegotiated? These are some of the questions I have dealt with in a study on Original Sin in Lutheran theology with the title "Outside Paradise."[1]

The study is part of a larger research project, which seeks to clarify and critically analyze the content of several central ideas in Lutheran theology and ethics. One aim is to analyze some important theological and ethical positions, which can be found in Martin Luther's own thoughts. These include his particular understanding of sin, justification, grace, morality, and vocation. Another aim is to analyze how these ideas have been further developed in later Lutheran tradition. A third aim is to critically assess different positions in Lutheran tradition and to constructively tackle the question as to what a fruitful formation of Lutheran theology and ethics might look like in today's post-Christian and multicultural society.

Sin is undoubtedly of crucial importance in Martin Luther's own theology. Luther believed that human nature is sinful, described as being without fear of God, without trust in God, and with **concupiscence**. Luther described Original Sin in his Lectures on Romans:

1. Granténn, *Utanför Paradiset*.

it is the propensity toward evil. It is a nausea toward the good, a loathing of light and wisdom, and a delight in error and darkness, a flight from and an abomination of all good works, a pursuit of evil.[2]

This became part of the Lutheran confession, as exemplified by Confessio Augustana's second article on Original Sin. But is it possible to talk about the dogma in a post-Christian society, and how should contemporary theology talk about Original Sin?

Through the development of historical critical methods in biblical exegesis and, likewise, critical methods in the natural sciences, certain aspects of the dogma have been challenged, like the existence of an ancient paradise, or the inheritance of sin from humanity's two ancestors, Adam and Eve. A literary understanding of the creation narrative does not correlate with the contemporary world view or understanding, and as a consequence the dogma of Original Sin faces the risk of becoming unintelligible. Modernity also challenges the notion of human nature as "sinful," on the basis that maybe it is society that makes people commit evil and selfish acts. In contemporary theology, sin is also understood to be something that permeates not only individuals but also social systems. The confession has a focus on individual sin and concupiscence, which, for a modern interpreter, seems to limit the understanding of Original Sin. Beyond the questions that address the intelligibility and scope of the dogma of Original Sin lies another important issue. The risk is that people cannot relate the dogma to their own experiences. People's existential questions nowadays center on meaningfulness and individual fulfilment, rather than on guilt before God, and this could result in the dogma on Original Sin becoming irrelevant. In sum, a post-Christian and pluralistic society challenges Lutheran theology to *renegotiate* its understanding of Original Sin. I use the term "renegotiate" to describe the *process* in which contemporary theology should respond to questions regarding intelligibility and relevance. A renegotiation occurs within a tradition when it meets new perspectives and challenges from outside the tradition in order to make it possible to continue to talk about theology in a way that makes it plausible—that is understandable and meaningful—in a post-Christian society.

One of the main questions is whether it is at all possible to formulate a Lutheran theology on Original Sin that appears reasonable today, with

---

2. Luther, *Lectures on Romans*, LW 25, 299. The original text is found in Luther, *Römervorlesung*, WA 56, 312: "Insuper et pronitas ipsa ad malum, Nausea ad bonum, fastidium lucis et sapientię, dilectio autem erroris ac tenebrarum, fuga et abominatio bonorum operum, Cursus autem ad malum."

"reasonable" being understood as "intelligible and relevant." Alternatively, should Lutherans abandon this old dogma? I am not prepared to lay it to rest. The main reason is that our experience tells us that things are not the way they could or should be. People can recognize themselves in Paul's reflection in Romans: "For I do not do the good I want, but the evil I do not want is what I do" (Rom 7:19). People experience themselves as rather ambivalent, and they cannot experience the world we inhabit in any other way, either—and that goes for all humanity. There is something ambivalent in the human situation that all religions and secular world views must face. A faith like Christianity, that confesses a good Creator God and wrestles with the existence of destruction and evil, needs to reflect upon these issues even further. Since the age of the Church Fathers different versions of the dogma of Original Sin have been developed and used to interpret the human situation in the face of sin and evil, and the dogma must therefore continue to be developed—I would like to phrase it renegotiated—not abandoned.

THE CHALLENGE FROM BIBLICAL EXEGESIS

Original Sin can be analyzed as a dogmatic system within Christian theology, and it can be described as a coherent interpretation of the negative ("evil") aspect of the general conditions for human existence. There is of course a positive ("good") aspect as well. We understand sin and evil dialectically against their alternatives: perfection, paradise, the Kingdom of God. These alternatives have one thing in common: we cannot find them either in nature or in history. We live "Outside Paradise." I use the word "we" to illustrate one important claim within the dogmatic system—universal validity. It is part and parcel of being human; it refers to a state connected to the human species and its members.

Although all living creatures experience nature as life-sustaining, it is also always experienced as hostile. Humans interpret these experiences and find nature ambivalent. That goes for their neighbors and themselves as well. Ambivalence permeates the human state or situation, with consequences like mistrust in goodness, anxiety, violence, and selfishness. Such mistrust, anxiety, selfishness, and violence threaten life and well-being, and they enslave people in an endless struggle for security for themselves and their loved ones. This is because of our common human capacity to interpret the state we live in, and the common capacity to long for a less ambivalent alternative. The capacity to imagine something entirely non-ambivalent—without pain, grief, selfishness, or death, for example—something that does not exist, and never has existed, in nature is a result of human cognitive evolution. However, it is not only a unique and common human capacity.

To be able to think about and long for a different state than we all experience also define us as human, because it has implications for human self-understanding. Not only do we experience our existence as situated "outside paradise" and act upon it, we also stand judged by the paradise we dream of, because we fall short of it. All interpretations of the human condition or state belong in this gap between the imagined perfect state, or longed for paradise, and the individual and shared experiences of imperfect state, as well as the ambivalence of the present and past situation.

Christianity confesses God as the good Creator, and human beings as created in God's image. God has a relationship with every human being. But there is brokenness in this relationship. In Christianity, the brokenness in the trustful relationship between humanity and God has been labelled sin, and the origin and universality of this mistrust or disbelief has been codified in the dogma of "Original Sin." The doctrine relates to biblical understandings of sin as resulting from being separated from God. According to the doctrine, this broken relationship with God is the result of human disbelief in a good Creator, and it results in death, enslavement and guilt before God and before creation.[3] According to the doctrine, sin entered the world as early as with the first humans. Nature is interpreted as "fallen" (from a state where there was no sin) while sin is portrayed as inevitable. This doctrine has played an important role in Christian and especially Lutheran theology. The Lutheran version of the doctrine of Original Sin can be described as the Lutheran tradition's interpretation of human experience of the ambivalence found within human existence. Original Sin is defined as *unbelief*—not believing in God or the goodness of God—and Original Sin has consequences. It results in death, selfishness, and worship of the creation rather than of the Creator. Sin becomes manifest not only in the life of the individual but also at group level, such as, for instance, in xenophobia and in environmental devastation.

Today, as I noted earlier, this doctrine faces challenges. The results of contemporary biblical exegesis are of particular importance, because of their fundamental relevance to any theology claiming to be Lutheran. The formal principle in Lutheran theology of *Sola Scriptura* can be interpreted to mean that no doctrine can stand without valid biblical support. Even with a more careful interpretation—that theological arguments must not deliver results contrary to Scripture—it is of crucial importance for Lutheran theology to pay attention to the relationship between biblical texts and doctrine.

---

3. In biblical narratives of how this relationship is restored, God is the actor. God is the giver of new life, the one who liberates from captivity and forgives sin. For example, the Pauline letters claim that Christ saves people from death (1 Cor 15:22), slavery (Rom 6:16), and guilt (Rom 3:23–24).

The issue here is that our understanding of what "valid" means in regard to biblical texts has changed significantly since the establishment of historical critical methods in biblical studies. If our understandings of central biblical texts change in a significant way, the dogmas relying on them might also need to be reinterpreted.[4]

The concept of sin is not something of minor importance in the Bible; it is central in the whole body of biblical texts. The word "sin" can refer to separate actions, e.g. breaking the law. However, a human being can also be a sinner, and sin can be described as a power. The Bible presents an account of how sin entered God's good creation in the third chapter of Genesis, and this is obviously a central text behind the dogma. In what way has our understanding of this chapter of the Bible changed? Old Testament scholars unite in describing the Eden narrative as a myth.[5] That means that it does not give a historical account of something that "really happened;" rather, it seeks to say something general about the human state. The mythical character of the first chapters of Genesis signifies that they deal with humanity as a whole, not with tangible historical persons. However, both Augustine and Luther took the historicity of Adam and Eve for granted (there was no alternative theory of the creation of humankind or any other life), and consequently portrayed our physical nature as bearer of sin's history. Augustine also made use of the knowledge of his time to explain how sin moved on to the next generation through procreation. Besides questioning the historical claim of the creation story, exegesis shows that the historical "fall" from original perfection or innocence into a state of corruptibility that Augustine and Luther read into the text does not occur in the narrative in Genesis 3; rather, the corruptibility of humans is a precondition for the temptation to act against the will of God. Both of these exegetical claims are of importance for Lutheran theology on Original Sin.

Starting with the claim that Genesis 3 (as a part of the pre-history found in Genesis 1–11) is myth, not history, this deserves some attention. Human beings do not live outside history. Ruling out Adam and Eve as historical figures leaves theology with having to find another history for the beginning of mankind, and another historical account of how sin entered God's creation. Does the doctrine of Original Sin stand or fall with the existence of Adam and Eve and the Paradise as historical facts? This appears not to be the case in Lutheran theology. The theologians Ted Peters and Wenzel van Huyssteen, among others, have pointed to the decisive human

---

4. For a discussion of the relevance of exegesis for dogmas, see Schleiermacher, *The Christian Faith* (1830) §25.

5. Westermann, *Genesis 1–11: A Commentary*. Mettinger, *The Eden Narrative*.

ability to imagine a life in paradise, maybe in a distant pre-history, maybe in a coming New Jerusalem (Rev 21), as sufficient for a theology on sin and grace in Lutheran theology. According to these theologians, there is no need for an ancient historical paradise in order for there to be a longing for an existence in paradise. Both Peters and van Huyssteen conduct dialogue with contemporary natural science when they reflect on sin and grace. Science tells us that humans evolved in history, together with the rest of the living world. Evolution shaped the human brain, and human cognitive capacities. At some time in human history, cognitive evolution allowed for humans to start reflecting on the ambivalence they experienced in life, in relation to a longed for alternative, not found in nature. In the course of history, humans started to view themselves as living "outside paradise," to long for "paradise," and to conceptualize this in terms of sin and grace.[6]

For contemporary Lutheran theology on sin, this means that focus in the dogma of Original Sin should shift from the origin (of the first) sin or the hereditary component of sin towards the universal and inevitable aspects of sin. The interpretation suggested by Peters and van Huyssteen also makes it easier to integrate faith and science, since a scientific world view includes an understanding of the human species as evolved in history, rather than as created at a specific point in history.

THE CHALLENGE FROM EVOLUTIONARY THEORY

However, much larger issues than the temporal location of paradise arise if theology starts dealing with the second exegetical claim—that there is no fall in the narrative found in Genesis 3. The "Fall from Life to Death" is the classical basis behind the doctrine of Original Sin, which portrays death and suffering as God's righteous judgment on human sin. Originally, the world was not characterized by death or suffering; the Creator and the creation were good. In order to face this challenge, it is helpful to take a closer look at the scientific description of the biological history of the creation, something that is also called for by the fact that evolutionary biology intensifies the problem of evil. The theory of evolution tells us that all living beings have a common ancestor, and life has diversified from this ancestor into all species that live or have lived on planet Earth. The species are constantly and gradually changing, and the mechanism for this gradual change is selection within varieties within a population, a variation nowadays known to be genetic. Some variants reproduce more successfully than others because they have a genetic make-up adapted to their environment. The key mechanism of evolution is called natural selection, and it is defined as the gradual

---

6. Peters, "The Evolution of Evil"; Van Huyssteen, *Alone in the World*.

process by which biological traits become either more or less common in a population as a function of the effect of inherited traits on the differential reproductive success of organisms interacting with their environment. This mechanism is not teleological. Furthermore, death is integral to multicellular life and extinction is integral to the evolution of species. Selection always occurs at the level of the individual, meaning that one successful strategy for individuals to survive and reproduce is to behave in ways that secure your own existence, to be "selfish."

Taking evolutionary theory seriously thus means several things for theology. How does God create through evolution? Several models have been developed, such as theistic evolution, process theology, and natural theology. What is more important is how theology understands God as Creator in light of the so called "theodicy of nature"—the unfeeling brutality of evolutionary history, and the in-built problem of extinction. A believer can find it hard to accept that natural selection is the handiwork of a personal, good, and loving Creator God. More specific challenges face the doctrine of Original Sin. What about death? Death cannot be said to be a consequence of "the fall," it is constitutive of life itself. There is also no clear point in history where sin entered. If sin is understood as mistrust in the goodness of creation, it may well be that as soon as human beings evolved a capacity to reflect upon the ambivalent state of their existence, unbelief or mistrust occurred. Taking today's evolutionary science seriously not only rules out the fall as a historical event, but also challenges understandings of creation as good. One can sum up all these questions in one major challenge. Why did God choose to create a universe with laws knowing that they would not only make evolution possible but also with it the problem of natural evil, death, extinction, mistrust, and sin caused by natural selection and the ambivalent state it puts human beings in?

Ted Peters is among those who have responded to this challenge. For Peters, as for me, it is clear that the scientific explanation cannot replace the doctrine of Original Sin, since the historical and natural theory, although it can provide an explanation for the origin of sinfulness, cannot provide any explanation or understanding of the human longing for redemption, or, in Christian words, human relationship with God in Christ. He concludes that you cannot discuss natural evil in the context of the theology of creation. It must move into a theology of redemption. He suggests an expansion of Luther's "Theology of the Cross," to include not only humanity but also nature in God's redemptive work through Jesus Christ.[7] According to the theology of the cross, the glory of the Creator is hidden behind suffering

---

7. Peters, "Grace, Doubt, and Evil"; Peters, *The Evolution of Terrestrial and Extraterrestrial Life*.

and death. Luther says about the person seeking God: "It does him no good to recognize God in his glory and majesty, unless he recognizes him in the humility and shame of the cross. (. . .) God can be found only in suffering and the cross."[8] God shares in our suffering, and also in the suffering of nature, Peters claims. The resources to expand theology from human history to nature's history are found in the recognition of Christ as the firstborn of the whole creation, and in viewing his cross as applying to the natural domain. God shares in the suffering of the world, and includes the creation in God's promise of a New Creation.[9]

In summary, science, both in the shape of historical critical method in biblical exegesis, and natural science, challenges Lutheran theology to renegotiate its understanding and interpretation of the doctrine of Original Sin. But renegotiation is sufficient; science in no way rules out the doctrine. On the contrary, evolutionary science gives support to the notion that human existence is ambivalent, and also to the claim that finding the state you live in as a human being ambivalent has universal validity. Exegetical scholarship supports an understanding of the narrative of Adam and Eve as myth. That means that it says something important and universal about humanity. Such a renegotiation of the doctrine also has the benefit of correlating with a modern world view and it makes the doctrine of Original Sin more intelligible.

THE CONTENT OF ORIGINAL SIN RENEGOTIATED

Contemporary Lutheran theologians should not only revisit Luther and his theology of the cross to increase the intelligibility of the doctrine of Original Sin; they could also learn something from Luther regarding the relevance of their work. Luther took cause against indulgences and the mediatorial function of the Church because guilt and forgiveness were the dominant existential questions and experiences of his time, including for him personally.

In Luther's time the basic feeling in religion was fear, the devil was real, and the common belief was that God punished people with pestilence, famine, and war. After his own experience of a loving God, Luther engaged in strategic and cognitive work in order to accomplish an emotional turn from fear to joy, and from anxiety to trust, claims Luther scholar Birgit Stolt.[10] Contemporary theology must work in the same way and face the issues of importance to people, especially those that connect to people's experiences. If sin before God coupled to a fear of Judgment Day has given way to experi-

---

8. Luther, *Heidelberg Disputation*, LW 31, 52–53.
9. Peters, *The Evolution of Terrestrial and Extra-terrestrial Life*.
10. Stolt, *Lasst uns fröhlich springen*.

ences connected to the meaning of life and individual perfection, as I have discussed elsewhere, would not an expansion of Lutheran theology into a broader understanding of sin and grace be rather helpful when dealing with the challenges of pluralism found in late modern society?[11]

Although some decades have passed since Reinhold Niebuhr grappled with the understanding of sin in Lutheran theology, I find his reflections on these themes relevant. With an economy in crisis, increasing nationalism and group egoism, it can be said that similar challenges face people now as in the 1940s. His interpretation of the doctrine of Original Sin is also compatible with modern biblical exegesis. His dialectical method allows for critique of theological traditions as well as identification and critique of contemporary manifestations of Original Sin.[12]

Niebuhr discusses the ambivalence in the human situation as finite freedom. The issue of freedom represents another theological approach to the problem of sin, besides the tradition of the "fall." How can human freedom be exercised in God's creation? The ability to strive beyond the historical existence that freedom entails tempts humans to think too much about themselves, and the root of sin thus lies in the human situation itself, because this freedom is restricted, chiefly by death. It results in anxiety, in itself an ambivalent concept, because it not only tempts people to sin, it is also a precondition for human creativity and curiosity. Niebuhr defines the problem of meaning as the basic problem in religion today. Meaning is threatened by death. Faced with their mortality, humans become anxious, and start to seek power to guarantee their own security, inevitably at the expense of other life, including non-human life. Although the questions relating to a lack of meaning differ, the attempts to solve them have the same outcome—sin. Furthermore, collective sin expressed in pride exceeds those of the individual, Niebuhr argues:

> In its whole range from pride of family to pride of nation, collective egotism and group pride are a more pregnant source of injustice and conflict than purely individual pride.[13]

The church is no exception—it can become a vehicle for collective egoism. All human knowledge is also permeated by sin, according to Niebuhr. Nor

---

11. See Grantén, "Religioners bidrag till samtal i det offentliga rummet: om människovärde och kroppslig perfektion."

12. Niebuhr, *The Nature and Destiny of Man: A Christian Interpretation*. For example, Niebuhr talks about interpretations of death as a punishment for sin as a chronological mistake. Niebuhr, *The Nature and Destiny of Man: A Christian Interpretation*, vol. 1, 174.

13. Ibid., 213.

does sin decrease through increased knowledge of what is right and wrong. Humans regularly fail to recognize the limits of knowledge, including scientific knowledge. Finally, moral pride can even make virtue a vehicle for sin, and sinners claim to have some special knowledge or moral superiority that justifies the sin and egoism. Interestingly, Niebuhr finds Luther's comment on the unwillingness to recognize oneself as a sinner as the final form of sin as valid now as in Luther's day.[14] In short, there is plenty for contemporary Lutheran theology to address.

Niebuhr provides some criteria on how to recognize sin. It must connect to the human situation of anxiety; anxiety manifested in avoidance of dependence on others, striving to escape mortality and denial of judgment. Strategies to escape from anxiety necessarily lead to injustice and oppression. Niebuhr's ability to stand at a critical distance from the tradition allowed him to see clearly that Lutheran theology was lacking in its ability to identify sin in relation to the fourth commandment, something that had devastating consequences in his own time.[15] Lutheran theology must be able to harbor not only individual, but also collective and structural sin.

Niebuhr's analysis is especially helpful when it comes to the quest for inner and outer perfection that permeates so much of society today. People should stay happy, young and healthy, popular, and become famous, and if they do not succeed in their efforts to achieve these states, no one is to be blamed but the individual. Anxiety permeates this quest, and the message runs counter to the gospel; and Niebuhr is the first to recognize that the world is still in great need of the gospel. The gospel is grace, understood in Christianity both as God's forgiveness of human sin and as new life in Christ. Niebuhr would like to see a renewed synthesis between these two aspects of grace, mainly because we must recognize that life in history is filled with indeterminate possibilities, while on the other hand every effort to eliminate the final corruption of history must be disavowed.[16] Interestingly, such a development has occurred in Lutheran theology in the last few decades.[17]

Thus, the abundance of sin does not mean that life outside paradise is of no importance to Niebuhr. On the contrary, he contributes a great deal when it comes to the crucial question of how we can live together in a good and righteous way in a pluralistic society. Niebuhr introduces the

---

14. Ibid., 200.

15. Ibid., 269.

16. Niebuhr, *The Nature and Destiny of Man: A Christian Interpretation*, vol. 2, 207.

17. See for example Mannermaa, *Christ Present in Faith: Luther's View of Justification*. I would still argue that the first aspect, the forgiveness of sin, should have priority in Lutheran theology.

very helpful distinction between principle and practice.[18] Transcending sin is possible in principle, through grace, but not in practice. In the same way as there is no area of life that is not permeated by sin (that is no areas or experiences where anxiety is completely transcended, except in principle), there is no area of life where grace does not impinge. The *simul justus et peccator* expressed in history fulfils and negates the Kingdom of God; Christ is what we ought to be and also what we cannot be, Niebuhr claims.[19] To solve this paradox, Niebuhr calls for increased dialogue with one another, especially with those not belonging to one's own group, in order to reach good approximations of Christian love manifested as justice and equality, something that is as urgent for a post-Christian society as it was in Niebuhr's day. There is a method suggested: a willingness to entertain views, which oppose our own, without making an effort to suppress them, and an ability to remain true to and to act upon our best convictions.[20]

A renegotiation of the doctrine of Original Sin regarding human freedom and the possibility of justice and equality along Niebuhr's line of thought thus has certain interesting consequences. Luther's own theology became relevant in his day because he tackled the basic feeling in religion: fear of God's punishment. In order to stay relevant, Lutheran theology today should also address the basic feeling in contemporary religion, namely lack of meaning. The unwillingness to acknowledge the finiteness and dependence of the human situation must accordingly be addressed by Lutheran theology, not solely as manifested in guilt, but also in anxiety, unbelief, despair, lack of love, and injustice. At the same time, Niebuhr reminds us, the avoidance of belief in God as the judge of sinners is in itself a proof of Original Sin: unbelief in God as a Creator and Lord. Tolerance coupled to faithfulness to one's own tradition as a method for living life together in a pluralistic society also seems to be of importance for Lutheran theology today.

Christian ethics must also recognize that sin is inevitable. This does not make people less Christian according to the Lutheran tradition, though. The inevitability of sin and the knowledge of inevitability do not mean that we lack responsibility because we live with an awareness of who we are as sinners coupled with a vision of ourselves in paradise.[21] At the same time Niebuhr points out that although all human beings are sinners, there is nevertheless an ascertainable inequality of guilt among us. Niebuhr criti-

---

18. Niebuhr, *The Nature and Destiny of Man: A Christian Interpretation*, vol. 2, 204.
19. Ibid., 204.
20. Ibid., 236.
21. Niebuhr, *The Nature and Destiny of Man: A Christian Interpretation*, vol. 1, 279.

cizes orthodox Lutheranism for its blindness to the prophetic judgment in Scriptures that fall upon the rich, the powerful, the wise, and the righteous. These are human beings who, through power and position, become guilty of pride and injustice.[22]

Taken together, Niebuhr's analysis is helpful when contemporary Lutheran theology deals with manifestations of sin in modern society. There is, of course, a need to develop it further, for example in relation to gender issues. However, I still find the identification of meaninglessness and anxiety in relation to human finitude as valid today as when he wrote his magnum opus. Development in human technology and humanity's increased power to change and even abuse the entire ecosystem of planet Earth make the need for relevant theological response to sin ever more called for.

LUTHERAN THEOLOGY REMEMBERING THE PAST AND LIVING THE FUTURE

The renegotiation of the doctrine of Original Sin made necessary by challenges like applying a scientific world view, recognizing expanded manifestations of sin, and accepting biblical scholarship also raises questions within the larger framework of the research project. Is it possible to talk about doctrines in Lutheran theology at all in a post-Christian society? Can Lutheran theology, still remembering the past, keep its identity and face the future? What is of importance for the heritage, development, and relevance of Lutheran theology?

First, it is true that the doctrine of Original Sin is largely rejected by people nowadays, and not only this doctrine. The whole Christian drama is rejected by people, partly because of the *incredible* character of the doctrines regarding creation, fall, or atonement, in which it is expressed. The credibility of the doctrines is challenged because the pre-modern world view they rely on is replaced by a modern, scientific one, and because biblical exegesis presents theology with new facts. To meet the incredibility challenge, any dogma should be able to harbor up-to-date biblical scholarship, and strive to get into a dialogue with the world view shared by people today.

Secondly, Lutheran theology must realize that there is a larger challenge than an outdated world view, or poorly reflected Bible interpretations. People are actually more certain of the complete *irrelevance* of these doctrines than of their incredibility. A Lutheran doctrine of Original Sin in a post-Christian society must therefore first and foremost be able to connect to people's experiences and the existential questions of its time in order to become or remain relevant and meaningful. In my study, the contrast

---

22. Ibid., 223.

between our individual situation (as well as with the state of the communities we belong to) and the paradise we long for proved to be decisive to human self-understanding. To talk about human beings as sinners is therefore in accordance with common ambivalent human experience.

However, if theology hangs on to a reduction of Original Sin, turning it into something like an abstract, and inherited corruptness, it risks making the doctrine both incredible and irrelevant. If Lutheran theology addresses questions of meaning, stands up for the good based on its own beliefs but in a spirit of tolerance, and, last but not least, acknowledges what human beings long for, the talk about sin and grace is of central importance to people. Life and history are not meaningless or evil; neither is the world illusory in the Lutheran tradition. Reformation insights today must on the whole be related more dialectically to the range of human experience, rather than what the Reformation succeeded in doing.

At the same time, a doctrine must be true to its heritage. In other words, it should be able to be recognized as Lutheran. In what way and to what degree the history of a doctrine is binding for contemporary theology is a much discussed topic. As evident from this chapter, I look upon new knowledge of biblical texts as well as knowledge of the world and human beings as an appeal to make the interpretations within Lutheran theology more adequate in relation to the tradition's central beliefs, or, as I have put it, to start a renegotiation. The central belief in Lutheran theology is that justification by grace alone, through faith alone in Christ's righteousness alone, is the core of the Christian faith, around which all other Christian doctrines are centered and based. From this core follows a view of humans as ambivalent—they are both sinners and righteous at the same time. In my renegotiation of the doctrine of Original Sin, the *simul justus et peccator* of the Reformation stands firm because it is both a universal and common human experience, and a central Lutheran belief. Moreover, it is because of this firmness that towards the end of my project I decided to keep the Swedish term *arvsynd* (from the German *Erbsünde*), meaning "inherited sin." This was not because Augustine was right about Original Sin being transmitted through generations through sexual intercourse, but to point to the universality of sin. Members of the human species all share the same state, experience the ambivalence of existence, and fall into unbelief or mistrust in the goodness of God. In Niebuhr's words, this is inevitable, but not necessary.[23]

Taken together it is important to work with the criteria of intelligibility, meaningfulness, and recognizability. This could make for a development

---

23. Ibid., 150.

of contemporary Lutheran theology that remains true to its heritage, meets people's existential questions, and thus remains relevant. My study on Original Sin shows that there was surprisingly little that needed to be done; accepting contemporary biblical scholarship, reflecting theologically upon the origin of humanity and human ambivalence, and making some analysis of where sin is particularly visible today, in order to translate this ancient dogma into a post-Christian situation.

BIBLIOGRAPHY

Granténm, Eva-Lotta. *Utanför Paradiset: Arvsyndsläran i nutida luthersk teologi och etik*. Stockholm: Verbum, 2013.

———. "Religioners bidrag till samtal i det offentliga rummet: om människovärde och kroppslig perfektion." In *Religionens offentlighet: Om religionens plats i samhället*, edited by Hanna Stenström, 217–28. Skellefteå: Artos, 2013.

Luther, Martin. *Heidelberg Disputation* (1518). LW 31. St. Louis: Concordia, 1957.

———. *Lectures on Romans* (1515–1516). LW 25. St. Louis: Concordia, 1972.

———. *Römervorlesung* (1515–1516). WA 56. Weimar: Hermann Böhlaus Nachfolger, 1938.

Mannermaa, Tuomo. *Christ Present in Faith: Luther's View of Justification*. Minneapolis: Fortress, 2005.

Mettinger, Tryggve N. D. *The Eden Narrative: A Literary and Religio-historical Study of Genesis 2–3*. Winona Lake: Eisenbrauns, 2007.

Niebuhr, Reinhold. *The Nature and Destiny of Man: A Christian Interpretation*. Vol. 1: *Human Nature*. Vol. 2: *Human Destiny*. 1941. Louisville: Westminster John Knox, 1996.

Peters, Ted. "The Evolution of Evil." In *The Evolution of Evil*, edited by Gaymon Bennett et al., 19–52. Göttingen: Vandenhoeck & Ruprecht, 2008.

———. *The Evolution of Terrestrial and Extra-terrestrial life: Where in the World is God*. Kitchener: Pandora, 2008.

———. "Grace, Doubt, and Evil." In *The Gift of Grace: The Future of Lutheran Theology*, edited by Niels Henrik Gregersen et al., 307–25. Minneapolis: Fortress, 2005.

Schleiermacher, Friedrich. *The Christian Faith*. 1830. Edinburgh: T. & T. Clark, 1999.

Stolt, Birgit. *"Lasst uns fröhlich springen": Gefühlswelt und Gefühlsnavigierung in Luthers Reformationsarbeit*. Berlin: Weidler, 2012.

Van Huyssteen, Wentzel. *Alone in the World: Human Uniqueness in Science and Theology*. Grand Rapids: Eerdmans, 2006.

Westermann, Claus. *Genesis 1–11: A Commentary*. Minneapolis: Augsburg, 1984.

8

Lutheran Spiritual Theology in a Post-Christian Society

KARIN JOHANNESSON

Many scholars studying how religious faith develops around the world today emphasize one important transition. Linda Woodhead and Paul Heelas, following the philosopher Charles Taylor, characterize this ongoing transformation as a spiritual revolution.[1] It reveals itself, *inter alia*, as a growing interest in a multifaceted variety of activities associated with various religious traditions that have one important thing in common. They have traditionally been conceptualized as spiritual training since they have been assumed to contribute to a more flourishing relationship with God or a deeper contact with a spiritual reality. Yoga, pilgrimages, and meditation are examples of such undertakings.

Spiritual exercises are a prominent feature both within the Christian and non-Christian traditions. The Greek term *askesis* is frequently used as a Christian designation of this kind of training and the growth sought is set apart, in turn, as the human being's sanctification or *Heiligung*.[2] Consequently, present-day Christian congregations can easily draw upon resources within their own heritage and put them to use so as to offer a way of being religious that might appeal to contemporary people living in the Western world. However, it is not at all obvious that this opportunity is open to Christian congregations belonging to the Lutheran tradition. The reason

---

1. Heelas and Woodhead, *The Spiritual Revolution*, 1–11, 72–73, 78.

2. In what follows, I use the term *asceticism* and the expressions *spiritual training* and *spiritual exercises* as synonymous.

for this is, quite simply, that their portal figure, Martin Luther, fought forcefully against the belief that human undertakings such as spiritual exercises can support a person's relationship with God. Instead, he emphasized the life-threatening dangers that accompany the assumption that there is such a possibility. As a result, it is quite easy to make use of Martin Luther's theological perspective in order to criticize or denounce present-day interest in spiritual training.

My aim in this chapter is not to elaborate such an argument. Instead, I want to highlight three possible lines of reasoning that all end up with the conclusion that certain activities stand out as recommendable spiritual training even in light of Luther's explication of the Christian faith. My motivation for undertaking this assignment is twofold. First, I believe that Luther is not as reluctant to encourage asceticism or spiritual training in general as he is routinely claimed to be. Secondly, I believe that if Lutheran congregations are to survive in the future, they have to offer what people today can conceptualize as valuable opportunities to grow spiritually. Based on that assumption, I find it interesting to investigate what kind of spiritual training Lutheran congregations might encourage, endorsed by Luther's theological work, and how they might present the value of such training. In that sense, what I am aiming for is a Lutheran theology that clarifies the content and function of recommendable asceticism.

Since spiritual training is set apart by its contribution to the practitioner's religious development, each of the three lines of reasoning that I will be investigating is based on an exposition of Luther's understanding of sanctification. The first option is put forward by the Finnish professor Tuomo Mannermaa (born 1937). The second is offered by Arvid Runestam (1887–1962), a distinguished representative of Swedish Luther renaissance. The third option is articulated by Professor Rudolf Hermann (1887–1962), a prominent scholar of the German Luther renaissance. My reason for choosing to present and analyze these three options is that, in my opinion, they are the most promising accounts of Luther's understanding of the Christian believer's sanctification that are available to a contemporary Lutheran theologian who wants to argue in support of the view that it is possible to encourage some kind of spiritual training without jeopardizing Luther's most fundamental insights. My judgment is based on four considerations. First, Mannermaa, Runestam, and Hermann all aim at presenting a historically adequate account of Luther's theology that might evoke people's faith in more recent times. Secondly, they discuss Luther's conception of sanctification at length. Thirdly, they emphasize that Luther's conception of sanctification is of crucial importance within his overall theological perspective. Fourthly, each of them explicate Luther's understanding of the Christian believer's growth in faith, i.e. her sanctification, in a way that enables us to demarcate some kind of spiritual training that is worth encouraging.

I will present the three options in sequence. I will begin with the interpretation of Luther that Mannermaa elaborates and end with the alternative presented by Hermann. When discussing each option I will first summarize the conception of sanctification that its proponent attributes to Luther. Then I will clarify the understanding of recommendable spiritual training that the conception in question generates. Lastly, I will evaluate the different options. My evaluation will form a line of reasoning in support of the conclusion that the explanation of Luther's understanding of sanctification that Hermann elaborates is to be preferred. My argument in favor of Hermann's interpretation of Luther is basically that there are certain flaws in the options put forward by Mannermaa and Runestam that speak against them. Hermann's account is superior since it corrects those errors.

SANCTIFICATION ACCORDING TO MANNERMAA

Tuomo Mannermaa's key claim is that the leading idea in Luther's theology is his insistence on Christ's real presence in faith. According to Mannermaa, this presence implies that the believer becomes one person with Christ and, consequently, that she is made holy as he is holy, i.e. she is divinized or sanctified. Accordingly, Mannermaa portrays Luther's conception of sanctification as corresponding to the notion of *theosis*, i.e. divinization, a notion that is accentuated in the Ancient Church as well as in the Eastern-Orthodox Christian tradition.

Mannermaa maintains that Luther scholars tend to be quite ignorant of the fact that Luther understands the believer's becoming one with Christ in faith as a radical ontological change. For this reason, according to Mannermaa, they regularly misconstrue Luther's notions about sanctification/divinization. Primarily, their misreading is due to their tendency to use a latter-day philosophical perspective, namely neo-Kantianism, when they elucidate Luther's theology. In particular, this criticism is directed against scholars representing what is known as the Luther renaissance, a research era that had its prime time during the first decades of the twentieth century and was highly influenced by the Kant renaissance that flourished at that time. Arvid Runestam and Rudolf Hermann belong to this school of thought.

According to Mannermaa, neo-Kantianism is mainly set apart by the claim that we can only know reality through the effects it has on us.[3] Man-

---

3. Mannermaa, "Why is Luther so Fascinating?" 4–9. Cf. Saarinen, *Gottes Wirken auf uns*, 229–31.

nermaa argues that Luther asserts that the believer's divinization/sanctification is ontologically real in a more substantial sense than neo-Kantianism allows for since Luther assumes that the believer's union with Christ is a state of affairs in reality even if it has no effect discernible to human beings. Consequently, neo-Kantianism prohibits a historically adequate account of Luther's theology and conceals the fact that the believer's ontological unity with Christ is the focal point that Luther's theology revolves around.

Mannermaa elaborates on his argument in support of the opinion that the believer's divinization/sanctification is Luther's main concern by calling attention to Luther's use of the distinction between *favor* (grace) and *donum* (gift). He emphasizes that, according to Luther, Christ is not only God's favor, i.e. an external/imputed righteousness that belongs to Christ and is attributed to the believer, but also a gift (*donum*), i.e. God's presence within the Christian believer. Since Christ is a divine person, Mannermaa argues, the notion of Christ as a gift means that the believing subject becomes a participant in that divine nature. Consequently, when Christ in faith gives himself in a real way to the Christian, it brings about her participation in the divine life. This participation, in turn, is characterized by Luther, as Mannermaa reads him, as a mystical union that brings forth the believer's continuous transformation into the likeness of Christ.[4] This union implies that the Christian believer has a spiritual existence (*esse gratiae*) that is absolutely real. Mannermaa depicts this reality as "real-ontic." The real-ontic unity between Christ and the Christian entails that God changes the human being ontologically by making her righteous, according to Mannermaa's interpretation of Luther. Accordingly, she is not only considered to be righteous (although she is not). She is, in fact, righteous since her self/I, i.e. her personal identity as a spiritual being, is united with Christ. Christ and the believer are one person. Consequently, they share every personal quality and have the capacity to act jointly in order to fulfill God's will.

In light of his elaboration of Luther's understanding of Christ's real presence in faith, Mannermaa argues that Luther, contrary to later Lutheranism, gives equal emphasis to the "forensic" and the "effective" aspects of justification. This implies that justification and sanctification, rather than being two distinct states, are intertwined with one another and come about simultaneously. Consequently, the doctrine of justification and notions about sanctification constitute one whole in Luther's theology. Christ as united with the Christian is simultaneously the imputed, alien righteousness

---

4. Mannermaa, "Justification and *Theosis* in Lutheran-Orthodox Perspective," 32; Mannermaa, *Christ Present in Faith: Luther's View of Justification*, 19, 22, 66–67; Kärkkäinen, *One with God: Salvation as Deification and Justification*, 45, 50; Stjerna, "Luther, Lutherans, and Spirituality," 39. Cf. Peura, "Christ as Favor and Gift (*donum*)," 60.

that justifies the believer by protecting her against the wrath of God (the forensic aspect) and a transforming gift that renews the believer by making her righteous (the effective aspect).[5]

According to Mannermaa's explication of Luther's theology, Christ can permeate the believer as a transforming gift to a greater or lesser extent, i.e. her divinization or sanctification may be more or less extensive. However, in most cases this process will be invisible to humans—the sanctified person herself included—since the Christian believer's spiritual existence is mostly hidden to everyone but God.[6] Mannermaa highlights this invisibility in his criticism of Luther scholarship influenced by neo-Kantianism. I will be making clear that this invisibility is the main reason for me not supporting the conclusion that Mannermaa's interpretation of Luther is the best option available for Lutheran theologians who want to argue in favor of the opinion that certain activities stand out as recommendable spiritual training in light of Luther's explication of Christian faith. In brief, my objection is that we are unable to make the claim comprehensible that a reality exists, which it is possible for us to identify only in exceptional cases. In other words, the notion that such a reality exists is philosophically untenable. Before elaborating on this line of reasoning, I will examine the understanding of recommendable spiritual training that Mannermaa's work results in.

A BROAD AND A NARROW UNDERSTANDING OF SPIRITUAL TRAINING

As I made clear at the outset, recommendable spiritual training is per definition set apart by the fact that it contributes to the believer's sanctification. Consequently, if a person's sanctification is usually invisible, the appropriate delineation of promotable asceticism will mostly be undetectable. For that reason, Mannermaa's explication of Luther's theology results in the conclusion that although there are actions that contribute to the believer's deification, i.e. actions that Christ as *donum* accomplishes in and through the believer and the outcome of which is an increasing divinization, we cannot usually tell whether a certain action belongs to this category or not. However, what we do know, according to Mannermaa, is that Luther assumes that the word and the sacraments establish a real-ontic unity between Christ and

---

5. Mannermaa, "Justification and *Theosis* in Lutheran-Orthodox Perspective," 28, 38; Mannermaa, *Christ Present in Faith*, 46, 49, 54, 57; Peura, "Christ as Favor and Gift (*donum*)," 47–48, 67; Kärkkäinen, *One with God*, 53–54, 62, 65; Stjerna, "Editor's Introduction," xii.

6. Mannermaa, *Christ Present in Faith*, 40, 73, 75; Peura, "Christ as Favor and Gift (*donum*)," 48; Kärkkäinen, *One with God*, 46, 59.

the Christian.[7] Consequently, Mannermaa's work results in both a very broad understanding of spiritual training and a very narrow demarcation of recommendable asceticism. The broad understanding entails that every action that Christ as *donum* accomplishes in and through a Christian believer may be depicted as spiritual training, be it a visit to an elderly relative, an hour of physical exercise with the local soccer team, or cooking the family dinner. The narrow demarcation, however, clarifies that since we only know for sure that reading/listening to the Word and receiving the sacraments contributes to the Christian believer's spiritual existence, such activities as studying the Bible, paying attention to sermons, being baptized, or taking part in the Eucharist are the only undertakings that we undoubtedly and generally can conceptualize as recommendable spiritual training in light of Mannermaa's work.

AN OBJECTION CONCERNING ONTOLOGY

My main argument against Mannermaa's explication of Luther's views on sanctification is that the notion that there exists a "real-ontic" union between Christ and the Christian lacks comprehensible content. In my opinion, it is possible to explain what this union ontologically implies if we are allowed to employ neo-Kantian arguments and distinctions. However, Mannermaa's rejection of Luther research influenced by neo-Kantianism deprives us of this possibility. Consequently, we are stuck with an inexplicable notion of the real-ontic union.

In the absence of a precise and understandable clarification of the meaning of the term "real-ontic," we cannot evaluate Mannermaa's elucidation of Luther's understanding of sanctification.[8] Arguably, if Mannermaa did meet this criticism by clarifying that it implies that Christ is really present in the believer with the help of neo-Kantianism, the invisibility that Luther, according to Mannermaa, associates with the believer's spiritual existence would not necessarily seem as radical as Mannermaa suggests. This is due to the fact that Kant's work regularly inspires philosophers to argue that claims concerning what is real only make sense to us if the truth of the claims is at least in theory possible for us to discover.[9] For this reason, Mannermaa argues that every clarification of the term "real-ontic" that we can provide, using neo-Kantian distinctions and arguments, is not in

---

7. Mannermaa, *Christ Present in Faith*, 82–84. Cf. Peura, "Wort, Sakrament und Sein Gottes."

8. Kärkkäinen, *One with God*, 79. Cf. Hägglund, *Tro och verklighet*, 120; Appelqvist, "Finns det en föreställning om gudomliggörelse hos Martin Luther?" 67.

9. Johannesson, *God pro Nobis*, 160–62.

accordance with the history of ideas since Luther had a "deeper" or more substantial view on ontology than Kant's perspective allows for. However, I am of the opinion that if we cannot explain Luther's ontological claims in a way that we can understand today, we are not justified in concluding that Luther had a comprehensible ontological perspective. Furthermore, I believe that every ontological perspective that we can understand is, in some sense, neo-Kantian owing to the immense influence of the Copernican revolution that Kant brought about within the field of philosophy. As a result, every theologian aiming at presenting a historically adequate account of Luther's theology that might evoke people's faith today has to present an account that is, basically, neo-Kantian. This goes for Mannermaa as well.

SANCTIFICATION ACCORDING TO RUNESTAM

According to Arvid Runestam's exposition of Luther's theology, Luther understands sanctification as a certain extension of the freedom of the Christian. Runestam maintains that there are three different aspects to the freedom of the Christian. First, the Christian is religiously free, i.e. she is free from the law, from sin and from the belief that justification depends on her own actions, and, consequently, she is liberated to exercise the true worship of and communion with God. Secondly, the Christian is morally free. This moral freedom springs from the believer's religious freedom and it consists of her willingness and strength to do good deeds spontaneously. Thirdly, the Christian believer has a freedom to act or refrain from acting. Luther illustrates this freedom, according to Runestam, when he argues that occasionally it is up to the individual herself to decide what to do in a certain situation.[10] This third kind of freedom is important to note since it paves the way for Runestam's interpretation of Luther's understanding of the bondage of the will.

Influenced by the neo-Kantian philosophy of his day, especially the work of Wilhelm Windelband (1848–1915), Runestam finds it difficult to reconcile himself to the view that we humans, according to Luther, altogether lack the capacity to choose between faith/God/good and disbelief/the devil/evil. If we humans were deficient in that capacity, we would be puppets and not persons, in light of the neo-Kantianism that Runestam adheres to, since persons are set apart by their ability to make deliberate decisions. Furthermore, in view of the fact that puppets are unable to choose what they do, they lack moral responsibility. Consequently, Runestam maintains that moral behavior would not exist if it were true that we humans were

---

10. Runestam, *Den kristliga friheten hos Luther och Melanchton*, 1–3, 21, 23–26, 30, 32–36.

unable to choose between good and evil. Fortunately, Runestam argues, we do not have to conclude that Luther claims that we are basically puppets. Runestam's explication of Luther's reasoning about the bondage of the will explains why this is so.

Runestam depicts Luther's claims concerning the bondage of the human will as corresponding to his understanding of the freedom of the Christian. Although Runestam emphasizes that the bondage of the human will is an important presupposition for the Christian believer's religious freedom, he argues in support of the view that Luther attributes a good free will to the Christian believer that parallels the evil free will that he undoubtedly ascribes to human beings who are turned away from God. In both cases, this freedom is associated with a certain liberty that is of vital importance to Runestam, namely our psychological freedom, i.e. our ability to act according to and motivated by our own personality. Inspired by Wilhelm Windelband, Runestam characterizes a particular individual's personality as a cluster of *constant motives* that trigger off her actions. Unlike constant motives, *temporary motives* such as emotions that surge up at a particular moment are not expressions of a particular individual's personality, according to Windelband. Instead, they are a threat to her psychological freedom since they might hinder her constant motives/personality from finding expression in her actions.[11]

In light of the neo-Kantian accentuation of the human person's psychological freedom, Runestam wrestles with the question of whether, according to Luther, our psychological freedom is only a chimera. His conclusion is that it is not. We can be faithful to Luther, yet at the same time ascribe a genuine psychological freedom to the human being, to the sinner as well as to the Christian believer.[12] Runestam supports this conclusion by arguing that Luther understands the evil free will of human beings who are turned away from God as their self, their identity. Correspondingly, he understands the free will of the Christian believer as her self, her identity. Runestam refers to the Christian believer's self as her spiritual self and he portrays the psychological freedom that he associates with the believer's spiritual self as the freedom to act without selfish motives, or to act in order to overcome them. This freedom to act without—or against—egoistic intentions is the psychological freedom of the Christian and its growth is the aim of the recommendable spiritual training that Runestam identifies.[13]

---

11. Cf. Windelband, *Über Willensfreiheit: Zwölf Vorlesungen*, 83–94.
12. Runestam, *Viljans frihet och den kristliga friheten*, 18, 27, 38–39, 41, 47, 90, 95.
13. Ibid., 95, 197, 202–4.

TWO KINDS OF ASCETICISM

Runestam explicitly discusses the question of whether some kind of spiritual training stands out as recommendable in light of Luther's theology. His answer is in the affirmative and it rests on a certain explication of Luther's portrayal of the relationship between faith and good works. Runestam argues that the relationship between faith and good works in Luther's theology is so intimate that we have to understand it as reciprocal. This reciprocity implies that faith not only results in good works, i.e. that loving deeds automatically flow forth from the believer's heart, but that the opposite is also true: good works can result in faith since people can gain, regain or grow in faith as a consequence of their actions. This is true since loving deeds shape my heart just the same as unloving deeds infect my heart with sin. Consequently, a certain individual's caring actions can be a means of grace not only to others but also to the doer herself, i.e. my actions can spread or increase the gospel's reign in my life, Runestam explains, by helping me to keep my relationship with God open, by reviving my spiritual life and confidence and by leading me back into a position of faith in times of doubt or unbelief.[14]

Runestam himself explicitly emphasizes the value of two kinds of asceticism, namely what he identifies as *the asceticism of concentration*, i.e. practices that help an individual to focus on God and distinguish God's will for the world and in her life, and *the asceticism of reduction*, i.e. practices that help an individual to remain independent of things that stand out as unimportant in light of the gospel.[15] However, further actions can be characterized as part of a sound spiritual training by reference to Runestam's explication of Luther's theology. In fact, *any* action that springs forth from the believer's true (spiritual) self and promotes the gospel's reign in her life can be depicted as part of a recommendable asceticism. Furthermore, Runestam portrays human beings as being quite capable of discerning the real reasons behind their actions. Consequently, in most cases the doer herself can tell whether a certain action promotes the gospel's reign in her life or not, i.e. whether it is adequately differentiated as part of her spiritual training. The visibility that this implies is, I believe, philosophically an advantage. However, Runestam's optimism concerning our human capacity to know ourselves is quite problematic, in my opinion. My criticism of Runestam's Luther interpretation revolves around this appreciation of our human intellectual competence.

---

14. Runestam, "Opus instrumentale. Die Tat als Gnadenmittel," 81–86; Runestam, *Jagiskhet och saklighet*, 158–62, 164.

15. Runestam, *Kärlek, tro, efterföljd*, 204–9.

AN OBJECTION CONCERNING ANTHROPOLOGY

My main argument against Runestam's explication of Luther's views on sanctification concerns his characterization of the human person. Inspired by Windelband, Runestam portrays a human being's personality as her conscious and deliberate decisions. He assumes that every individual has a core identity which consists of her constant motives. This core identity is the cause of her actions and it is primarily associated with reason and rationality. Owing to his characterization of the human person along these lines, Runestam is unable to do justice to Luther's appreciation of the emotional elements of faith. As Birgit Stolt argues, according to Luther reason (*intellectus*) and emotion (*affectus*) are always intertwined in the life of a Christian believer.[16] Consequently, the anthropological perspective that Runestam attributes to Luther stands out as historically deficient.

Furthermore, Runestam's characterization of a human being's personality is difficult to reconcile with our present-day understanding of ourselves. Today, we usually assume that people are more complex and ambivalent than Runestam's perspective allows for. For example, we tend to think that our personality consists not only of rational choices but also of mixed emotions and subconscious motives, which influence our actions. Sigmund Freud, among others, has taught us that. Although it might be possible to improve on Runestam's interpretation of Luther by linking it to a more dynamic and multidimensional concept of a human being's personality, my conclusion is that in the absence of such an upgrading, Runestam's work is not the best available option for a theologian who wants to argue that certain activities stand out as recommendable spiritual training in light of Luther's theology.

SANCTIFICATION ACCORDING TO HERMANN

According to Rudolf Hermann's exposition of Luther's theology, Luther understands sanctification as a time concept (*ein Zeitbegriff*). More than anything else, this implies that he does not conceptualize sanctification as a quantity concept (*ein Massbegriff*). Hermann suggests that, according to Luther, to grow in faith is not to acquire something that can be likened to a greater spiritual muscle mass. Instead, a certain individual's spiritual development consists in her increasingly conscious and responsible participation in her dialogue with God. This dialogue, Hermann explains, is a necessary condition for every human being's existence and it begins when God calls a certain individual into being by creating her. It then evolves into a genuine

---

16. Stolt, "Luther's Faith of 'the Heart.'"

and redemptive communication when, in light of the Gospel, a person's response within this dialogue turns into a committed confession to Christ. When this happens, a new reality is created, according to Hermann. This reality is set up and manifested by a certain linguistic behavior, namely a particular verbal exchange between Christ and the human being. This conversation is governed by a specific set of basic rules that Hermann identifies. Essentially, those rules specify that the human being's most fundamental statement in this dialogue is her confession of sins. In turn, Christ's most important response is in his words of forgiveness.[17]

Hermann refers to this new reality as a certain time, namely God's time or eternity. This time or reality conveys communion with God, which is going to be fully realized in the world to come. At present, it is at hand in the proper dialogue between Christ and the Christian, i.e. a conversation governed by the basic rules that Hermann identifies.[18] In other words, it is realized in the Christian believer's communication with Christ in prayer. Consequently, it can be portrayed as *the heart's discourse with Christ.*

According to Hermann's interpretation of Luther, a Christian believer's sanctification implies that in a certain sense God's time, God's eternal reality, is stretched out in the believer's life by increasingly permeating her existence in earthly time. This development comes about, Hermann explains, when the human being responds to Christ in situations that occur by consciously relating herself and leaving her life to Him. In other words, Hermann portrays a person's sanctification as her discourse with Christ in further moments and in situations. More precisely, growth in a believer's faith implies that she includes additional aspects of her own life story in her dialogue with Christ by admitting that past transgressions belong to this narrative, i.e. by confessing her sins, and by committing herself to Christ in a particular moment.[19]

It is important to note that Hermann, in characterizing the Christian believer's sanctification as her dialogue with Christ in prayer, does not deny that this process is of importance not only to her verbal behavior but also to her non-verbal actions. Rather, it is the other way around. Hermann emphasizes that in a broader sense our deeds, including those actions that we accomplish by uttering words, can be conceptualized as replies in our dialogue with God. In addition, our actions are expressions belonging to further dialogues that we are engaged in. For example, when I take my sister's

17. Hermann, *Luthers These "Gerecht und Sünder zugleich"*, 78, 141, 191, 237, 258; Assel, *Der andere Aufbruch*, 482–84, Vollmer, *Gott Recht geben—im Gebet*, 77–78, 82, 237.

18. Hermann, *Luthers These "Gerecht und Sünder zugleich,"* 7, 229–30, 233, 282.

19. Vollmer, *Gott Recht geben—im Gebet*, 46, 134, 358, 370–71, 377.

dog for a walk, my doing so is a response to my sister (who asked me to walk the dog) and to the dog (who barked consistently before we went out). Furthermore, it is a response to God, who brought me into being with the intention of enriching the world. Because of this simultaneity and interconnectedness, every transformation in my discourse with God will influence my verbal and non-verbal responses in other conversations, for example my communication with my sister and my behavior towards her dog. In short, as my replies in my dialogue with God mature, this will have implications for my actions since God, by fostering our dialogue, will influence my way of living in a certain direction in order for me to be of use to God in God's overall ambition to save the world.[20]

Hermann's portrayal of the Christian believer's sanctification in terms of her dialogue with Christ entails that growth in faith is essentially associated with our language and a particular use of it. This intimate relation between the believer's verbal behavior and her sanctification implies, for one thing, that Hermann, contrary to Mannermaa, does not depict the Christian believer's spiritual life and existence as invisible to us humans. Since we are aware of our own verbal behavior, we can recognize God's time when it is at hand in a particular moment. Consequently, we are able to judge whether a particular claim concerning sanctification is justified or not. In short, we do have a criterion that we can use in order to demarcate between true sanctification and other personality developments. This I deem to be a huge advantage as regards Hermann's interpretation of Luther.

Furthermore, unlike Runestam, Hermann portrays a certain individual's personality as a dynamic cluster of different and constantly changing motives. His basic assumption is that a human being's personality is her current responses in the dialogues that she, in a particular moment, is engaged in. Since her dialogue with God is her most fundamental conversation, i.e. the discourse that her life depends upon, her response within this conversation is her core identity. A person's response to God, as well as her replies in every other dialogue that she is involved in, varies over time. This implies that the human being's core identity is continuously recreated during her life in earthly time.[21] However, according to Hermann, one fact about the Christian believer's reply to God will remain true throughout her life. Her response to God will be a multidimensional mix of trust/faith and distrust/unwillingness. This is what it means to be a sinner and to be righteous simultaneously.

20. Iwand, Review of Rudolf Hermann, *Willensfreiheit und Gute Werke im Sinne der Reformation*, 570.

21. Cf. Assel, *Der andere Aufbruch*, 488; Assel, "Einleitung," 31; Vollmer, *Gott Recht geben—im Gebet*, 75, 92–93.

Hermann emphasizes that, according to Luther, the human being's affirmative answer to God is never her own accomplishment. The bondage of the will implies that the human being is incapable of loving God. Furthermore, it implies that the human being can never remain in a particular moment. Every moment will pass and, consequently, every human being has to respond anew in the next moment by choosing some course of action.[22] This is also true of the Christian believer. The spiritual training that appears as recommendable in light of Hermann's interpretation of Luther is closely connected to Hermann's explication of Luther's understanding of the bondage of the human will since it consists in the believer's affirmative answer to God in further moments. The believer's positive response is characterized by Hermann as teamwork involving God as well as the Christian believer. They act simultaneously, in God's time, i.e. in a time other than our earthly time, in which a particular moment precedes or succeeds another moment. Their joint action is made possible in a very fundamental way by their access to certain linguistic resources. Accordingly, this access is decisive for the spiritual training that stands out as recommendable in light of Hermann's clarification of Luther's conception of sanctification.

PRAYER TO CHRIST AND SPIRITUAL THEOLOGY

Inspired by Hermann's interpretation of Luther, we can portray a particular linguistic exchange, namely the believer's prayer to Christ, as recommendable spiritual training. Consequently, promoting spiritual training implies teaching other people, and learning from other people, how to maintain such a conscious dialogue as that which Hermann portrays as generating a new reality. Since this new reality is associated with a specific communication, i.e. a certain use of language, recommendable spiritual training is basically about language acquisition. It mainly involves intentionally relating oneself to Christ in further situations by praying in accordance with the insight that the human being's most basic reply in this dialogue is her confession of sins, though the conversation contains significantly more statements than the believer's prayer for forgiveness.

In light of Hermann's explicit words of warning against a particular misunderstanding more precisely the belief that spiritual training can generate something measurable, praying to Christ appears as the only asceticism that can be encouraged without risk of misunderstanding. Furthermore, on the basis of Hermann's interpretation of Luther, elaborating on sound teachings about the Christian believer's growth in faith that remedies

---

22. Hermann, "Die Lehre vom Willen," 154–55. Cf. Assel, *Der andere Aufbruch*, 392–93; Assel, "Einleitung," 24.

frequent confusions about asceticism appears to be a major undertaking for the Lutheran theologian. To carry out that task is to get involved in a theological sub-field that I believe is of immense importance today, owing to the growing interest in activities that have traditionally been conceptualized as spiritual training, namely *spiritual theology*.[23] The fact that Hermann's explication of Luther's theology encourages such work speaks in its favor and is a further reason for me to conclude that Hermann's clarification of Luther's conception of sanctification is to be preferred by a Lutheran theologian who wants to encourage spiritual training.

CONCLUSION

Hermann's line of reasoning, as well as those of Mannermaa and Runestam, results in the conclusion that certain activities can be characterized as recommendable spiritual training in light of Luther's explication of Christian faith. Consequently, a contemporary Lutheran theologian who wants to respond to today's growing interest in spirituality by recommending some kind of spiritual training can give content to and argue in support of such an approach by using any of these three explications of Luther's concept of sanctification. However, in my opinion, the option that Hermann advocates is a preferable point of departure since, as I have argued above, there are vital flaws inherent in the other two. The ontological outlook that Mannermaa attributes to Luther is quite incomprehensible. The anthropological perspective that Runestam associates with Luther's theology is, in turn, outdated. Hermann, on the other hand, elaborates a comprehensible and philosophically tenable ontological position as well as a dynamic characterization of the human person's identity. Consequently, his explication of Luther's understanding of sanctification is the best option available to a theologian who wants to argue in support of the view that there are activities that we can identify as recommendable spiritual training without jeopardizing vital elements in Luther's theology. According to Hermann's interpretation of Luther, praying to Christ in accordance with certain basic rules contributes to growth in the Christian believer's faith. As a result, such praying is spiritual training.

A present-day Lutheran theologian who formulates a considered answer to the question of what helps people make progress in their spiritual life will be involved in the discipline of spiritual theology.[24] This field of research has long since been neglected by Lutheran theologians, most ob-

---

23. This sub-field is introduced, *inter alia*, in McGrath, *Christian Spirituality*. A classic Catholic textbook is Aumann, *Spiritual Theology*.

24. Allen, *Spiritual Theology*, 18.

viously due to the fact that scholars tend to assume that Luther is of the opinion that the believer is not capable of doing anything to contribute to her spiritual growth.[25] In light of today's growing interest in spirituality, some scholars—correctly, in my opinion—argue that this is a disadvantage that has to be addressed if Lutheran traditions are to prosper in the future.[26]

My intention in this chapter is to encourage and facilitate a discussion addressing this particular shortcoming. In light of Mannermaa's, Runestam's and Hermann's elaborate explications of Luther's understanding of sanctification, certain activities undoubtedly stand out as recommendable spiritual training. Consequently, these three theologians and our critical reflection on their work smooth the way for a Lutheran spiritual theology. Such a theology is, I believe, of vital importance to the continued existence of Lutheran traditions in a post-Christian society characterized by, *inter alia*, an increasing interest in spiritual training. Accordingly, Lutheran theologians ought to pay this field of research the attention it is due.

BIBLIOGRAPHY

Allen, Diogenes. *Spiritual Theology: The Theology of Yesterday for Spiritual Help Today*. Cambridge: Cowley, 1997.

Appelqvist, Thomas. "Finns det en föreställning om gudomliggörelse hos Martin Luther? 'Den nya finska tolkningen av Luther' och en kritisk diskussion av dess betydelse i nutida teologi." *Svensk Teologisk Kvartalskrift* 86 (2010) 59–69.

Assel, Heinrich. *Der andere Aufbruch: Die Lutherrenaissance*. Göttingen: Vandenhoeck & Ruprecht, 1994.

———. "Einleitung." In Rudolf Hermann. *Religionsphilosophie: Gesammelte und nachgelassene Werke V*, edited by Heinrich Assel, 9–37. Göttingen: Vandenhoeck & Ruprecht, 1995.

Aumann, Jordan. *Spiritual Theology*. London: Sheed & Ward, 1980.

Heelas, Paul, and Linda Woodhead. *The Spiritual Revolution: Why Religion is Giving Way to Spirituality*. Oxford: Blackwell, 2005.

Hermann, Rudolf. "Die Lehre vom Willen." In *Luthers Theologie: Gesammelte und nachgelassene Werke I*, edited by Horst Beintker, 145–68. Göttingen: Vandenhoeck & Ruprecht, 1967.

———. *Luthers These "Gerecht und Sünder zugleich": Eine systematische Untersuchung*. Güthersloh: C. Bertelsmann, 1930.

Hägglund, Bengt. *Tro och verklighet: Tre studier i 1900-talets teologihistoria*. Skellefteå: Artos och Norma bokförlag, 2007.

Iwand, Hans J. Review of Rudolf Hermann:, *Willensfreiheit und Gute Werke im Sinne der Reformation*. *Theologische Literaturzeitung* 54 (1929) 567–70.

Johannesson, Karin. *God pro Nobis: On Non-Metaphysical Realism and the Philosophy of Religion*. Leuven: Peeters, 2007.

---

25. Stjerna, "Luther, Lutherans, and Spirituality," 39.
26. Cf. Yeago, "The Promise of God and the Desire of our Hearts," 21–30.

Kärkkäinen, Veli-Matti. *One with God: Salvation as Deification and Justification.* Collegeville: Liturgical, 2004.
Mannermaa, Tuomo: *Christ Present in Faith: Luther's View of Justification.* Minneapolis: Fortress, 2005.
———. "Justification and *Theosis* in Lutheran-Orthodox Perspective." In *Union with Christ: The New Finnish Interpretation of Luther,* edited by Carl E. Braaten and Robert W. Jenson, 25–41. Grand Rapids: Eerdmans, 1998.
———. "Why is Luther so Fascinating? Modern Finnish Luther Research." In *Union with Christ: The New Finnish Interpretation of Luther,* edited by Carl E. Braaten and Robert W. Jenson, 1–20. Grand Rapids: Eerdmans, 1998.
McGrath, Alister E. *Christian Spirituality: An Introduction.* Oxford: Blackwell, 1999.
Peura, Simo. "Christ as Favor and Gift (*donum*): The Challenge of Luther's Understanding of Justification." In *Union with Christ: The New Finnish Interpretation of Luther,* edited by Carl E. Braaten and Robert W. Jenson, 42–69. Grand Rapids: Eerdmans, 1998.
———. "Wort, Sakrament und Sein Gottes." In *Luther und Ontologie: Das Sein Christi im Glauben als Strukturierende Prinzip der Theologie Luthers,* edited by Anja Ghiselli, Karl Kopperi, and Rainer Vinke, 35–68. Helsinki: Luther-Agricola-Gesellschaft, 1993.
Runestam, Arvid. *Den kristliga friheten hos Luther och Melanchton.* Stockholm: Svenska kyrkans diakonistyrelses bokförlag, 1917.
———. *Jagiskhet och saklighet: Till läran om rättfärdiggörelsen genom tron.* Stockholm: Svenska kyrkans diakonistyrelses bokförlag, 1944.
———. *Kärlek, tro, efterföljd: Om moralens anpassning efter verkligheten.* Stockholm: Sveriges kristliga studentrörelses förlag, 1931.
———. "Opus instrumentale: Die Tat als Gnadenmittel." *Zeitschrift für systematische Theologie* 18 (1941) 76–95.
———. *Viljans frihet och den kristliga friheten: En undersökning i Luthers teologi.* Uppsala: Författaren, 1921.
Saarinen, Risto. *Gottes Wirken auf uns: Die Transzendentale Deutung des Gegenwart-Christi-Motivs in der Lutherforschung.* Stuttgart: Franz Steiner Verlag, 1989.
Stjerna, Kirsi. "Editor's Introduction." In *Christ Present in Faith: Luther's View of Justification,* written by Tuomo Mannermaa, xi–xix. Minneapolis: Fortress, 2005.
———. "Luther, Lutherans, and Spirituality." In *Spirituality: Toward A 21st Century Lutheran Understanding,* edited by Kirsi Stjerna and Brooks Schramm, 32–49. Minneapolis: Lutheran University Press.
Stolt, Birgit. "Luther's Faith of 'the Heart': Experience, Emotion, and Reason." In *The Global Luther: A Theologian for Modern Times,* edited by Christine Helmer, 131–150. Minneapolis: Fortress, 2009.
Vollmer, Reinhard. *Gott Recht geben—im Gebet: Zur anthropologischen Bedeutung der Rechtfertigungslehre bei Rudolf Hermann und Hans Joachim Iwand.* Bad Salzuflen: MBK Verlag, 2006.
Windelband, Wilhelm. *Über Willensfreiheit: Zwölf Vorlesungen.* Tübringen: Mohr, 1918.
Yeago, David S. "The Promise of God and the Desire of our Hearts: Prolegomena to a Lutheran Retrieval of Classic Spiritual Theology." *Lutheran Forum* 28 (1996) 21–30.

9

Lutheran Theology and Dialogical Engagement in Post-Christian Society

JAMES M. CHILDS, JR.

In Canadian philosopher Charles Taylor's massive and highly regarded work, he has examined the impact of a long and continuing process of secularization on our views of religion in society.[1] In the societies of the Western world we commonly see secularization as implicated in the development of our post-Christendom age and the emergence of post-Christian society. Post-Christendom and post-Christian are not terms that Taylor employs. However, he sees one expression of secularity to be the public sphere "emptied of God or any reference to ultimate reality" and the norms of our various spheres of activity devoid of any reference to God or religion.[2] These traits are characteristic of what Douglas John Hall has called the disestablishment of Christianity in his definition of post-Christendom.[3] Then there is Taylor's additional definition of secularity as consisting in "the falling off of religious belief and practice, in people turning away from God and no longer going to church."[4] Clearly this is a phenomenon we would associate with a post-Christian society and it accords with the definition given by Netherlands missiologist, Stefan Paas:

> So, I propose that when missiologists use the term "post Christian," they do not refer to the secularization of institutions, but

---

1. Taylor, *A Secular Age*.
2. Ibid., 2.
3. Hall, *The Cross in Our Context: Jesus and the Suffering World*, 160–62.
4. Taylor, *A Secular Age*, 2.

to changes in the beliefs, motivations and practices of people. Post-Christian societies are societies where so many individuals have declined from Christian beliefs and practices that Christians have become or are becoming a minority. Also, it could signify the diminishing importance and relevance of Christian beliefs and practices on the motivational level, even if people do not leave the church formally.[5]

Paas would have us remember that the secularization of institutions we associate with post-Christendom does not mean that the society is post-Christian. The United States is a case in point. At the same time, the continuing linkage of church and state in European countries does not obviate a post-Christian situation.

While the challenges to the Christian witness of a post-Christian situation might appear more daunting than those in which the impact of secularization is primarily in the realm of public spaces, secularization has had other consequences that affects all Western societies. Taylor argues cogently that the secularization of public spaces has created a situation in which there are a "plurality of options" and in which belief in God is not axiomatic.[6] Paas, following Taylor, speaks of this aspect of secularization as "pluralisation." The collapse of the sacral union between church and state opens the door for new religious "providers." In this regard, then, virtually all Western societies, including the United States are secular. By contrast the Islamic societies of the Middle East are not.[7]

The plurality of options, the emergence of new religious providers in secularization-as-pluralisation can mean humanistic and atheistic alternatives to formal religious traditions but it can also mean a variety of religious traditions, expressive of increasing multiculturalism, vying for adherents and cultural and political influence in a wide open field. It is the secular as pluralistic that Taylor wants to examine.

The situation of pluralisation as Taylor describes it may well fit the state of affairs that Jürgen Habermas has described as "post-secular." For Habermas a post-secular society is one "in which religion maintains a public influence and relevance, while the secularist certainty that religion will disappear worldwide in the course of modernization is losing ground."[8] Ingolf Dalferth adds this:

---

5. Paas, "Post-Christian, Post-Christendom, and Post-Modern Europe," 3–25.
6. Taylor, *A Secular Age*, 3.
7. Paas, "Post-Christian, Post-Christendom, and Post-Modern Europe," 8.
8. Quoted in ibid., 16.

> Post-secular societies are neither religious nor secular. They do not prescribe or privilege religion, but neither do they actively refrain from doing so. They are neither for not against religion(s), whether in the private lives of their citizens or in the public realms (. . .) Religion in whatever form has become a matter of indifference.[9]

However, Habermas maintains that a context of indifference does not mean religion is impotent. While rationality in public discourse is still privileged, Habermas believes that cultural and religious pluralism require the voice of religion in civic debates on urgent moral matters such as abortion, stem cell research, immigration, climate change, etc. At the same time religious participation needs to be self-reflexive concerning their own beliefs and the challenges of communication.[10]

In sum, the age of Christendom is clearly past and the marks of a post-Christian situation are evident in a number of Western societies, but the secularization that underlies both these developments has also led to a pluralistic state of affairs in which it is possible to imagine Habermas's vision of a post-secular society. However, whether we identify a society as post-Christian or post-secular, it is clear that the Christian witness is being challenged in seemingly unprecedented ways.

Not the least of these challenges is finding a common language for the meaningful sharing of beliefs and values. The reality of pluralisation brings to mind the commonly held view of our Western societies as "post-modern." The situation is one of lacking an overarching meta-narrative, a unitive account of reality that provides a framework of commonly held meaning and values. In the bygone era of Christendom the Christian narrative could provide that. Moreover, as Alasdair MacIntyre pointed out, the Enlightenment hope for reason's capacity to provide a universal language and rationale for the resolution of moral issues has been a failure. This failure has left us with what he described as an "emotivist" society in which matters of ethics are matters of feeling that have no claim on any but those who share those feelings.[11] Though written over thirty years ago, MacIntyre's thesis retains cogency and finds echoes in the post-modern emphasis on the relativity of moral judgments to the particularities of socio-cultural location.

---

9. Dalferth, "Post-Secular Society," 324.
10. Dillon, "Can Post-Secular Society Tolerate Religious Differences?" 146.
11. MacIntyre, *After Virtue*, 11–12.

DIETRICH BONHOEFFER AND THE "WORLD COME OF AGE"

Historically and theologically Dietrich Bonhoeffer's Tegel theology is an appropriate point of departure for the engagement of Lutheran theology and ethics in our present secular age. Bonhoeffer approached the reality of advancing secularity with neither handwringing alarm nor passive capitulation. Rather, he saw the possibility for regaining the integrity of the Christian witness.

For Bonhoeffer the movement toward human autonomy that marks secularization has been underway for centuries but is now reaching a state of completion.

> Human beings have learned to manage all important issues by themselves, without recourse to 'Working hypothesis: God.' In questions of science or art, as well as in ethical questions, this has become a matter of course (. . .) but in the last hundred years or so, this has also become increasingly true of religious questions; it's becoming evident that everything gets along without 'God' and does so just as well as before. As in the scientific domain, so in human affairs generally, 'God' is being pushed further and further out of life.[12]

Bonhoeffer considered the Christian apologists' efforts to invoke a need for God in light of death and guilt to be a pointless attempt to make people depend upon things they are no longer dependent upon. Furthermore, it is unchristian "because it confuses Christ with a particular stage of human religiousness (. . .)"[13] God is not a stopgap whom we recognize only in our dying, our suffering, and our sin. God wants to be recognized in the midst of all our life.[14]

There follows then these oft quoted comments from his July 16, 1944 letter to Bethge:

> We cannot be honest unless we recognize that we have to live in the world—'*etsi deus non daretur.*' And this is precisely what we do recognize—before God! God himself compels us to recognize it. Thus our coming of age leads us to a truer recognition of our situation before God. God would have us know that we must live as those who manage their lives without God (. . .) The same God who makes us live in the world without the working

---

12. Bonhoeffer, *Letters and Papers from Prison*, 425–26.
13. Ibid., 427.
14. Ibid., 406.

> hypothesis of God is the God before whom we stand continually (. . .) God consents to be pushed out of the world and onto the cross; God is weak and powerless in the world (. . .) Christ helps us not by virtue of his omnipotence but rather by virtue of his weakness and suffering! This is the crucial distinction between Christianity and all religions. Human religiosity directs people in need to the power of God in the world, God as *deus ex machina*. The Bible directs people toward the powerlessness and the suffering of God; only the suffering God can help (. . .) the world's coming of age, which has cleared the way by eliminating a false notion of God, frees us to see the God of the Bible who gains ground and power in the world by being powerless.[15]

It is questionable to draw too close a comparison between Bonhoeffer's time and ours but surely his comments on the world come of age resonate. One is also aware of the varied interpretations theologians have made of his work, but it at least seems clear that here Bonhoeffer is advancing a strong theology of the cross as the spiritual core of the church's vocation in a world come of age.[16] The church is called to solidarity with the suffering, a participation in Christ, the man for others. The Lutheran theme of the theology of the cross blends readily with the Lutheran tradition of vocation: "The church is the church only when it is there for others (. . .) It must tell people in every calling what a life in Christ is, what it means "to be there for others." Humility and modesty are among other companion virtues that must replace hubris and the worship of power.[17] Douglas John Hall, a distinguished Reform theologian who has made Luther's theology of the cross a central theme in his own theology, is worth quoting at this juncture.

> The *theologia gloriae* confuses and distorts because it presents divine revelation in a straightforward, undialectical, and authoritarian manner that silences argument, silences doubt—silences therefore, real humanity. It overwhelms the human with its brilliance, incontestability, its certitude. Yet just in this it confuses and distorts, because God's object in the divine self-manifestation is precisely not to overwhelm but to befriend.[18]

Bonhoeffer's earlier words in *Discipleship* against the backdrop of an increasingly virulent National Socialist ideology come readily to mind.

15. Ibid., 478–79.
16. See the discussion of his theology of the cross in Rasmussen and Bethge, *Dietrich Bonhoeffer*, especially 107.
17. Bonhoeffer, *Letters and Papers from Prison*, 503.
18. Hall, *The Cross in Our Context*, 20.

> The idea requires fanatics, who neither know nor respect resistance. The idea is strong. But the Word of God is so weak that it suffers to be despised and rejected by people. Likewise the witnesses to the Word are weaker than the propagandists of an idea. But this weakness liberates them from the sick restlessness of the fanatic; they suffer with the Word. (. . .) This weak Word, which suffers contradiction by sinners, is the only strong merciful Word that can make sinners repent from the bottom of their hearts. The Word's power is veiled in weakness.[19]

Here Bonhoeffer captures some of the contextual implications of the theology of the cross along with an allusion to one aspect of Luther's ideas about the "hidden God."

THE CHURCH FOR OTHERS AND THE "TWO KINGDOMS" TRADITION

For Bonhoeffer and other Lutheran theologians of the twentieth century the idea of a Lutheran social ethic of active engagement with the world, a "church for others," had to contend with the dualistic interpretations of Luther's two realms doctrine.

The influential nineteenth century essay by Christian Ernst Luthardt exemplifies that dualistic element of post-reformation Lutheran tradition:

> To begin with, the Gospel has nothing to do with outward existence but only with eternal life, not with external orders and institutions which could come into conflict with the secular orders but only with the heart and its relationship to God, with the grace of God, the forgiveness of sins, etc. (. . .) Thus, Christ's servants, the preachers, likewise have no reason to espouse these secular matters but are only to preach grace and forgiveness of sins in the name of Christ.[20]

Luthardt's statement alludes to an important dimension of the two kingdoms tradition, the notion of the "orders of creation," divinely instituted structures encompassing, family and marriage, work, government, and church. The idea that such secular orders as they appear in history were established by God in creation leads logically to the sort of "hands off" conservatism we read in Luthardt and those who shared his position. The secular orders are of the left hand rule of God, to be supported by Christians

---

19. Bonhoeffer, *Discipleship*, 173.
20. Quoted in *Two Kingdoms and One World*, 83–84.

while the mission of the church is the proclamation of the gospel and the nurture of members in the faith.

For Bonhoeffer there was the additional problem of the orders being co-opted by National Socialist ideology and the Reich's Kirche in its support of the National Socialist regime. However, his thought goes beyond response to his immediate historical and cultural context. He substitutes the idea of "mandates" for "orders." Theses mandates relate to the same structure of society as the orders. However, they are mandates from God in relation to these human activities and not to be confused with any historically established human order.

> The divine mandates depend solely on God's *one* commandment as it is revealed in Jesus Christ. They are implanted in the world from above as organizing structures— 'orders'—of the reality of Christ, that is, of the reality of God's love for the world and for human beings that has been revealed in Jesus Christ. They are thus in no way an outgrowth of history; they are not earthly powers but divine commissions.[21]

Bonhoeffer thus chooses a Christocentric focus over the creation oriented tradition. And this Christocentric vision brooks no dualistic version of the two realms.

> There are no two realities, but *only one reality*, and that is God's reality revealed in Christ in the reality of the world. Partaking in Christ we stand at the same time in the reality of God and in the reality of the world. The reality of Christ embraces the reality of the world in itself. (. . .) It is a denial of God's revelation in Jesus Christ to wish to be 'Christian' without being 'worldly,' or [to] wish to be worldly without seeing and recognizing the world in Christ. Hence there are not two realms, but only *the one realm of the Christ-reality [Chrituswirklichkeit]*, in which the reality of God and the reality of the world are united.[22]

While there is no want of theologians who see the construal of Luther's two-kingdoms thought in the Luthardt tradition as a distortion of Luther's intentions, there are also some who, though they reject that dualism, see the seeds of it in Luther's thought. Helmut Thielicke has seen what he regards as three potential dangers in Luther's doctrine of the two realms: bifurcation, secularization, and harmonization. Bifurcation is the separation of the two realms into the personal versus the official, leading to a "double morality."

---

21. Bonhoeffer, *Ethics*, 390.
22. Ibid., 58.

Secularization removes the gospel from the world; the world is divided into autonomous spheres of activity under the rule of totally secular authorities. Harmonization refers to the impression Luther sometimes gives that the two kingdoms stand side by side in mutual harmony, each having different laws from the other.[23] In all three of Thielicke's categories there is a personal vs. social duality and a quietistic relationship of the church to the world.

Thielicke himself sees the orders as "orders *of* history" (*Notordnungen,* "emergency orders") rather than orders of creation and, therefore fluid and subject to criticism and change. Moreover, on balance he also sees an antidote to dualism in Luther's writings with particular reference to *love* and *vocation.* Thielicke speaks of an objective and subjective link that holds the two kingdoms together. The objective link is God's love, which is operative in both modes of divine rule; in the left hand rule of the orders of earthly authority and in the right hand rule of the gospel. The subjective link is the love with which the people of God respond in both their immediate relationships with their neighbors and in service to their neighbors as fulfillment of their vocation in the orders of earthly authority. Love is the determinative principle in both realms. [24]

The critical role of love finds expression in this statement from Karl Holl: "By interpreting the orders of secular life as means for the exercise of love, and by charging Christians to keep improving them in this sense, [Luther] demonstrated the possibility of retaining love as the ruling motive of every situation and every moment."[25] Then there is this from Gustaf Wingren's study, *Luther on Vocation*:

> It is the neighbor who stands at the center of Luther's ethics (...) Vocation and the law benefit the neighbor, as does love born of faith (...) love born of faith and the Spirit effects a complete breakthrough of the boundary between the two kingdoms, the wall of partition between heaven and earth, as did God's incarnation in Christ.[26]

For Luther in Wingren's view and for Wingren himself, vocation is grounded in his theology of creation. God creates continually in this world in and through our vocation as God's people at work in the world for the good.[27]

---

23. Thielicke, *Theological Ethics,* vol. I, 364–73.
24. Ibid. 373–78.
25. Holl, *The Reconstruction of Morality,* 133.
26. Wingren, *Luther on Vocation,* 46.
27. Ibid., 27. Wingren sees in Luther the same objective and subjective link of divine love uniting the two realms as does Thielicke. He goes on to say, "Through the work in man's offices, God's creative work goes forward, and that creative work is love, a

This correlates with his conviction that Luther did not see laws as a static given at the dawn of creation and immutable ever since.

> The doctrine of creation which was dominant in Europe a generation ago, especially in Germany, proceeded from a premise which Luther consistently rejected—the premise that God's creating action took place 'in the beginning' and that consequently God had once been Creator but now was something else (i.e., Savior).[28]

Again, for Wingren, as for Luther, God is continually creating. For Luther the law must "accommodate itself to the situation." The laws represented movement in society for Luther.[29] Law as an evolving servant of the common good, an ongoing expression of *creatio continua*, into which Christians are called as their vocation, is a theology of engagement with the world in contrast to the commitment to the status quo characteristic of dualistic versions of the two realms tradition.

In a manner congenial to the eschatological perspective we are about to pursue, Wingren speaks of deeds of healing and proclamation as together containing promises of the future kingdom. "Healing and proclaiming have, therefore, the same character: both give something now, and, as a result, of what they give now, both contain promises of the future."[30] Moreover, Wingren argues, the church, if it is to be true to Jesus, "the man for others," to use Bonhoeffer's phrase, it does not cast its lot as an honored institution of the establishment but, "The church's influence is most pure and genuine when it moves in where individuals are threatened, and where they do not get support from anyone else."[31] Wingren thus adds to our fund of Lutheran theologies of engagement with the world in solidarity with the needs of humanity and all creation.

Wolfhart Pannenberg has been among the most prominent of recent Lutheran theologians to bring an eschatological perspective to the critique of two kingdoms quietism. Pannenberg has observed that, "Like Augustine before him, Luther did not do justice to the positive relationship between hope for the Kingdom of God and the themes of political life, but instead

---

profusion of good gifts. With persons as his "hands" or "coworkers," God gives his gifts through the earthly vocations, toward man's life on earth."

28. Wingren, *Credo*, 63.

29. Ibid.

30. Ibid., 86. Wingren sees the works of the Son as a continuation of the creation toward its divinely intended fulfillment.

31. Ibid., 87.

regarded the latter as only an emergency measure against sin."[32] Pannenberg recognizes the validity of Luther's distinctions between the roles of church and government. Luther's realism is essential in our not-yet world of enduring violence and injustice in which secular force is necessary; it remains a hedge against the unrealistic enthusiasm for social transformation. Yet Pannenberg laments that "nowhere in Luther can we find any inspiration to transform political conditions by the powerful vision of the eschatological vision of the Lordship of Christ which already illumines the present world."[33] It is to that vision that we now turn.

THE THEOLOGY OF THE CROSS AND VOCATION IN ESCHATOLOGICAL PERSPECTIVE

To live out the theology of the cross in our post-Christian or post-secular world come of age is to abandon any remaining triumphalist vestige of Christendom. The vocation of the church is one of service in solidarity with human need and indeed the needs of a threatened creation. As we have seen, prominent Lutheran theologians of the twentieth century have freed the two kingdoms tradition for active engagement in the world on behalf of justice, peace, and the common good.

The theologies of hope most prominently developed by Pannenberg and Jürgen Moltmann have introduced a renewed eschatological perspective that values history in its biblically grounded vision of God as the world's future. It is a theological vision that can take the church even deeper into engagement with the world.

It is incumbent upon any ethical system that it answers the question, "What is the Good?" From our eschatological vantage point I would argue that the ethical quest of the "church for others" is informed by the "good," proleptically revealed in the Christ event as the promise of the eschatological reign of God. The values that comprise that eschatological good are life and wholeness for the entire creation, peace, equality (justice), community and unity (reconciliation), joy, and freedom from all bondage to sin and evil (personal, social, and political). Christians pursue these values not in progressivist optimism but in the faith and hope of the promised future of the resurrected Christ, the gospel. Thus, Christian activism on behalf of the good is gospel witness, a testimony to the hope within us. The Christian community, which has seen in the Christ this revelation of God's future, has its vocation to be *a people of anticipation* running ahead to meet it in faith active in love seeking justice. As I have written previously,

32. Pannenberg, *Ethics*, 129.
33. Ibid., 130.

> When Christians stand for the value of all life by standing against the wanton use of abortion or by standing for the acceptance, rights, and opportunities of the disabled, they anticipate the fullness of life that is part of the gospel promise of the reign of God. When Christians become advocates for a public policy that can help provide a greater measure of health care for all people. (...) they are acting in anticipation of the wholeness that is part of the gospel promise for the reign of God. When Christians become active agents of reconciliation at every level of life from nuclear family to international family, they anticipate the promise of peace that is part of their hope for the dominion of God. When Christians oppose racism, sexism, and other isms that exclude and denigrate people for what they are, they anticipate the value of equality that is part of our hope for the future reign of God. When Christians actively care for the earth and love the creation as God does, they anticipate the wholeness, life, and peace of the new creation when the wolf will lie down with the lamb and hurt and destruction will end forever (Is.11:6–9). When Christians reach out to people in their addictions and in their inner turmoil or when they actively address all forms of oppression, they anticipate the freedom from bondage that is God's future for us. When Christians do these and many more things that we could name, they sow the seeds of joy in anticipation of the new heaven and new earth of God's coming reign when every tear will be wiped away and death, pain, and sorrow will be no more (Rev. 21:1–4).[34]

In an earlier essay on the influence of Augustine, Pannenberg observed that Augustine's ethics were marked by a dualism and pessimism regarding the world, producing what Pannenberg called an "otherworldly distortion." Eschatological hope in this account is to be with God in God's transcendent otherness and separateness from the world. However, if, along with biblical eschatology, we understand God to be the future of the world, then the promise of eschatological hope is for the transformation and fulfillment of all creation. Ethical striving in and for this world becomes more meaningful in light of its future in God. We are converted to the world. Thus, Pannenberg states, "The most constructive consequence of this conversion into concern for the world is the Christian idea of love that affirms the present world in transforming it."[35]

---

34. Childs, *Ethics in the Community of Promise*, 26–27. I am deeply influenced by Pannenberg's eschatological theology and doctoral mentor Carl Braaten who instructed me in the theology of hope.

35. Pannenberg, *Theology and the Kingdom of God*, 110–12.

Anticipation as the hallmark of the Christian community's vocation captures the proleptic character of the world's existence.[36] In an eschatological perspective, the realism of Luther's two realms doctrine is preserved in the tension between the future revealed and present in Christ's victory and the present of brokenness and unbelief. The existential tension of the individual as *simul justus et peccator*, projected on the large screen of human history shows the very pattern of the world's proleptic existence; God's kingdom is coming as the world's destiny while yet the world resists, preferring what it believes to have in its possession to what it can hope for in openness to God's future. In this in between time, the theology and spirituality of the cross remain for the people of hope.

Bonhoeffer rejected the idea of God as a stopgap to be invoked primarily to deal with guilt and death. Douglas John Hall has expressed sentiments that also challenge us to go beyond thinking of Christ's atoning work as solely a matter of delivery from the guilt of sin and the fear of death.

> Until the postmodern, Post-Christendom church has found a way of addressing this (. . .) most complex and damning anxiety, that of meaninglessness and emptiness, we will not have spoken to the predicament that is dominant here and now—and into the foreseeable future.[37]

Atonement theology has in the main focused on Christ's sacrifice effecting our delivery from sin and death. That remains the faith of believers in our day, as Hall himself recognizes. It is at the core of Christian faith. That said, Hall's challenge remains for our secular world; to ask how Christ's redemptive work speaks also to the aporia of our day.

The overarching meta-narrative of Christendom no longer holds sway. We also recall Alasdair MacIntyre's trenchant analysis of the failure of Enlightenment hopes for reason to provide a cogent universe of meaning. We are left with an "emotivist" society that lacks a moral center. Or, as Taylor put it, the world is open to any number of different "providers" offering meaning and seeking our loyalty. For some the outcome of secularization is the exhilarating attainment of human freedom—everything is wide open for individuals to chart their own course. That may work well for those with the wherewithal to create their own world of meaning and personal purpose. But most of us are not so free and many have hardly any wherewithal.

---

36. "The idea of anticipation received its classic expression in the word of Jesus: The Kingdom of God is at hand. It is here and yet it is not here. The metaphor "at hand" has the same double meaning as the metaphor "anticipation" (. . .) possessing and yet not possessing at the same time." Tillich, *The Protestant Era*, 171.

37. Hall, *The Cross in Our Context*, 132.

Most simply have to deal with the day to day issues of survival, a challenge common not only to the poor. For many who must simply deal with life's joys and sorrows and responsibilities and try to make something of them our "post" situation may make them feel like they are drifting at sea with neither a rudder nor an anchor.

To be sure, the promise of Christ's saving work will continue to speak powerfully to the human situation in every age. However, atonement also confers a calling to be the people of anticipation who live for the world, having seen in Christ its future. We are not simply saved *from* but saved *for*. This engagement with the needs of the world we live in strikes me as powerful witness to the meaningful life of hope directed to the well-being of the "others." It is a life of self-giving love that flows from the freedom born of Christ's atoning work that has bestowed on us a self to give. Luther's comments in *The Freedom of a Christian* come to mind:

> (. . .) as our heavenly Father has in Christ freely come to our aid, we ought also to help freely our neighbor through our body and its works, and each should become a Christ to the other that we may be Christ to one another and Christ may be the same in all, that is, that we may be truly Christians.[38]

Moreover, this life of self-giving love is not simply a solo performance but one in which we participate together as the church.

DIALOGICAL ENGAGEMENT

For "the church for others," the people of anticipation, to engage our pluralistic world dialogue is essential. Dialogue is appropriate for a theology of the cross that eschews triumphalism's desire to control and claim absolute knowledge. There is also a close correlation between dialogue in the spirituality of the cross and the situation of anticipation; to have and yet not have is to live in a Law-Gospel tension that cannot sustain rigid and intolerant dogmatism. It is essential for dialogue that there be a genuine readiness to see dialogue partners as equals and dialogue as mutually beneficial. It is a path of discovery that has the capacity for better understanding and even resolution of differences. It can also lead to the discovery of shared values that might form the basis of cooperative action for the common good.

The church is free in the promise of the gospel to participate in the give and take quest for the discovery of shared values that can guide action for the common good. The church also brings its realism to the dialogue in a world that has forever been fraught with ambiguity and conflicting claims.

---

38. Luther, *The Freedom of a Christian*, LW 31, 367–68.

This perspective, well grounded in Lutheran theology and ethics, fits nicely with Charles Taylor's advice that both faith and humanism should approach future dialogue with "humility" and "realism."[39] For the church in particular Taylor says it must be ready to listen to all voices and open to its own voice to be changed by that listening.[40]

For many Christians such openness may be threatening. The fear is that the world will set the church's agenda in ways that violate the core values of the faith. Concerns of that sort have certainly arisen in matters of sexual morality, the endless debate about abortion, and the question of war. For this reason dialogue within the community of faith is an essential corollary activity to participation in public discourse. In the final analysis commitment to dialogue rejects any sort of sectarian withdrawal from the threats of a changing world but neither is it ready to simply accommodate to cultural pressures. It is the nature of dialogue to bring one's honest convictions to the table while remaining open to new discoveries.

But is dialogue in matters of ethical import even possible in our "post" age? One might argue in response that, though the diversity of our situation makes dialogue more difficult, it also makes it essential if there is to be any shared moral vision for the common good. Moreover, the Christian faith professes a view of the good that is far from sectarian or parochial. The vision of the good revealed as the values marking God's future for the world is a source of hope and guidance for the church's activism on their behalf. For a world indifferent to the faith such values as life, freedom, peace, and justice nonetheless resonate with the deepest longings of humanity. So also a faith-based care for the creation correlates with secular concerns for the preservation of its intrinsic and instrumental values. Furthermore, while the Decalogue has been seen in positive terms to express aspects of neighbor love it is also readily formulated to correlate with commonly held ethical principles and with documents such as the United Nations' *Universal Declaration of Human Rights*.[41] In my own work I have argued that the general rules of respect for autonomy, justice, sanctity of life, truth-telling, and promise-keeping—principles commonly held in secular moral discourse—can be rooted in the Decalogue and expressive of love's conduct toward the neighbor.[42] It is reasonable to think that we have a sufficient number of shared values and principles to make public dialogue possible.[43] Further-

---

39. Taylor, *A Secular Age*, 674–75.
40. Ibid., 753–55.
41. Harrelson, *The Ten Commandments and Human Rights*, 192–93.
42. Childs, *Ethics in the Community of Promise*, 111–77.
43. Gustaf Wingren sees the necessity of Christian and non-Christian cooperation

more, given our Lutheran belief in civil righteousness, there is a built in theological hope and expectation that a broad coalition of persons of good will can come together on behalf of those values.

That said, dialogue may not always be possible in search of a broadly shared moral vision even when the church accommodates its own ethical claims to the language of secular culture. For post-modernists like Michel Foucault, a true disciple of Nietzsche, for whom all truths were illusions, the absence of objective knowledge that is value free means that efforts to benefit humankind in general are not possible. Gains for the good are possible only for particular groups.[44] Such is the nature of moral discourse in a pluralistic world. Despite sharp differences in outlook, one is reminded of Reinhold Niebuhr's observation that groups do not vote against themselves in matters of public policy. Thus, injustice may only be mitigated by oppressed elements attaining some balance of power. Although Christians have no illusions that such gains have anything to do with agape love, they are driven by love to participate in whatever serves justice. Dialogue may not always be possible but the voice of service is audible and clear.

Pluralisation includes a multireligious society as another dimension of our post-Christian or post-secular age. Here too dialogue among the faiths and dialogue's demeanor of mutual respect are important, not to obliterate differences between these traditions, but to "forge a positive ethos of public engagement between alternate faiths."[45] For Christians in what he calls our globalizing age, Paul Ricoeur maintains it is a matter of seeking out "the fresh forms of poverty which occur in any period (where poverty includes all forms of deprivation, oppression and injustice)."[46] Christians can bring that commitment to the conversation among the faiths for the development of a shared religion of service.[47]

---

in dealing with the ethical issues of today's growing environmental crisis. Such cooperation, consistent with his grounding of ethics in creation, should be based on commonsense deliberation drawn from nature. Wingren, *The Flight from Creation*, 83.

44. See Grenz, *A Primer on Postmodernism*, 123–38.

45. Dallmayr, "Post-Secular Faith: Toward a Religion of Service," 33–34.

46. Ibid., 32.

47. Michelle Dillon, while applauding the religious tolerance and capacity for interfaith dialogue she sees in Habermas and Taylor, believes that the matter is more complicated than they imagine and less likely to eventuate in reflexive self-reflection than they would hope. Dillon, "Can Post-Secular Society Tolerate Religious Differences?," 149–52.

CONCLUSION

Lutheran theologian Ted Peters has written an insightful and dialogical discussion of Christian witness in our pluralistic world of atheists, Muslims, and others. He concludes by saying that what is essential is to affirm that the God in whom Christians trust is gracious and to do the works of love that flow from that faith.

> Although Christian theologians should feel responsible to address the epistemological concerns raised by atheism, pluralism, and Islam, the indispensable role played by discipleship in knowing God needs to find its place. In an era where a violent world is scrambling painfully to find a road to peace, perhaps the road of discipleship which begins with a commitment to a loving peace might lead to a more illuminative understanding of God.[48]

I have stressed *dialogical* engagement with the world as adjunct to the theology of the cross in the witness of service. Thus, dialogue where possible is valuable for the benefits already mentioned but not as an end in itself. From the church's vantage point it is the servant of the Christian witness of compassionate solidarity with human need and the needs of the planet. This is the vocation of the "church for others." Indeed, I believe that engagement with the needs of the world, though often confrontational, is also itself dialogical. Such engagement, marked by a spirituality born of the theology of the cross is ready to give of itself in love and, while doing so, to discover a deeper understanding of what love entails through its self-reflexive participation in the realities of our world.

We must also be clear about the distinctiveness of the Christian witness in this dialogical engagement. I have argued that the eschatological values revealed as the "good" have resonance with human experience in general and can form the basis dialogue outside the faith and with other faiths. However, there is also distinctiveness to the Christian ethical witness that has been implicit in the foregoing and must now be made explicit.

Ethics is more than stated values and cognate principles of obligation; it is rooted in more fundamental beliefs about the truth of existence that are the shaping force of the character that grounds the moral life of individuals and communities. These fundamental belief's find expression in Luther's theology of the cross and the freedom of the Christian in the gospel, in Bonhoeffer's Christological account of the mandates and, most of all for

---

48. Peters, "Christian God-Talk While Listening to Atheists, Pluralists, and Muslims," 101.

Bonhoeffer, in his Tegel theology of Christ the "man for others" who calls for a church for others in a seemingly godless world. Out of this ground of divine grace and power grows the openness of faith active in love seeking the good for all. For the Christian community in the world, the ethical life begins with God's grace rather than our task. For Christians love and its related principles is not merely an obligation; it is deep in the character of faith that makes it the motive of the moral life and provides a sense of vocation that gives meaning to life. This vocation furthermore is a calling to witness. The values of God's eschatological future revealed in the person and work of the Christ are promises that, as Pannenberg put it, convert the faith community to the world. Thus, love's striving for these values on behalf of the neighbor and the world is not only obedience to the love commandment; it is also a witness to the gospel hope that is at the core of Christian faith.

A church for others living out its vocation of service and solidarity in the theology of the cross, sustained by faith and hope is equipped for participation in our pluralistic post-Christian /post-secular world. It is free in faith to engage the complex ethical dialogue and debate of our diverse societies with compassionate concern for life, freedom, peace, and justice; free to let discipleship be its most eloquent statement. It is called to be a beacon of hope.

BIBLIOGRAPHY

Bonhoeffer, Dietrich. *Discipleship*. DBW 4. Edited by Geffrey B. Kelly and John D. Godsey. Minneapolis: Fortress, 1996.

———. *Ethics*. DBW 6. Edited by Ilse Tödt, Ernst Feil, and Clifford Green. Minneapolis: Fortress, 2005.

———. *Letters and Papers from Prison*. DBW 8. Edited by John W. de Gruchy. Minneapolis: Fortress, 2010.

Childs Jr., James M. *Ethics in the Community of Promise: Faith, Formation, and Decision*. 2nd ed. Minneapolis: Fortress, 2006.

Dalferth, Ingolf U. "Post-Secular Society: Christianity and the Dialectics of the Secular." *Journal of the American Academy of Religion* 78:2 (2010) 324.

Dallmayr, Fred. "Post-Secular Faith: Toward a Religion of Service." *American Theological Inquiry* 2:1 (July 15, 2008) 26–36.

Dillon, Michelle. "Can Post-Secular Society Tolerate Religious Differences?" *Sociology of Religion* 71:2 (2010) 139–156.

Grenz, Stanley J. *A Primer on Postmodernism*. Grand Rapids: Eerdmans, 1996.

Hall, Douglas John. *The Cross in Our Context: Jesus and the Suffering World*. Minneapolis: Fortress, 2003.

Harrelson, Walter. *The Ten Commandments and Human Rights*. Philadelphia: Fortress, 1980.

Holl, Karl. *The Reconstruction of Morality*. Edited by James Luther Adams and Walter F. Bense. Minneapolis: Augsburg, 1979.

Luther, Martin. *The Freedom of a Christian* (1520). LW 31. St. Louis: Concordia, 1957.

MacIntyre, Alasdair. *After Virtue*. Notre Dame: University of Notre Dame Press, 1981.

Paas, Stefan: "Post-Christian, Post-Christendom, and Post-Modern Europe: Towards the Interaction of Missiology and the Social Sciences." *Mission Studies* 28 (2011) 3–25.

Pannenberg, Wolfhart. *Ethics*. Philadelphia:Westminster, 1981.

———. *Theology and Kingdom of God*. Philadelphia: Westminster, 1969.

Peters, Ted. "Christian God-Talk While Listening to Atheists, Pluralists, and Muslims." *Dialog: A Journal of Theology* 46,2 (Summer 2007) 91–101.

Rasmussen, Larry and Renate Bethge. *Dietrich Bonhoeffer: His Significance for North Americans*. Minneapolis: Fortress, 1990.

Taylor, Charles. *A Secular Age*. Cambridge, MA; London: The Belknap of Harvard University Press, 2007.

Thielicke, Helmut. *Theological Ethics*. Vol. 1. Edited by William H. Lazareth. Philadelphia: Fortress, 1966.

Tillich, Paul. *The Protestant Era*. Edited by James Luther Adams. Chicago: University of Chicago Press, 1957.

Two Kingdoms and One World. Edited by Karl Hertz. Minneapolis: Augsburg, 1976.

Wingren, Gustaf. *Credo: The Christian View of Faith and Life*. Minneapolis: Augsburg, 1981.

———. *The Flight from Creation*. Minneapolis: Augsburg, 1971.

———. *Luther on Vocation*. Philadelphia: Muhlenberg, 1957.

10

Physicality as a New Model for Lutheran Ethics in a Multicultural Global Community

RICHARD J. PERRY, JR.

In this chapter I explore the practice of physicality by some African and European American elders within the Lutheran communion. My claim is that this practice establishes a new model for Lutheran ethics in a multicultural global community. Physicality I define as "the act of intentionally placing one's body into public spaces as a means of expressing concerns for justice in the world."[1] At the core of physicality is God's justifying grace. These elders carried their bodies, anchored by their faith in a justifying God, from the sanctuary of their churches to the streets where God was also active with demonstrators for justice.

I will pursue my argument by first setting the context for this chapter. 2013 was a year of commemorations for a number of important civil rights activity which occurred fifty years ago. After setting the context, I suggest a framework for pursuing the theme of "Remembering the past—living the future." The central question is, why do we need to look back in order to go forward? My short answer is, for Lutherans ethics to have an impact in a multicultural global world, the witness of African American and European

---

1. It has been suggested to me that "physicality" could be broadened to include what individuals did other than participating in marches. I agree. Some individuals challenged racial injustice by not going to work, by financially supporting civil rights activities, performing other tasks needed for a successful campaign, and expressing their views through written means. My focus, however, is on one particular form of expression of physicality; namely, the public practice of engaging in nonviolent direct action.

American Lutherans who served in the African American community needs to be recovered and transmitted to the contemporary and future church as an ethical method. Then I pursue a theological and anthropological foundation for conceptualizing physicality. I suggest that the Christian doctrine of incarnation (including the *imago dei*), God coming into the world in a human body and entering into the pains, joys, and struggles of humankind, focuses on the concreteness of physicality. I also appropriate the thinking of Anthony Pinn (who follows Mary Douglas, a cultural anthropologist) who suggests a material and symbolic understanding of African American bodies. Following that discussion, I will explore The Rev. Dr. Martin Luther King, Jr.'s book *Why We Can't Wait*[2] where he discusses presenting one's body as a means of publicly expressing a desire for justice in the world. The ensuing discussion moves to a description of the activity of several Lutheran elders who practiced physicality. The final section follows Luther's cathetical question, what does this mean for Lutheran ethics in a multicultural global community?

In sum, my purposes are threefold, (1) to contribute a reflection on the 50th anniversary commemoration of the Birmingham Civil Rights Movement and the "March on Washington for Jobs and Freedom," (2) to recover the legacy of some Lutheran elders who practiced physicality, and (3) to suggest that there are a plurality of ways of expressing Lutheran ethics in a multicultural global world. Ultimately, the question of this chapter is, can where God's people choose to publicly place their bodies for expressing God's desire for justice in the world be a new model for contemporary Lutheran ethics in a multicultural global world? But, first I want to look at the context which shapes my thinking.

A YEAR OF COMMEMORATIONS

Commemorations of civil rights activity proliferated throughout 2013 in the United States of America. The year began with the 150th anniversary of the Emancipation Proclamation which "freed" African slaves from the yoke of slavery.[3] Festivities continued with the marking of the 50th anniversaries of the "March on Washington for Jobs and Freedom" and the stirring "I Have A Dream" speech delivered by the Rev. Dr. Martin Luther King, Jr.[4] The tragic murder of Medgar Evers in Mississippi, the vicious bombing of the Sixteenth St. Baptist Church which killed four innocent African American young women, and the murder of two African American young men

2. King, *Why We Can't Wait*.
3. *The Emancipation Proclamation*.
4. King, "I Have a Dream."

in Birmingham, Alabama were also commemorated.⁵ 2013 was a year of jubilation and challenge, especially in the area of racial justice. The primary focus of this chapter will be Birmingham, Alabama which was a bastion of segregation, racism, and where Lutherans were involved.

The jubilation experienced during some of these events reveal how much progress has been made in the struggle for racial justice in Alabama, America, and across the globe. As one participant in the Birmingham Movement said,

> Black people were in bondage and had to go through a period of preparation in order to recognize and realize the blessings that God had bestowed upon us. We still have not accomplished all we can accomplish, but we have come a long way. *And it's only through the grace of God that we are as far along as we are.*⁶

Only through God's grace! The 1963 Birmingham Movement and the broader Civil Rights Movement brought a new sense of power to African Americans and others in their pursuit of racial justice.

Racial justice is still a challenge facing America. The killing of unarmed African American young people, the revoking of several parts of the 1965 Voting Rights Act, states enacting laws to suppress voting by communities of color, and racial profiling reveals America still faces vastly different perceptions and experiences of race. According to a 2013 Pew Research Center survey, more than 45 percent of African Americans surveyed (Whites and Hispanics 32 percent and 43 percent respectively) thought more work had to be done to achieve racial equality.⁷ The euphoria surrounding many of the celebrations was tempered by the challenge to make real racial justice and equality in America.

Commemorations, though, are vital religious, spiritual, and cultural practices. Complete with colorful pageantry, fiery sermons and speeches, a tasty cuisine, and joyful music, they preserve the memory of important contributions of named and unnamed individuals. They deepen a community's faith in God and Jesus Christ who journeys with God's people on their path to justice and freedom. They provide a sense that "trouble don't last always." Hope abides. In the midst of these festivities, individuals and communities create space to look back, rediscover important values, contemplate the actions of ancestors and elders, and speak about new directions.

---

5. Wright, *1963: How the Birmingham Civil Rights Movement Changed America and the World*, 65–82.

6. Ibid., 93 (emphasis added).

7. Gao, "On MLK Day, racial equality found wanting."

There is more to the celebrations of the civil rights movement activities of 1963. A common thread emerges. That thread is the willingness of African and European Americans choosing to publicly place their bodies into demonstrations as a method of concretizing God's desire for justice and equality in the world. During 1963, the global community witnessed African Americans being treated to a vicious type of violence never before witnessed since the atrocities of lynching. Through the use of fire hoses, dogs, and beatings, the police force of Birmingham sought to repress the nonviolent public voice for justice and equality. Simply put, while exercising their citizenship rights to free assembly and expression, the bodies of African American nonviolent protesters (especially women and children) were treated as non-bodies and without basic citizenship rights. Now that the context has been set (1963 Birmingham, Alabama), why would Lutherans globally look back in order to go forward?

LOOKING BACK, GOING FORWARD IN FAITH

The 1963 Birmingham Civil Rights Movement was not unlike other campaigns of the broader Civil Rights Movement. The faith foundations were prominent from the beginning. At the outset of the Birmingham Movement, volunteers were required to sign a "Commitment Card" which listed "Ten Commandments." Three of those commandments focused on Jesus, God, and prayer.[8] Grounded in the Black Religious Tradition, typically experienced in the mass meetings which were held, one of the gifts of the Civil Rights Movement was passing on a *religious* and *spiritual* heritage which incorporated the practice of physicality. In other words, signing the commitment card represented an obligation to embrace a specific way of life, public nonviolent direct action protest or resistance, as a way of securing racial justice in society. The ethos of the mass meetings and the Birmingham Movement serve as a conduit for why, I believe, Lutherans go back to move into the future. Three sources contribute to this framework: The Bible, cultural symbols, and a doctrinal perspective.

The principle biblical text for the claim I am asserting as a basis for why Lutherans need to look back in order to go forward is Deuteronomy 6:4–12. In that passage Moses, who serves as the voice of God, gives the Israelites several commandments which are to be taught to the children, love of God and loving God with one's whole being. The elders were to recite these two commandments.

There are two issues in this passage. First, the tradition or heritage of the Israelites may be lost. The children may become disconnected from

---

8. King, *Why We Can't Wait*, 63–64.

that heritage and thus the promises of God would be lost. Consequently, the elders are charged with telling the children the story of God's liberating activity and commandments wherever they found themselves located. The children needed to remember that everything their community has are gifts from a faithful God. A second issue, although implicit, is whether the children would receive what the elders have to share with them. The multicultural global Lutheran communion must look back and recover the whole of the Lutheran heritage and enter into dialogue with the diversity of Lutherans. The dialogue is not so much lecturing the new voices at the table but appreciation for each other and the particularity of the heritage they share. The Lutheran heritage, like the heritage of the Israelites, is worthy of repeating and transmitting to succeeding generations. The whole story, however, has to be told.

A second dimension of this framework is cultural symbols. Commemorations are more than an exercise in nostalgia. Remembering our past includes embracing cultural symbols which are transmitted by the ancestors and elders. Cultural symbols reflect the complex interplay between context and history. This interplay forms our reality and perspective about God, Jesus Christ, ethical principles, and morality. And cultural symbols are particular; that is, each culture has symbols and aphorisms which transmit deeply held beliefs.

The Akan of Ghana have a wonderful symbol, which has been embraced by some parts of the African American community, called the Sankofa bird. The Sankofa bird has a long neck which stretches backward to its tail. Standing on one leg with an egg in its mouth, it is walking or flying forward. The proverb associated with the Sankofa bird literally means "it is not taboo to go back and fetch what you forgot."[9] Going back and getting the history, knowledge, and wisdom of African American Lutherans and those who served in the African American community is crucial because they are the bearers of the community's heritage and tradition. What the ancestors and elders "know" and how they exercise their agency in the midst of struggle serves as a foundation for contemporary consideration of physicality as a new model for contemporary Lutheran ethics. I contend that Lutherans ethics in a global multicultural world are incomplete when it does not know, include, and transmit the ethical method and moral wisdom of the whole global multicultural community.

Completing this threefold framework for looking back and going forward is the doctrine of justification by grace through faith. The Lutheran communion holds the belief that God's justifying grace, embodied in the

---

9. "The Meaning of the Symbolism of the Sankofa Bird."

person of Jesus Christ, is central to its interpretation of the Hebrew Bible, the New Testament, and its existence in the world as the Body of Christ, the church. One cannot argue with what Martin Luther discovered in the Bible. Luther's desire to find a gracious and liberating God in the midst of an oppressive context, led him to discover God's grace was freely given and apprehended by faith alone without human works or merit. "By faith alone, not by faith formed by love, are we justified" Luther wrote in a lecture on Galatians.[10] And in that great passage in Romans 3:28, Luther embraces the words of the Apostle Paul, "For we hold that a person is justified by faith apart from works prescribed by law." The human being is a forgiven creature as a result of God's gift of grace and who apprehends this forgiveness in faith.[11] The fruit of faith is serving the neighbor in love, what we Lutherans normally express as our faith being active in love. This maxim becomes a regulating principle for social ethics from a Lutheran perspective. The 1963 Birmingham Movement would test the adequacy of faith being active in love.

CONCEPTUALIZING PHYSICALITY

I think it is important to recognize that whenever people, who are marginalized or oppressed by race, class, gender, or any other socially constructed barrier, speak or act they are bringing ethical method and principles to the forefront of Christianity in ways never thought or experienced. Their social location and lived experience is valuable because it is outside the experience and knowledge of the dominant culture. Here I want to privilege conceptualization of physicality on the basis of the behavior of those who adopted nonviolent direct protest or resistance during the Birmingham Movement as a means of securing racial justice. I begin with an understanding of the body.

One of the key Christian doctrines is the incarnation. Theologically, physicality begins with God's action. The gospel of John proclaims, "In the beginning was the Word, and the Word was with God, and the Word was God (. . .) And the Word became flesh and lived among us, and we have seen his glory, the glory as of the father's only son, full of grace and truth" (John 1:1, 14). God's Word entered into the human situation in a human body. As the gospel story in Matthew records it, God's Word (the *Logos*) manifested itself during a particular political era (the reign of King Herod), in a particular place (Bethlehem), as a particular body (male), and into a particular religious orientation (Jewish). By entering into the human

---

10. Luther, *Lectures on Galatians*, LW 26, 137.
11. Kolb and Wengert, *The Book of Concord*, 38, 39.

condition in human form, Jesus connected with the tension between what the world determined to be salvation and what God determined to be salvation. That is to say, Jesus took on the pains, joys, and struggles of human bodies by living with the people. As the bodies of the people were assaulted and marked by socially constructed barriers, Jesus' body was also marked. Yet, Jesus continued to act through miracles, healing, and proclaiming the coming of God's kingdom. Jesus through his ministry transformed public space dominated by sin and evil by practicing physicality.

Physicality may in some sense, therefore, be considered embodiment. Sometimes these two words are employed to communicate similar meanings. Physicality implies a body taking action and reflecting something. Embodiment, on the other hand, connotes "one that embodies something."[12] For example, human beings were created in the image of God. The human being embodies the image of God. Yet, the body does not do something.

Anthony Pinn offers a perspective on embodiment much closer to what I mean by physicality. Anthony Pinn's theological project is grounded in notions of the body and embodiment as a starting point for theology. Following the thinking of cultural anthropologist Mary Douglas,[13] the conceptual foundation for embodiment "is the suggestion that black bodies are material, real, but what is meant by this and what is known/experienced about this body is not possible outside discourse (knowledge) generated in connection to power relationships."[14] Materiality and symbol are critical because they represent social spaces.

> The body occupies a social space whose texture and tone cannot be fully assessed only through the workings of spoken language, but we must be sensitive to the physical placement, condition, and actions of real and specific bodies.[15]

A crucial point is made here regarding physicality; namely, physicality is a broader concept than embodiment. The body is more than a reflection of something. Physicality is a body moving into social spaces.

This is an interesting point when considering physicality as a new model for Lutheran ethics. It is common knowledge that African Americans encountered social spaces which had ordinances, rules, and laws preventing free movement of their bodies. Segregation in the southern part of the United States prohibited African Americans from eating in public

12. "Embodiment."
13. Douglas, *Natural Symbols*.
14. Pinn, *Embodiment and the New Shape of Black Theological Thought*.
15. Ibid., 9.

restaurants, staying in hotels, going to segregated schools, going to movie theatres, receiving services at hospitals, and the most hideous experience, not being able to get a drink of water. The life and movement of African American bodies were controlled by members of the European American community. Physicality, therefore, is about occupying those social spaces where the visible laws of segregation were felt, experienced, and reinforced by custom. Occupying those spaces meant transforming them into places of freedom and justice. This is the challenge Martin Luther King, Jr. faced upon arrival in Birmingham.

MARTIN LUTHER KING, JR. AND PHYSICALITY

Birmingham 1963 can be identified as the site of victory for a way of life, nonviolent direct action. The people and leadership of the Birmingham Movement injected into the African American protest tradition a method for seeking racial justice in society. The practice of physicality was clearly expected of the leaders of the Movement. When it came time for a public witness against segregation and for racial justice, Martin Luther King, Jr. struggled internally with this decision. This struggle came at the onset of whether to disobey a law or court injunction during the Birmingham Movement. After intense debate and a period of prayer, Martin Luther King, Jr. said, "Ralph Abernathy and I would *present our bodies* as personal witnesses in this crusade."[16]

I contend that physicality was a part of the strategy of nonviolent movement in Birmingham. According to King, "there are four basic steps: collection of the facts to determine whether injustices exist; negotiation; self-purification; and direct action." After failed attempts at negotiation with White leaders of Birmingham, King was clear, "We had no alternative except to prepare for direct action, whereby we would *present our very bodies* as a means of laying our case before the conscience of the local and national community."[17] King and the other leaders were committed to practicing physicality as an act of faith in God's grace. Nonviolent direct action, therefore, became a way of life rather than merely a tactic for accomplishing a goal. This method was taught and transmitted to elders of the Lutheran communion who struggled to make racial justice real in their context.

---

16. King, *Why We Can't Wait*, 71.
17. Ibid., 78.

LUTHERAN MODELS OF PHYSICALITY

Central to my claim of physicality being a new model for Lutheran ethics in a global multicultural world is my assertion that it is context driven. When all non-violent methods of trying to secure justice (for example, negotiating with those in power) fails, physicality surfaces as an option. In a sense, this is what happened to some Lutheran elders. Physicality was their opportunity to show their faith in God by joining with other demonstrators in public spaces around Birmingham. Intentionally placing their bodies into those public spaces became a new method for expressing resistance to segregation and for justice. Andrew Schulze, Joseph Ellwanger, and Will Herzfeld, in many ways, reflected Martin Luther King, Jr. when he decided to go to jail in Birmingham.[18] Going to jail and joining in marches was a faith act![19]

There is a presupposition operating in describing the practice of physicality by some Lutheran elders. Andrew Schulze, Joseph Ellwanger, and Will Herzfeld were facing a problem which limited the life opportunities of African American people, racial segregation. I think Lutheran ethics should begin with concrete problems God's people experience through their public actions. A Lutheran ethic of this type, starting with physicality, moves from abstract solutions to concrete solutions.

This raises a second presupposition; namely, that there is diversity of opinion about the appropriateness of engaging concrete problems of God's people. While Lutherans would agree that, as believers we are "in the world but not of the world," how Lutherans engage the world is highly debated. For example, some Lutheran theologians and ethicists would argue that engaging the problems of the world and seeking solutions to those problems is tantamount to being "political." Political because Christians, especially Lutherans, will be exercising coercive power. Lutherans argue that God has two ways of ruling, law and gospel. The law, through its civic or political use is meant to restrain evil, sin, and bring order out of chaos. The gospel

---

18. The individuals highlighted here have several things in common. Two belonged to the Lutheran Church-Missouri Synod and one to the American Lutheran Church, a predecessor of the Evangelical Lutheran Church in America (ELCA). Second, they all pastored African American Lutheran congregations in the South. Third, they all had a working relationship with Martin Luther King, Jr. Finally, they all led interracial organizations.

19. In a discussion of an earlier version of this chapter it was noted that the Rev. Robert Graetz is also a person who actively participated in the Civil Rights Movement. Rev. Graetz, a White Lutheran pastor, served Trinity Lutheran Church, an African American Lutheran congregation in Montgomery, Alabama during the 1954 Montgomery Bus Boycott. Although Pastor Graetz had been admonished by his superiors to stay out of the public arena, he eventually became engaged in the struggle for racial justice. Graetz, *A White Preacher's Memoir: The Montgomery Bus Boycott*.

is directed to believers and forms them for service through their vocation individual vocations. Through preaching of the Word and celebrating the Sacraments, the church fulfills its mission. In part that mission is to hold the government accountable to its God given mission.[20]

Martin Luther offers an interesting insight about the relationship between the twofold governments as he calls the law and gospel. Writing in the treatise, "Temporal Authority: To What Extent It Should Be Obeyed," he says

> You suffer evil and injustice, and yet at the same time, you do resist it. In the one case, you consider yourself and what is yours; in the other, you consider your neighbor and what is his. In what concerns you and yours, you govern yourself by the gospel and suffer injustice toward yourself as a true Christian; in what concerns the person or property of others, you govern yourself according to love and tolerate no injustice toward your neighbor. The gospel does not forbid this; in fact, in other places it actually commands it.[21]

These are amazing words! The twofold governments are held together. What is amazing is the idea that as a Christian, believers suffer injustice that is meted out to them. At the same time, as a Christian, believers are to not tolerate injustice meted out to the neighbor. From my perspective, the practice of physicality is precisely what Martin Luther suggests in the above quote. With that said, I turn to a descriptive analysis of the practice of physicality by some Lutheran elders.

THREE LUTHERAN ELDERS: SCHULTZE, ELLWANGER, AND HERZFELD

Andrew Schulze was a German American who served several African American Lutheran congregations in the Lutheran Church-Missouri Synod. After a number of years of service in those, he accepted a call to serve as executive secretary of Lutheran Human Relations Association of America (LHRAA) headquartered in Valparaiso, Indiana. From this position, Schulze would challenge pastors and the Lutheran church to racially integrate their congregations.

Schultze's practice of physicality came in response to a 1962 nationwide call by Dr. Martin Luther King, Jr. for an interfaith non-violent protest in Albany, Georgia. In a very telling remark, Schulze wrote, "I have been

---

20. Benne, *The Paradoxical Vision*, Chapter 3.
21. Luther, "Temporal Authority," 111.

writing about this all this time, and if I can only write and I can't put *my body* where my words are, then I'm not much of a writer."²² Schulze then led a group to Albany, Georgia where he spent six days in jail! Schultze connected his writing with publicly participating in non-violent direct action recognizing that jail might be forthcoming.

The 1963 "March on Washington for Jobs and Freedom" was not lacking for Lutheran participation. Although Schultze was in Europe prior to the March, he arrived to join African and European American Lutherans in the march to the Lincoln Memorial. Hundreds of Lutherans from across the country came to Washington, D.C. and carried "Lutherans Marching!" and "Lutherans Human Relations Association" signs. Members of Lutheran congregations in Washington, D.C. made signs and fed marchers.²³ Martin Luther King, Jr. noted the support, endorsement, and participation of Lutherans when he wrote that the march included "thousands of congregations and ministers of the Lutheran and Methodist Churches."²⁴ Schultze armed with faith in a justifying God could practice physicality as a method for standing up for racial justice.

While Andrew Schulze was somewhat of a trailblazer among Lutherans and eradicating segregation and promoting racial justice, the Rev. Joseph Ellwanger was a compassionate pastor who joined marches in Birmingham and Selma, Alabama. A member of Lutheran Human Relations Association of America (LHRAA), Pastor Ellwanger served St. Paul's Lutheran Church, an African American congregation, in Birmingham. On September 15, four African American girls were killed when a bomb exploded at Sixteenth Street Baptist Church as they were preparing for morning worship. Among those who died was eleven year old Denise McNair. Denise McNair, along with her father, Christ McNair belonged to St. Paul's Lutheran Church.

Pastor Ellwanger was no stranger to marches. He was a member and leader of the Alabama Council on Human Relations. His role in the Birmingham Movement included planning the demonstrations with the leadership, including Martin Luther King, Jr. and others. Responding to Martin King's "Letter from Birmingham Jail," he along with a group of African American and European American pastors publicly supported demonstrations and march with members of St. Paul's.²⁵ Moreover, when requested

---

22. Galchutt, *The Career of Andrew Schulze, 1924–1968*, 179. Galchutt is quoting from Karl Lutze, Oral History Collection, 32 (emphasis added).

23. Pictures of Lutherans participating in the "March on Washington for Jobs and Freedom" are available online: http://www.flickr.com/photos/elcaarchives/sets/72157635276195810 (accessed 24/09/2013).

24. King, *Why We Can't Wait*, 123.

25. Interview with Rev. Joseph Ellwanger, conducted by Blackside, Inc.

by the McNair family to participate in the funeral service of the McNair's daughter, Ellwanger did. He was challenged, however, by a superior who counseled that it was inappropriate for him to participate. Pastor Ellwanger responded as any pastor would when a member is called to their eternal rest, "I am serving as pastor of the father of one of these girls. He asked me—he and his wife asked me—to lead their family in prayer before the funeral and to participate in the funeral, and I am going there as a witness to the Gospel; and I will be there."[26] Joseph Ellwanger certainly embodied Martin Luther's exhortation regarding Christians suffering injustice and not tolerating injustice to the neighbor.

The Rev. Dr. Will Herzfeld practiced a global form of physicality. A native of Alabama, Herzfeld knew well the pain and sorrow of segregation and how it affected African Americans. He served as pastor of Christ Lutheran Church in Tuscaloosa, Alabama from 1961–1965. During those years, Herzfeld became a close associate of Martin King. He was the founder and president of the Tuscaloosa chapter of the Southern Christian Leadership Conference (SCLC). He went on to lead the state chapter of SCLC.[27] Herzfeld was aware of not only racial injustice in his hometown and state, he was deeply concerned about the practice of sexism in the global Lutheran communion.

The global nature of Herzfeld intentionally placing his body into public spaces continued through his attendance and participation in the Lutheran church in Central Africa Republic's ordination of its first female pastor, Rachel Doumbaye. Herzfeld's observation of that event reflects his sense of justice. "One of the things ordination does is empower women, and women are not free in these societies," he said. "During the ordination, I could see the evangelical defiance on the face of all the women. They knew things had changed."[28] Herzfeld's public witness affirms the radical nature of God's justifying grace which leads the believer to have faith in God's power to lead one over society's desire for conformity and respectability.

LUTHERAN ETHICS: HEARING NEW VOICES

Martin Luther's cathetical question looms before us, what does this mean for the global Lutheran communion? If my argument is convincing that physicality is and can be a new model of Lutheran ethics for a multicultural global world, is it possible for Lutheran ethics to begin with actions of God's people and then reflecting on those actions? Is it possible in a world and

---

26. Kathryn Galchutt is quoting from Ziehr, *The Struggle for Unity*, 134–35.
27. Interview with Will Herzfeld, conducted by Lee H. Wesley, 26.
28. Basye, "People thought it was impossible," 49.

church, which has been shaped by the Enlightenment project (individualism), to welcome accounts of Lutheran ethics shaped by social spaces where some of God's people are marginalized and oppressed vis-à-vis social constructs (race, class, gender, sexual orientation, and geography) not of their making?

Ten years ago, the Lutheran World Federation launched a study team focused on Lutheran ethics at the intersection of living in the world. One of the results of the study team's deliberations was a call for a framework grounded in a "Lutheran grammar."[29] That Lutheran grammar is, of course, justification. However, there is a caveat. Is it possible for a universal Lutheran grammar to be accepted in specific and concrete situations which are different than Western Europe's living in the world? Yes, as long as there is acceptance of the difference articulated by specific people from a diversity of cultures.

Physicality seeks to move beyond abstract ethical principles and deciding prematurely the solutions to ethical matters. The emphasis here is twofold. First, there is a blending of the mind, body, and heart, a human person. As Luther expresses the wholeness of Jesus Christ, so the wholeness of human beings. "Similarly, body and soul present two distinct entities in a natural and sound person; yet the two constitute but one person, and we ascribe the functions, activities, and offices of each to the whole person."[30]

Second, physicality as a new model for Lutheran ethics surfaces an ethical method which is more descriptive than prescriptive. Lutheran ethics in a new grammar provides analysis of the behavior of God's people in particular contexts. In a word, Lutheran ethics gets into the messy lives of a diversity of people, as Jesus did. This necessitates a willingness to hear new voices who also have a deep faith in a God who justifies them before God and other human beings. Physicality is recognition that the specific other is real and a body which exists at the juncture of justice and injustice. Finally, physicality points to a plurality of ways Lutheran ethics can be done and expressed in a multicultural global world. The question is: Does God's Word which became flesh hold and bind those new voices in articulating a new understanding of Lutheran ethics?

CONCLUSION

This chapter sought to argue that some African and European American Lutheran elders have left a model for articulating Lutheran ethics in a global multicultural world. Physicality, intentionally placing one's body into social

---

29. Bloomquist, *Lutheran Ethics at the Intersections of God's One World*.
30. Luther, *Sermons on the Gospel of St. John. Chapters 14–16*, LW 24, 106.

spaces as a means of expressing justice, renews our contemporary and future witness for racial justice and equality. Physicality, with God's justifying grace at the core, emerges out of the lived experiences of poor and marginalized people. The legacy of the elders, globally, is worthy of emulating because it is our faith in God who calls us in our ministry of building a sustainable and just society for all people. Living in a global multicultural world means accepting a plurality of ways Lutheran ethics are expressed and practiced in society.

BIBLIOGRAPHY

Basye, Anne. "People thought it was impossible." *The Lutheran*, July, 2002.
Benne, Robert. *The Paradoxical Vision: A Public Theology for the Twenty-first Century*. Minneapolis: Augsburg Fortress, 1995.
Bloomquist, Karen L., editor. *Lutheran Ethics at the Intersection of God's One World*. Geneva: The Lutheran World Federation, 2005.
Douglas, Mary. *Natural Symbols: Explorations in Cosmology*. New York: Routledge, 1996.
The Emancipation Proclamation. Archives.gov Web site. Online: www.archives.gov/exhibits/featured_documents/emancipation_proclamation/ (accessed 01/01/2014).
"Embodiment." Merriam-Webster.com. Online: http://www.merriam-webster.com/dictionary/embodiment (accessed 02/03/2014).
Galchutt, Kathryn M. *The Career of Andrew Schulze, 1924–1968: Lutherans and Race in the Civil Rights Era*. Macon, GA: Mercer University Press, 2005.
Gao, George. "On MLK Day, racial equality found wanting." Online: http://pewresearch.org/fact-tank/2014/01/17/on-mlk-day-racial-equality-found-wanting/ (accessed 01/02/2014).
Graetz, Robert. *A White Preacher's Memoir: The Montgomery Bus Boycott*. Montgomery: Black Belt, 1998.
Interview with Rev. Joseph Ellwanger, conducted by Blackside, Inc. 13/11/1985. Online: Http://www.digital.wustl.edu/e/eop (accessed 02/03/2014).
Interview with Will Herzfeld, conducted by Lee H. Wesley. 21/01/1982. *Oral History from Will Herzfeld*. The Oral History of the Archives of Cooperative Lutheranism Record Group OH 1, Item 36, 1982, ELCA Archives.
King, Jr., Martin Luther. "I Have a Dream." In *A Testament of Hope: The Essential Writings of Martin Luther King, Jr.*, edited by James M. Washington, 217–20. San Francisco: Harper & Row, Publishers, 1986.
———. *Why We Can't Wait*. New York: The New American Library, 1963.
Kolb, Robert, and Timothy J. Wengert, editors. *The Book of Concord: The Confessions of the Evangelical Lutheran Church*. Minneapolis, MN: Fortress, 2000.
Luther, Martin. *Lectures on Galatians* (1535). LW 26. St. Louis: Concordia, 1963.
———. *Sermons on the Gospel of St. John. Chapters 14–16* (1537). LW 24. St. Louis: Concordia, 1961.
———. "Temporal Authority: To What Extent It Should Be Obeyed" (1522). In *Christian Social Teachings. A Reader in Christian Social Ethics from the Bible to the*

Present, edited by George W. Forell, 108–114. Minneapolis, MN: Fortress Press, 2013.
Pinn, Anthony. *Embodiment and the New Shape of Black Theological Thought*. New York: New York University Press, 2010.
"The Meaning of the Symbolism of the Sankofa Bird." DuBois Learning Center. Online: http://www.duboislc.net/SankofaMeaning.html (accessed 01/03/2014).
Wright, Barnett. *1963: How the Birmingham Civil Rights Movement Changed America and the World*. Birmingham: The Birmingham News Company, 2013.
Ziehr, Richard O. *The Struggle for Unity: A Personal Look at the Integration of the Lutheran Church in the South*. Milton, FL: CJH Enterprises, 1999.

PART THREE

Reformation as a Model
for Interpretation of the Present

11

Incarnate vs. Discarnate Protestantism

Martin Luther and the Disembodiment of Faith

NIELS HENRIK GREGERSEN

This chapter argues that Lutheran theology needs to reflect anew upon the *Gestalts* of Protestantism in a post-secular era. On the one hand, we have what I call a Protestantism without blood and flesh, in which faith is understood primarily as an individualized attitude of faith and inner freedom vis-à-vis church and society. On the other hand, we have a Protestantism of blood and flesh which knows that faith, hope, and love can only thrive in and through social forms of embodiment. The church, in this understanding, is a place in which a public understanding of the gospel is cultivated, and in which we are constantly reminded that the world of creation around us is "full of Bible," as Luther could express himself. On this view, faith can never be a purely private affair.

How is the relation between religion and the public realm perceived today? Some years ago I took a bus shuttle from Marina Hotel uphill to the Berkeley University Campus. During the ride I had a good conversation with another passenger. He was scouting for talents in biochemistry for pharmaceutical companies, and asked what I was doing. Well, I was in Berkeley to give lectures on science and religion. He hesitated a bit, and then remarked that while he had the deepest respect for spirituality and personal religion, he was critical of organized religion. "I feel something similar about science," I responded, "I find personal science very intriguing, but I'm more worried about organized science." Even though Americans are not used to the bite of Scandinavian irony, we subsequently had a sober discussion. The point I wanted to drive home was that our public discourse on religion should not follow other rules than discourse on societal issues in general. It would be curious if organizational aspects of religion are to be regarded with suspicion *a priori*, whereas the organization of science in universities and research centres would be judged on other standards. The idea of a private religion is probably as awkward as the idea of personal science or a non-public exercise of journalism. Personal and social forms of religion are always intertwined, directly or indirectly.

FAITH IN THE CONTEXT OF A FOUR-E ANTHROPOLOGY

In what follows my aim is to show how contemporary forms of Protestantism, like most other religions, operate in the creative zones of interpenetration between personal and organizational aspects of religion.[1] Before I go into the particulars of "internal" theological interpretations of embodied vs. disembodied forms of Protestantism, I begin with a broad "external" description of how religious faith may be understood as human phenomena on par with other human phenomena. Faith-traditions, I suggest, are explicable within the general trajectories of what may be termed a *four E-anthropology*. Faith-traditions of whatever sort are

- E*merging* out of evolution, channelled through long-lived but gradually changing traditions which serve as the "boundaries of our habitations,"[2]

- E*mbodied* in long-term habits of everyday life shaped by rituals and patterns of shared bodily movement and attention,

- E*mbedded* in linguistic traditions with a broad repertoire of publicly available semantic meanings and practical ways of orientation, and

- E*nvironmentally* sensitive to natural and social surroundings.

---

1. The term "interpenetration" is used by sociologist Niklas Luhmann about the reciprocal constitution of the psychological system of moods and thoughts and the social system of communication and action. The psychological and social systems are thus external environments to one another, without any direct input-output relations (in German: *Leistungen*). See Luhmann, *Soziale Systeme*, 289–90. For example, during a service the churchgoer's mind and moods may go in and out of the semantic world of the biblical texts, prayers and sermons. Nonetheless such "structurally coupled systems" eventually lead to overlapping correspondences (in German: *Überschneidungen*) between the psychological and the social system (292–93), for example in processes of mentally approaching or turning away from what is said and heard, in adherence or non-adherence, in attraction or repulsion.

2. Brown, *Boundaries of Our Habitations*.

As such, faith-traditions are both communally shared and personally enacted, but never in a one-to-one way. Ordinary people (and also religious professionals are ordinary people for the most of their time) live a life with a series of ephemeral feelings, wavering affectations and impulses for practical value-orientation, while also now and then practicing what is categorized as specific religious activities. Sometimes people also think about religious issues of meaning, especially in times of crisis or in states of wonder and reflection. But usually we live deeper than we think.

ORTHODOXIES AND POLYDOXIES

Accordingly, religious life is polymorphous in shape, just as also our religious reflections take a variety of forms in what the Jewish philosopher of religion Rabbi Alvin Jay Reines (1926–2004) has helpfully termed *polydoxy*.[3] For Reines, however, polydoxy is presented as a contrast term to orthodoxy, but this contrastive view is hardly in touch with the way religion is ordinarily lived. For *orthodoxy* is not the same as *monodoxy* but encapsulates a broad repertoire of semantic viewpoints, doctrines and assumptions, practices and attitudes, moods and affectations which are not equally shared by members of religious communities, even if some shared matrices of belief are usually present. I therefore prefer the term polydoxy as presented by Catherine Keller and Laurel Schneider in their *Polydoxy: Theology of Multiplicity and Relation* from 2011. As argued by Catherine Keller,

> Our experiment in polydoxy pits itself not against monotheism, not against orthodoxy, but against the temptation besetting both: that of a *monodoxy* that actually sabotages the full operation of its own trinitarian logic.[4]

The aim of Keller and Schneider is to present the idea of polydoxy as a revisionary program for constructive theology more than as a means for understanding contemporary religious life. Danish theologian Christine Johannesen-Henry, by contrast, uses polydoxy as a descriptive term when analyzing the flow of belief-formation among her contemporaries. The personal stories of Danish cancer survivors move in and out of Christian and non-Christian semantic repertories, interlacing very personal stories of grandparents, children, and friends (and the technicalities of chemotherapy) with the larger stories of what it means to a human individual, embedded in socio-material environments, while existentially confronted with the experience of death and dying. Nonetheless, many of the interviewed

---

3. Reines, *Polydoxy: Explorations in a Philosophy of Religion*.
4. Keller and Schneider, *Polydoxy: Theology of Multiplicity and Relation*, 94.

respondents report of a sense of transcendence and even of contact with deceased members of their family.[5]

If this is how everyday religion works in contemporary Western societies, I think it is wrong simply to contrast a fixed view of organized religion with the fluid forms of everyday polydoxy. Even if it is true that our religious mentalities are constantly changing (sometimes even changed with the suddenness of a conversion), organized forms of religion (say, a mass in the Uppsala Cathedral) will always host representatives of a polydox if not heterodox Christianity on the benches, while the attendants nonetheless presuppose the organized religion, either explicitly or implicitly, also when reacting against what may be perceived as problematic aspects of the institution of the Church of Sweden. As I have argued in an earlier book on *Twofold Christianity*, Nordic Protestantism hosts a creative symbiosis between what may be termed church-oriented Christianity and forms of Christianity living on the fringe of churches.[6] Both forms of Protestantism come in a multiplicity of forms, but never fully dissociated from one another. Since religions are emergent phenomena, they never arrive as fully new inventions. Traditions are at work also as matrices for expressing a sacred or secular discontent with established forms of religion. Sociologically speaking, the idea of a counter-cultural escape from tradition is a delusion.

Accordingly, too quick references to *religious pluralism* hardly catch the complexities of our religious situation today. Also religions make up a cultural history, in which some religions play a significantly stronger role than other religions. Wahhabism rules in Saudi Arabia, but in Western societies some religions also have a stronger representational stance than other religions. In the Nordic countries between 68 and 82 percent of the population were members of the Lutheran churches by 2012, and even though religious commitment vary enormously among the members, it would be wrong to dismiss this cultural embedment of religious life. Amalgamations of beliefs and practices may be the rule rather than the exception, but pluralism doesn't reign without constraints. Think, for example, of the widespread idea of a God as being essentially a loving God. Seen from the longer perspective of the history of religions this concept is quite rare; in view of human experiences of suffering and natural hazards, it may even be seen as counter-intuitive. Nonetheless, the wide majority of fluid religion in the West presupposes the matrix of orthodox Christian faith with its central

---

5. Johannesen-Henry, "Polydox eschatology," 107–29.

6. In Gregersen, *Den dobbelte kristendom*, I argued for such symbiosis of different forms of Christianity in the development of a Lutheran "folk church" identity in Denmark from the 1750's to the present. "Symbiosis" is here used as a biology-based metaphor for the co-existence of different mentalities in one and the same social body.

tenet that "God is love" (1 John 4). Certainly, there are mixed patterns of beliefs and practices and an overwhelming variety of distinct commitments, but no catch-phrase of pluralist religiosity can do the analytical work for contemporary theology without also attending to relatively shared patterns of belief and value orientation. Indeed, we do not only live in pluralistic society but are also, in a sense, "beyond pluralism." As argued by Graham Ward. "We have moved beyond pluralism, because there is no view from nowhere, no objective knowledge; the view from nowhere is itself a cultural ideology—often Western, white and male."[7]

INCARNATE AND DISCARNATE FORMS OF RELIGION: SOCIOLOGICAL OBSERVATIONS

More typical than pluralism for our contemporary Western attitude, I think, is the phenomenon of the *discarnation of belief*, especially in Protestant countries. In his opus magnum from 2007, *A Secular Age*, philosopher Charles Taylor has helpfully distinguished between various meanings of secularity.

- *Secularity1* means the retreat of religion from public life. From a general sociological point of view, this is the inevitable consequence of the differentiation taking place in modern Western societies since the age of mercantilism, pietism, and enlightenment.
- *Secularity2* refers to the decline in religious belief and practice, which was particularly felt in the century between 1870 and 1970, with forerunners in ancient scepticism and sequels in modern agnosticism and atheism.
- *Secularity3*, then, refers to the change in the conditions for having a religious engagement, a change of conditions on which Taylor focuses his analysis.[8]

Taylor insists that something new has taken place in our attitudes to religion. He agrees, however, with the analysis of Niklas Luhmann, José Casanova, and other sociologists of religion that the differentiation of society, which is part of modernity, does not necessarily lead to a privatization of belief.[9] On the contrary, the cases for a de-privatization of belief are many, not only in the Muslim world, but also in Hinduism, Buddhism, and Christianity (think of Gandhi, Dalai Lama, Desmond Tutu, or Tony Blair, to mention a few).

7. Ward, *Cities of God*, 237.
8. Taylor, *A Secular Age*, 423.
9. Ibid., 426.

Taylor also points to another feature of religion in modern society which he terms "excarnation," that is, the disembodying of spiritual life in the form of "the transfer of our religious life out of bodily forms of ritual, worship, practice, so that it comes more and more to 'reside in the head.'"[10] This excarnation is the point of departure for everyday secularity (*Secularity3*). Religious commitments are thus less stable and have less prior probability than in earlier societies, in which religion was ingrained in daily life, incarnated in liturgies, festivals, carnivals, icons, home altars, etc.

However, the question is whether Taylor is right that the excarnation of belief has become a general condition of having a religious mentality. It seems to me that we today can mention many cases of a *re-ritualization*. Drives towards religious ritualization often come up in states of crises. Some examples from Denmark and Norway: The fire on the ship Scandinavian Star in 1990, leading to the death of 159 passengers, gave rise to the establishment of a corps of emergency pastors (today 42 pastors) in the Evangelical-Lutheran Church in Denmark; a common memorial service was held, the first of its kind in Denmark. The Estonia disaster in 1994 (with 852 casualties) led to several mourning ceremonies for friends and family members. The same happened in the year 2000, when 9 participants were tramped down at the Roskilde Festival; the service in Roskilde Cathedral was even shown in public television. Also the Breivik massacre on 77 young persons on July 22, 2011, led to a wide number of national mourning ceremonies in the cathedral of Oslo, and in many other national churches all over the country.

Most people are in need of cognitive orientation and affective accompaniment, and rituals are a well-winnowed way of marking out existentially significant events in the public realm. Rituals function, as Niklas Luhmann points out, as *symbiotic mechanisms* that offer a security in view of the insecurity of faith as a "symbolic medium of communication." As a symbolic medium faith is supposed to be available for use whenever needed, in principle like money in the monetary system, or power in the political system. But as Luhmann further argues, every symbolic medium of communication needs to be backed up by a material basis of *real assets*: Political governance through military and other forms of power; science by empirical observation; intimate love through sexual intercourse and other forms of corporal intimacy; monetary systems through gold and property.[11] In this sense one might say that religion without rituals is similar to marriage without sex. It

---

10. Ibid., 613.
11. Luhmann, *Funktion der Religion*, 144.

can work, and it does work to a certain extent and for a certain period, but it does work less well than it could have done.

Furthermore, in his posthumous work, *Die Religion der Gesellschaft* from 2000, Luhmann argues that the concept of secularization needs to be defined relative to the observers. As part of a secular meta-narrative in the vein of *Secularity2* (the decline in religious belief and practice), reference to secularization was part of the expectation of religion's extermination in a foreseeable future. The so-called "new atheism" of Richard Dawkins, Christopher Hitchens, and others may in part stem from a deep frustration that religions after all haven't gone away, but sometimes even gain a new momentum. Accordingly, the concept of secularization may be part of an "observation of the observation" of the relation between religion and its environment, seen from a disappointed religious (or atheist) viewpoint.[12] Religious practitioners tend to see others as "secular," when they do not attend church life. Similarly, the idea of secularization sometimes is frequently used by secular sociologists who don't understand, as put by Luhmann, that "sleeping late on Sunday" doesn't mean "refusing the sacrament."[13]

But also today religions continue to host a sense of an *attunement* to realms of reality not empirically detectable, be it in terms of the future, in terms of a transcendent realm of values, truths and beauties, or in terms of a feeling of being encompassed by the comprehensive reality called God. Here comes to the fore not so much the embodied aspects of religion, but an awareness of the wider environment of human existence. In *Public Religions in the Modern World*, José Casanova puts it as follows:

> Religion always transcends any privatistic, autistic reality, serving to integrate the individual into an intersubjective, public and communal 'world.' Simultaneously, however, religion always transcends any particular community cult, serving to free the individual from any particular 'world,' and to integrate the same individual into a transsocial, cosmic reality.[14]

We here arrive at a view closely connected to Charles Taylor's observation that religion "saturates" reality while being "side-lined" from public incarnations.[15] Protestantism (and some strands of Catholicism) live quite comfortably with the secular fact that the church cannot, and shouldn't, fill out the world, but in a sense *must* be side-lined to exist alongside other social institutions. Protestant churches tend not to have very definite views

12. Luhmann, *Die Religion der Gesellschaft*, 282.
13. Ibid., 283.
14. Casanova, *Public Religions in the Modern World*, 216.
15. Taylor, *A Secular Age*, 816.

on cinemas and soccer games, or poker. However, streams of worldly reality may still be "full of God," as already phrased by the pre-Socratic philosopher Thales.[16]

In spite of all religious disembodiment, the world still affords the presence of events and processes that continue to trigger a religious sensibility. The sun still rises, the air in the lungs still feels refreshing, birds continue to sing, cats still move elegantly, children are born and grow up, people mourn about their lost friends, family life still goes on despite crises, and the neighbour still continues to be annoying as well as sometimes a positive surprise. Even if religion may no longer be necessary from the perspective of the other functions of society, such as legal or scientific institutions, religion deals with experiences in the midst of society, which are more than necessary for human survival: Cognitive complexities beyond rational comprehension; moral demands beyond reasonableness; and with the aesthetic excess of reality; intimations of transcendence. At the same time, however, the disembodiment of faith also offers ample space for a disengagement from faith.

This raises a question to future ways of developing Protestant traditions. Crudely put: Should Protestant mentality in general, and the Lutheran tradition in particular, define itself as the archetype of a disembodied faith, a religious *mentalité* of reserve and freedom from all external constraints? Or should Protestantism, and the Lutheran traditions in particular, cultivate different expressions of belief—*emerging* out of the semantics and pragmatics of particular traditions open to reality, *embodied* in audible words, visible signs and touchable gestures, *embedded* culturally in both institutionalized and fluid religion, and having a sense of an *environment*, a world of creation larger than our individual bodies, larger than the congregational bodies of the churches and larger than the cultural horizons of contemporary consumer societies?

VARIETIES OF PROTESTANTISM WITHOUT FLESH AND BLOOD

My perceptive reader will now probably have guessed the overall direction of my own answers to these questions.[17] As there is an embodied Protes-

16. Aristotle, *De anima* 411 a7. Recently, Casanova has argued that it is typical for Nordic Protestantism that there is no clear boundary between the secular and the sacred in contrast to the Southern European Catholic pattern of a *laïcité* vis-à-vis the Church, see Casanova, "The Two Dimensions, Temporal and Spatial, of the Secular: Comparative Reflections on the Nordic Protestant and Southern Catholic Patters from a Global Perspective," 21–33.

17. The following argument is further developed in Gregersen, "Protestantisme med kød og blod," 253–70.

tantism of flesh and blood, there is a Protestantism *without* flesh and blood, which appear wherever one seeks to identify the idea of Protestantism with reference to essential principles. We see this tendency in both G.W.F Hegel and the later Schleiermacher. Let me begin with G.W.F. Hegel's (1770–1831) stunning statement in his *Lectures on the Philosophy of History*: "This is the essence of the Reformation: Man is in his very nature destined to be free."[18] It is noteworthy that this concern is defined without any basis in the actual writings of the Reformers, who rather say the opposite, namely that human beings can only become free through the liberating work of the Holy Spirit. Pursuing Hegel's line of thought even more radically, F.C. Baur (1792–1860) speaks of the *disparity* between Catholic and Protestant principles. In Protestantism, we find "the *autonomy* of the subject in contrast to all the *heteronomy* of the Catholic concept of the church."[19] Protestantism is here regarded as a form of consciousness in the cultural arena without any particular content or church affiliation.

Friedrich Schleiermacher, as always, is more cautious but still on the same plane when arguing for the principal distinction between a Protestant and a Catholic attitude:

> [T]he antithesis between Protestantism and Catholicism may provisionally be conceived thus: the former makes the individual's relation to the church dependent on his [or her] relation to Christ, while the latter contrariwise makes the individual's relation to Christ dependent on his [or her] relation to the church (1831, § 24).[20]

According to Schleiermacher, Protestantism eliminates the church as a necessary mediator between the believer and God. The church's fellowship is the *result* of the fact that people believe in God through Christ; the church is not the necessary *presupposition* for faith. Schleiermacher thus leaves the door ajar for the possibility that Christianity can grow out beyond the church—for why cannot the individual's relationship to God be realized outside the church? In a sense, Schleiermacher was fully right on this. In the Protestant world, it is indeed possible to understand oneself as a believer also after leaving the church. We find a later echo of this understanding of

---

18. Hegel, *The Philosophy of History*, 417. German original in Hegel, *Vorlesungen über die Philosophie der Geschichte* in *Sämmtliche Werke* Bd. 11, 524: "Dies ist der wesentliche Inhalt der Reformation: der Mensch ist durch sich selbst bestimmt frei zu sein."

19. Baur, *Die Epochen der kirchlichen Geschichtsschreibung*, 257.

20. Schleiermacher, *The Christian Faith*, 102. German original: Schleiermacher, *Der christliche Glaube nach den Grundsätzen der evangelischen Kirche im Zusammenhange dargestellt*, vol. 1, 137.

the Protestant principle of individuality in Max Weber's sociology of religion. In *Wirtschaft und Gesellschaft*, he made his famous thesis of a *Verspraclichung des Sakralen* with reference to both Buddhism and Christianity.[21]

The Protestant liberal theologian Ernst Troeltsch coined the distinction between Old Protestantism and New Protestantism in order to argue that the Christian religion had grown beyond the walls of the uniform confessional church, a uniform church still presupposed by Friedrich Schleiermacher. As a historian, Troeltsch was fully aware that the Hegelian interpretation of Luther is untenable. He acknowledges that the Reformation had a Janus face, with one side facing back to the Middle Ages and the other facing forward to prepare the way for modernity. He even defines the distinction between the two as "old Protestantism" presuming a uniform confessional church and modern Protestantism growing *beyond* this church form, with Schleiermacher's Preussian *Unions-Theologie* marking the border between old, *church-oriented* Protestantism and modern *cultural* Protestantism. In consequence, the traditions of Hegel and of Schleiermacher concur in pursuing the *principles* of Protestantism. Paul Tillich's concept of the "principle of Protestantism" is grown in the same mould.[22]

It's an irony of history that also the strongest proponents of Lutheran restoration dogmatics in the nineteenth century theology continued the search for principles of Protestantism. The two Reformation principles were formulated by August Twesten (1789–1876): Scripture as the *formal principle* and Justification by Faith as the *material principle*. Twesten argues that this distinction expresses the interaction between the objective side (the Bible alone) and the subjective side (the principle of faith).[23] We find similar formulations in conservative Hegelianism, for example in the German Isaak August Dorner and in the Dane H.L. Martensen.[24] As Jan Rohls

---

21. Weber, *Wirtschaft und Gesellschaft*, 283: "Der Buddhismus bestand, soweit die Laien in Betracht kamen, ursprünglich lediglich in Predigt, und in den christlichen Religionen bedeutet sie um so mehr, je vollständiger die magisch-sakramentalen Bestandteile eliminiert sind. Am meisten daher innerhalb des Protestantismus, wo der Priesterbegriff gänzlich durch den Predigerbegriff ersetzt ist." I owe this quote to my colleague, Prof. Bent Flemming Nielsen.

22. Tillich, *The Protestant Era*, chapter 11. Tillich, however, knew that Protestantism cannot do without some form of sacramental awareness.

23. To the best of my knowledge the two principles were first formulated by August Twesten in *Vorlesungen über die Dogmatik der evangelisch-lutherischen Kirche*, vol. 1, 257–264.

24. Martensen, *Den christelige Dogmatik*, 33: "What the Reformation wanted was neither exclusively the Objective or the Subjective; it was the free union of the Objective and the Subjective, of the content of faith and the intensity of faith" (§ 21; my translation). A similar position is already found in Dorner, "Das Prinzip unserer Kirche nach dem inneren Verhältniss der materialen und formalen Seite desselben zueinander,"

matter-of-factly notes, "The proclamation of a Protestant principle served as a means for finding a common fundament behind the doctrinal differences between Lutherans and Reformed."[25]

Principles, however, can't stand alone. Not even a Protestantism without blood and flesh can do without hagiographies and iconic representation. On entering the imposing cathedral in Berlin, built by the unionist Emperor Wilhelm II and completed in 1905, we are facing a peculiar iconography: We are confronted with statues of Luther and Calvin on their high pedestals in the nave—like cherubim guarding the entrance to the high altar where Christ sits enthroned in the background. But if we look beyond these statues we see a similar statue of Zwingli on Luther's right hand (even though they were ardent enemies), while a statue of Melanchthon, Luther's right hand man, stands inappropriately on Calvin's left. The position of the icons of faith suggests that despite clear *disagreements* in real life, the four could all agree on a few basic "Protestant" principles. Apparently the minimalism of the Protestant principles served to keep the actual differences at arm's length.

A PROTESTANTISM OF FLESH AND BLOOD

Are we placed in another situation today? I think we are. We nowadays need to articulate an evangelical theology with a quite different sense of body and sociality. By "flesh and blood," however, I do not mean so much the physical body *per se* (in German rendered as *Körper*) as the fact that we as living bodies (in German: *Leiber*) are always embedded in a natural world full of meanings. We live and breathe in a world of nature, and we also live in a world of meanings, in which words, signs, and gestures have significance to us, even beneath our conscious awareness. A Protestantism of flesh and blood is an evangelical theology that is aware of the fact that our understanding of Christianity cannot be detached from the pre-lingual signs and body-based expressions of our human existence.

In this view, information and meaning belong to the nature of reality. As biocultural beings, we are constantly in the process of interpreting a world which is forever richer than we can conceive of.[26] The bandwidth of potential information requires of us to have a trusting attitude to reality. At one and the same time, reality is iconically close in the way it impacts

---

published in extended form in Dorner, *Gesammelte Schriften aus dem Gebiet der systematischen Theologie, Exegese und Geschichte*, 49–150.

25. Rohls, *Protestantische Theologie der Neuzeit*, vol. I, 573.

26. This is the main thesis of Davies and Gregersen, *Information and the Nature of Reality: From Physics to Metaphysics*.

on our awareness of being present (here, not elsewhere) while also prompting us towards horizons of potential meanings (out there, or in the future), meanings which cannot be seen with the naked eye or touched with the bodily senses.

This intertwinement of physicality and meaning comes to the fore in Martin Luther's theology of creation as well as in his Eucharistic theology. In what follows I hope to show that central aspects of Luther's theology can indeed be expressed through the Four E-anthropology sketched out above. The easiest point to make regards the notion of evolutionary emergence. The Reformation was intended as a *re-formatio* and not as a *novitas*, and was indeed emerging out of the traditions of the ancient and medieval church. Luther was not a man of modernity, as supposed by Hegel, but a man of the late Middle Ages, as evidenced by contemporary historians.[27] But what about the three other E's: embodied, socially embedded, and environmental?

LUTHER'S ENVIRONMENTAL ANTHROPOLOGY

My aim is not here to promote Luther as a forerunner for a modern ecological theology. But that nature is central to his understanding of Christian life is easily found in his theology of creation.[28] Having rejected natural theology (not least in *The Heidelberg Disputation* 1518), he begins doggedly to formulate a theology of creation. Already in his attack on Emser in 1521, he is arguing that "all God's activity and all God's creatures are purely living signs and divine word."[29] Certainly, God is not to be found in nature but in the Word and the sacraments; yet the whole world is "full of Bible."[30] Luther develops this line of thought in his sermons and lectures, and in particular those on Genesis, the Psalms of David, and the preaching of Jesus. In his *Lectures on Genesis* on Gen 1:11, for example, Luther can say that "any bird whatever and any fish whatever are nothing but nouns in the divine rule of language."[31] The message is actually quite simple and one also articulated

---

27. See, for example, Leppin, *Martin Luther*.

28. See Gregersen, "Grace in Nature and History: Luther's Doctrine of Creation Revisited," 19–29.

29. Luther, *Auf das überchristlich, übergeistlich und überkünstlichen Buch Bocks Emsers zu Leipzig Antwort*, WA 7, 614–98 (650): "all gottis werck und creaturn [sind] eytel lebendig tzeychen und wort gottis."

30. Luther, *Predigten des Jahres 1544*, Nr 16, WA 49, 434: "Also ist unser Haus, Hof, Acker, Garten und alles vol Bibel, Da Gott durch seine Wunderwerck nicht allein prediget. Sondern auch an unsere Augen klopffet, unsere Sinne rüret und uns gleich ins Herz leuchtet, so wirs haben wollen." See overview in Groh, *Schöpfung im Widerspruch. Deutungen der Natur und des Menschen von der Genesis bis zur Reformation*, 541–98.

31. Luther, *Lectures on Genesis*, LW 1, 49; WA 42, 36–37.

in his Catechisms, namely that God's goodwill and mercy is channeled into his creation without our merit. As the sun rises on both good and evil (Matt 5:45), so we receive the divine blessings from God through the creatures. "Creatures are only the hands, channels, and means through which God bestows all blessings. For example, he gives to the mother breasts and milk for her infant (...)"[32]

In his preaching, Luther can therefore take his starting-point wherever he likes: in the sacraments, in the preaching of Jesus, in the letters of Paul, in the Psalms of David, or in ordinary experience. For David invites us to "the beautiful song of praise" (*Das schöne Confitemini*), as Luther calls his exposition of Psalm 118 in July 1530. Already in the first verse ("O give thanks to the Lord, for he is good; his steadfast love endures forever!"), he takes God's creation as his starting-point. God demonstrates his favor to all people beyond all measure, for

> He is the Creator of our bodies and souls, our Protector by day and by night, and the Preserver of our lives. He causes the sun and the moon to shine on us, fire, air, water, and the heavens to serve us. He causes the earth to give food, fodder, and wine, grain, clothes, wood, and all necessities. He provides us with gold and silver, house and home, wife and child, cattle, birds, and fish. In short, who can count it all? And all this is bountifully showered upon us every year, every day, every hour, and every minute.[33]

Luther's argument does not lead along the path of reasoning from the structure of creation to the assumption of God, as in natural theology. Due to the blindness of human sin, we fail to *notice* the overwhelming gifts of God, and this blindness furnishes us with an illusion so thorough that we do not realize it:

> What is a kingdom compared with a sound body? What is all the money and wealth in the world compared with one sunlit day? (...) What would our magnificent castles, houses, silk, satin, purple, golden jewelry, precious stones, all our pomp and glitter and show help us if we had to do without air for the length of one Our Father.[34]

For Luther creation was not only an objective fact. It's God's living work, given to human beings for appreciation. We live in a world of signs that

---

32. Luther, *The Great Catechism*, 389.
33. Luther, *The Beautiful Confitemini*, LW 14, 47–48; WA 31, 69–70.
34. Ibid., LW 14, 48; WA 31, 70–71.

contains a message to which we must respond—in the gratitude of faith or in the indifference of neglect. Just as the face of the flower stretches to the light of the sun and its roots to the water of the earth, so do we seek light, so do we drink when we are thirsty, so do we seek each other's company, and so on.

"[A]ll this universe is perfused with signs," as Charles Sanders Peirce said.[35] As human beings we live in a biophysical world of meaning inclined towards creativity, continuation, and growth, as we ourselves are inclined towards fellowship and care for each other. Accordingly, human beings don't exist as individual islands. We live in the created world of flesh, blood, and meaning in the three life-spheres: the great drama of nature itself, the medium-size sphere of our social life, and in the small sphere of individual existence. None without the other!

LUTHER'S EMBODIED ANTHROPOLOGY

We do not have to read many pages of the young Luther's sacramental theology before we meet the triad of sign (Lat. *signum*, Ger. *tzeychen*), meaning (Lat. *res*, Ger. *bedeutung*) and use (Lat. *utilitas*, Ger. *geprauch*) of faith:

> These three parts must be found in every sacrament. The sacrament must be external and visible, having some material form or appearance. The significance must be internal and spiritual, within the spirit of the person. Faith must make both of them together operative (*zu nutz*) and useful (*yn den prauch*).[36]

Significantly, the sacramental signs comprise not only the water of baptism or the bread and wine of the Eucharist but also the word and social act of which the natural elements are part. In the case of *baptism*, Luther writes: "The sign consists in this that we are thrust into the water in the name of the Father and of the Son and of the Holy Spirit; however, we are not left there but drawn out again. This accounts for the expression: *aus der Taufe gehoben*. The sign must thus have both its parts: the putting in and the drawing out."[37] Thus the sign is not the physical element alone, but the entire social act of baptism.

The same emphasis on the sociality of the sign is also found in his sermon on the Eucharist from 1519. Again it is not just the bread and wine that constitute the elements but the fact that bread and wine are "used in

---

35. Peirce, "The Basis of Pragmaticism in the Normative Sciences," 394.
36. Luther, *The Blessed Sacrament of the Holy and True Body of Christ, and the Brotherhoods*, LW 35, 49; WA 2, 742.
37. Luther, *The Holy and Blessed Sacrament of Baptism*, LW 35, 30; WA 2, 727.

eating and drinking, just as the water of baptism is used by immersion or pouring."[38] We here notice the pragmatic orientation of Luther's theology of baptism and Eucharist. The sign of the Eucharist is the entire meal, including the related words of Christ, not just the elements. Moreover, the meaning (*bedeutung*) and effect (*werck*) of the sacraments reach beyond the visible act and into the entire story that God and humankind share. We who are present at a baptism or a Eucharist know that part of the story is incomplete or absent. The meaning is only present in anticipation, since we only abstain from sin at our death:

> The significance of baptism is a blessed dying into sin and a resurrection in the grace of God, so that the old man, conceived and born in sin, is there drowned, and a new man, born in grace, comes forth and rises.[39]

In this connection Luther emphasizes that although the act of baptism (the sign) lasts only a few moments, its spiritual meaning "lasts as long as we live and is completed only in death."[40] Similarly, the meaning of the Eucharist institutes a fellowship with Christ and all other believers, reaching beyond death. Thus presence and absence condition each other: Christ's real presence is the pre-condition for a future story which can only be anticipated in faith, but not be grasped by any rational prognosis.

Accordingly, we may express the distinction and coordination between baptism and Eucharist in terms of bodily absorption. In baptism, we are absorbed into the body of Christ: *we in him*! But in the Eucharist, he is entering our bodies: *he in us*!

LUTHER'S ANTHROPOLOGY OF SOCIAL EMBEDMENT

Whereas baptism is the sacrament for the complete life-story of the individual, the Eucharist is the sacrament of fellowship: "The significance or effect (*die bedeutung odder das werck*) of this sacrament is fellowship of all the saints."[41]

There is thus a spatial sense to the Eucharist, since it directs us into the fellowship of love with all believers, while there is a predominantly time-related horizon linked to baptism, since its meaning is only fulfilled once

---

38. Luther, *The Blessed Sacrament of the Holy and True Body of Christ, and the Brotherhoods*, LW 35, 49; WA 2, 742.

39. Luther, *The Holy and Blessed Sacrament of Baptism*, LW 35, 30; WA 2, 727.

40. Ibid., LW 35, 30; WA 2, 728.

41. Luther, *The Blessed Sacrament of the Holy and True Body of Christ, and the Brotherhoods*, LW 35, 50; WA 2, 743.

the old Adam finally dies in order to be transformed into the new Adam through the grace of the resurrection. In baptism *faith* stands at the center, in the Eucharist *love*, for this is a "sacrament of fellowship, love, and unity."[42]

The meaning of the Eucharist cannot therefore be distilled from the full context of the Eucharistic meal. It cannot be captured in purely linguistic form as sentences, nor can it be owned as a floating spiritual "attitude." The Eucharist has no benefit or effect whatsoever if its participants isolate their relationship to God from fellowship with those in need: "For the sacrament has no blessing and significance unless love grows daily and so changes a person that he is made one with all others."[43]

Luther's sacramental theology exemplifies what I mean by a Protestantism of flesh and blood. At the center is not the physical body but the social body, which is made up of the fellowship with other believers and all suffering people. It is also a Protestantism that exists only insofar as it is lived: it cannot exist simply in a consciousness relation to God. For the same reason it is a very challenging Protestantism, beyond all confessional self-righteousness. For it is only those who believe and contribute that are "Christians" in Luther's sense. And who would dare to burst as having faith and love in contrast to "the others" that don't? The evangelical concern that surfaces in Luther's theology therefore cannot be reduced to a "position"—least of all a minimalist Protestantism whose principles could be learned and appropriated in twenty minutes. It is a way of life.

CONCLUSION

What I have done in this chapter is to exercize a two-fold move. I began with the contemporary status of religion in everyday life, particularly within my own North-Western orbit, and then moved backwards through the minimalist versions of Protestantism in the nineteenth century to Martin Luther's interpretation of the Christian faith as thoroughly embodied in the three life-circles of the human person, the social realm and the wider drama of creation. From here I then moved forward to our time. While I have argued that the basic contours of Luther's theology can be explicated within a contemporary bio-cultural world view encapsulated in the Four E-anthropology, I am fully aware that the insights of a genuinely incarnate understanding of evangelical faith for today will require systematic efforts not achievable within this brief essay.[44]

42. Ibid., LW 35, 61; WA 2, 750.
43. Ibid., LW 35, 58; WA 2, 748.
44. I can refer here to collective efforts in this direction, including Gregersen, Holm, Peters, Widmann, *The Gift of Grace*; Helmer, *The Global Luther*; and Bloomquist, *Transformative Theological Perspectives*.

My main point has been to argue that a Protestantism that choses to define itself on the basis of its principles rather than its primary manifestations in time and space risks a trivialization of Luther's theological concerns. Once upon a time there may have been pedagogical considerations behind those principles. Imagine a cultural context where both theologians and the laity were familiar with the Biblical traditions and the day-to-day life of the church, even to excess. In such context, a Protestantism of principles may have been experienced as a relief from the overload of tradition, as it was the case perhaps until the 1950s. Nineteenth century "liberal" theologians and twentieth century "dialectical" theologians were all children of an overtaxed pietism, and were ready to oppose it with reasoned principles and reductive formula.

However, we no longer live in a culture in which the Lutheran churches seem to be insistent about very much—for the simple reason that in the meantime the ensemble of secularization and post-secularity has gained ground, and the churches will have to address a variety of audiences. In this new situation, Protestant principles become a rather unworldly and dull affair—having lost their earlier educational purposes and liberating functions. Just as Christianity is found as a *lived* religion, never as an abstraction, so also faith is always lived in the framework of the Four E's: as *emerging* from tradition, as *environmentally* sensitive, as socially *embedded*, and as psychosomatically *embodied*.

Certainly, even a compendious Four E-anthropology can only serve as a framework for rethinking the particular insights coming from Martin Luther's theology of blood and flesh. What lies within the framework has always to be rediscovered and rearticulated anew. The Reformation is never a *fait accompli*.

BIBLIOGRAPHY

Aristotle. *De anima*. Oxford Classical Texts. Oxford: Oxford University Press, 1956.

Baur, F.C. *Die Epochen der kirchlichen Geschichtsschreibung*. Tübingen, 1852. Online: www.bibliolife.com/opensource (accessed 20/11/2013).

Bloomquist, Karen L., editor. *Transformative Theological Perspectives*. Minneapolis: Lutheran University Press, 2009.

Book of Concord: The Confessions of the Evangelical Lutheran Church. Edited by Robert Kolb and Timothy J. Wengert. Minneapolis: Fortress, 2000.

Brown, Delwin. *Boundaries of Our Habitations: Tradition and Theological Construction*. Albany: State University of New York Press, 1994.

Casanova, José. *Public Religions in the Modern World*. Chicago: University of Chicago Press, 1994.

———. "The Two Dimensions, Temporal and Spatial, of the Secular: Comparative Reflections on the Nordic Protestant and Southern Catholic Patters from a

Global Perspective." In *Secular and Sacred?: The Scandinavian Case of Religion in Human Rights, Law and Public Space*, edited by Rosemarie van den Breemer, José Casanova, and Trygve Wyller, 21–33. Göttingen: Vandenhoeck & Ruprecht, 2014.

Davies, Paul, and Niels Henrik Gregersen, editors. *Information and the Nature of Reality: From Physics to Metaphysics*. Cambridge: Cambridge University Press, 2010. Reprinted as Cambridge Canto Classics, 2014.

Dorner, Isaak August. "Das Prinzip unserer Kirche nach dem inneren Verhältnis der materialen und formalen Seite desselben zueinander." 1841. In *Gesammelte Schriften aus dem Gebiet der systematischen Theologie, Exegese und Geschichte*, 49–150. Berlin: Hertz, 1883.

Gregersen, Niels Henrik. *Den dobbelte kristendom*. Herning: Poul Christensens Forlag, 1996.

———. "Grace in Nature and History: Luther's Doctrine of Creation Revisited." *Dialog: A Journal of Theology* 44:1 (2005) 19–29.

———. "Protestantisme med kød og blod." *Dansk Teologisk Tidsskrift* 73:4 (2010) 253–70.

Gregersen, Niels Henrik, Bo Holm, Ted Peters, and Peter Widmann, editors. *The Gift of Grace: The Future of Lutheran Theology*. Minneapolis: Fortress, 2005.

Groh, Dieter. *Schöpfung im Widerspruch. Deutungen der Natur und des Menschen von der Genesis bis zur Reformation*. Frankfurt am Main: Suhrkamp, 2003.

Hegel, G. W. F. *The Philosophy of History*. New York: Dover, 1956.

———. *Vorlesungen über die Philosophie der Geschichte*. 1837. In *Sämmtliche Werke*, vol. 11, edited by Hermann Glockner. Stuttgart: Bad Cannstadt, 1971.

Helmer, Christine, editor. *The Global Luther: A Theologian for Modern Times*. Minneapolis: Fortress, 2009.

Johannesen-Henry, Christine Tind. "Polydox eschatology: Relating systematic and everyday theology in a cancer context," *Studia Theologica* 66:2 (2012) 107–29.

Keller, Catherine, and Laurel C. Schneider, editors. *Polydoxy: Theology of Multiplicity and Relation*. New York: Routledge, 2011.

Leppin, Volker. *Martin Luther* (Gestalten des Mittelalters und der Renaissance). Darmstadt: Wissenschatliche Buchgesellschaft, 2006.

Luther, Martin. *Auf das überchristlich, übergeistlich und überkünstlich Buch Bock Emsers zu Leipzig Antwort* (1921). WA 7. Weimar: Hermann Böhlaus Nachfolger, 1897.

———. *Lectures on Genesis* (1535–1538). LW 1. St. Louis: Concordia, 1958; WA 42, Weimar: Hermann Böhlaus Nachfolger, 1911.

———. *Predigten des Jahres 1544*, nr 16. WA 49. Weimar: Hermann Böhlaus Nachfolger, 1913.

———. *The Beautiful Confitemini* (1530). LW 14. St. Louis: Concordia, 1958; WA 31. Weimar: Hermann Böhlaus Nachfolger, 1913.

———. *The Blessed Sacrament of the Holy and True Body of Christ, and the Brotherhoods* (1519). LW 35. Philadelphia: Fortress Press, 1960; WA 2. Weimar: Hermann Böhlau, 1884.

———. *The Great Catechism* (1529). In *Book of Concord: The Confessions of the Evangelical Lutheran Church*, editors Robert Kolb and Timothy J. Wengert. Minneapolis: Fortress Press, 2000.

———. *The Holy and Blessed Sacrament of Baptism* (1519). LW 35. Philadelphia: Fortress Press, 1960; WA 2. Weimar: Hermann Böhlau, 1884.

Luhmann, Niklas. *Funktion der Religion*. Frankfurt am Main: Suhrkamp Verlag, 1982.

———. *Soziale Systeme: Grundriss einer allgemeinen Theorie*. Frankfurt am Main: Suhrkamp Verlag, 1984.

———. *Die Religion der Gesellschaft*. Frankfurt am Main: Suhrkamp Verlag, 2000.

Martensen, H. L. *Den christelige Dogmatik*. 1849. Edited by Alfred Th. Jørgensen. København: Gad, 1904.

Peirce, Charles Sanders. "The Basis of Pragmaticism in the Normative Sciences." In *The Essential Peirce. Selected Philosophical Writing*s, vol. 2 (1893–1913), edited by The Peirce Edition Project. Bloomington: Indiana University Press, 1998.

Reines, Alvin J. *Polydoxy: Explorations in a Philosophy of Religion*. Amherst: Prometheus, 1987.

Rohls, Jan. *Protestantische Theologie der Neuzeit*. Vol. I. Tübingen: Mohr-Siebeck, 1997.

Schleiermacher, Friedrich. *The Christian Faith*, edited by H. R. MacIntosh and J. S. Stewart. Edinburgh: T. & T. Clark, 1989.

———. *Der Christliche Glaube nach den Grundsätzen der evangelischen Kirche im Zusammenhange dargestellt*. 1831. Berlin: Walter de Gruyter, 1960.

Taylor, Charles. *A Secular Age*. Cambridge: Belknap Press of Harvard University Press, 2007.

Tillich, Paul. *The Protestant Era*. Chicago: The University of Chicago Press, 1948.

Twesten, August. *Vorlesungen über die Dogmatik der evangelisch-lutherischen Kirche*. Hamburg: F. Perth, 1826. Online: www.openlibrary.org (accessed 20/11/2013).

Ward, Graham. *Cities of God*. London: Routledge, 2000.

Weber, Max. *Wirtschaft und Gesellschaft*. Tübingen: Mohr-Siebeck, 2002.

12

Contra Philosophos

The Lutheran Reformation as Critique of the Rationality of Modernity

KNUT ALFSVÅG

MODERNITY AND *VIA MODERNA*

A number of scholars have noted the continuity between the late medieval movement called *via moderna* and typically modern philosophical emphases.[1] Until the fourteenth century, it was commonly accepted in European thought that human beings' position as a part of the universe made it impossible for them to get to know reality in its totality. This necessitated the use of a variety of rhetorical strategies in exploring the world, conceptual analysis being but one of them, and not necessarily the most appropriate one. The *via moderna* establishment of univocity as the epistemological ideal changed this. The understanding of the knowing subject as itself a part of the field of investigation was then replaced by a strict difference between the experiencing subject and the world experienced. This made possible the precise analysis that the natural sciences have since employed with great success.

The expansion of knowledge thus established came with a price, though. While the idea of univocity, that is, the exact correspondence between fact and concept, undoubtedly allowed for a high level of precision, it also decreased the significance of the fields of knowledge that were not

---

1. For a summary of this argument, see Hyman, *A Short History of Atheism*, 67–80.

so easily reducible. This has probably been most conspicuous in the field of theology; while the former approach, both in its Greek and Christian instantiations, was founded on an understanding of the divine origin of the universe, of which human beings found themselves to be a part, God was now reduced to being a part of the world of which the human was lord through the capacity for definite and experience-based knowledge.[2] The roles of God and human were thus switched; while premodern theology was theology proper in the sense that it had a deep appreciation of God as the origin and foundation of the world, the inherent theology of modernity implies the divinization of the human, the outcome of which has been the emphasis on the human individual as the significant point of orientation for any relevant world view. However, as humans are unfit for the role the divine, this has led to a proliferation of world views that have reduced politics to power struggle[3] and morality and religion to matters of private choice.[4]

One of the earliest critics of this development was Martin Luther, his works before the indulgence controversy consisting of long lists of complaints concerning the inconsistencies of the *via moderna* movement. Scholars have disagreed, however, on the significance of this critique. While the Roman Catholic scholar Louis Dupré has seen in Luther one of the main attempts at letting the world keep its "transcendental moorings" against the onslaught of modernity,[5] scholars like Alasdair MacIntyre and John Milbank have been considerably more reserved. According to Milbank, Luther left *via moderna* epistemology largely in place, just tacking his "grace alone" emphasis on as an afterthought.[6] Furthermore, MacIntyre charges Luther himself with being the forerunner of modernity by emphasizing the "grace alone" aspect to the extent that the rationality of the world is lost; in his view, it is but a short step from Luther's understanding of human sinfulness

---

2. According to ibid., xvii: "The self becomes the *subject* that applies the disciplines of reason and science to the world, which is thereby conceived to be the *object* of that activity. This was in marked contrast to the model that prevailed in medieval theology. (. . .) This includes God, who now becomes an object of thought."

3. This is the gist of the argument in John Milbank's famous *Theology and Social Theory*.

4. This is a main point, e.g., in Heelas and Woodhead, *The Spiritual Revolution*.

5. Quotation taken from Dupré, "The dissolution of the union of nature and grace," 102. The argument is developed more in detail in Dupré, *Passage to Modernity: An Essay in the Hermeneutics of Nature and Culture*. Dupré finds similar attempts in the work of Nicholas Cusanus, Erasmus(!), Calvin, and Cornelius Jansen.

6. Milbank, "Knowledge," 23–24.

to Hobbes' understanding of society as nothing but a power struggle between incurable egoists.[7]

Who is right? Does Luther establish a significant critique of the theology inherent in *via moderna* epistemology, or is he rather to be seen as someone who promoted the modern project more or less against his will? Moreover, if his theological project is a critical one in this sense, is his critique something that still makes sense, or should it interest us mainly as a historical phenomenon? In this essay, I will try to answer these questions. Among the vast body of Luther texts, I will concentrate on the disputations, both because his early disputations aptly summarize his critique of *via moderna* and because his later disputations are a good starting point for a discussion on his more mature epistemology and anthropology.

LUTHER'S DECONSTRUCTION OF *VIA MODERNA*

The starting point of Luther's *Disputation on the power of humans without grace*[8] of 1516[9] is that the biblical understanding of human beings as created in the image of God implies that any attempt by humans at making it on their own is to be considered as vanity,[10] which, through the work of humans, extends to all other creatures.[11] For Luther the relationship to God is thus the key to understanding human beings in a way that implies that God's grace is the precondition for the appropriate realization of humanity and creatureliness. This is applied as a critique of the idea that humans can do what is good on their own, and of the understanding of salvation as dependent on humans contributing to the best of their ability. No names are mentioned as the target of the critique, but William Ockham (1287-1347) provides one of the significant quotes for what Luther rejects.[12]

---

7. MacIntyre, *A Short History of Ethics*, 121-24; MacIntyre, *After Virtue*, 53-55.

8. Luther, *Quaestio de viribus et voluntate hominis sine gratia*, WA 1, 145-51; Luther, *Luther deutsch: die Werke Martin Luthers in neuer Auswahl für die Gegenwart*, LD 1, 345-54. Translations from Luther's works in the following are my own.

9. On the historical context of the disputation, see Lohse, *Martin Luther's Theology*, 98. The theses were written and defended by one of Luther's students, but closely follow what Luther had taught in the classroom.

10. "The human, who by reason of its soul is God's image and thus suitable for God's grace, will, left to its own natural powers, subject any creature it uses to vanity, seeking only its own and what belongs to the flesh." Luther, *Quaestio de viribus et voluntate hominis sine gratia*. WA 1, 145:10-13; LD 1, 345.

11. "The old human, vanity of vanities and universal vanity, makes also the other creatures, that otherwise are good, to be vain." Ibid., WA 1, 145:29-30; LD 1, 346. As argument Luther refers to Rom 8:20, which in *Vulgata* reads: "For the creature was made subject to vanity" (Douay-Rheims translation).

12. "Homo, quando facit quod in se est, peccat, cum nec velle aut cogitare ex seipso

The critique is considerably more explicit in *Disputation against scholastic theology*[13] of 1517[14]. Here Duns Scotus (1266–1308) and Gabriel Biel (1410–1495)[15] are attacked for the idea that the human will by nature can conform to what is right,[16] though Luther pauses to assert that he does not thereby subscribe to the Manichaean understanding of humans as naturally evil.[17] Luther considers the *via moderna* argument that humans can love God as they can love other things to be absurd.[18] In Luther's view, humans cannot on their own love anything as they should; even an ordinary sign of human goodwill like friendship is thus seen by Luther as an act of divine grace.[19] It is even less likely that they can love God; on the contrary, sinful humans consistently covet the position of God for themselves.[20]

Luther thus consistently and explicitly attacks the *via moderna* understanding of the natural as neutral and the corresponding understanding of God as an entity among other entities. For Luther, God is the foundation of all that there is with the implication that nature is either conceived as graced by God or finds itself in opposition to him. Ockham is thus quoted and criticized for his view that humans can be accepted by God without justifying grace; for Luther, anyone who is outside the grace of God sins constantly.[21] The significance of the understanding of God as the foundation

---

possit" (The human, when it does what it has in itself, sins, because it cannot either want or think from itself)." Ibid., WA 1, 148:14–15; LD 1, 350. On Ockham's position in this respect, see Hägglund, *History of Theology*, 200. Luther's expression "either want or think" refers to Phil 2:13.

13. Luther, *Disputatio contra scholasticam theologiam*, WA 1, 224-28; LW 31, 9–16.

14. Now Luther himself is the author; see Lohse, *Martin Luther's Theology*, 98–99.

15. Luther studied Biel's works closely and had according to Melanchthon more or less memorized them; see Lohse, *Martin Luther's Theology*, 23.

16. "6. It is false that the will by nature can conform to what is right. Against Scotus and Gabriel. 7. But without the grace of God, it necessarily produces an act that is deformed and evil." Luther, *Disputatio contra scholasticam theologiam*. WA 1, 224:17–19; LW 31, 9.

17. "8. But it does not follow that it is naturally evil, that is, by nature belonging to the evil, as taught by the Manichaeans." Ibid., WA 1, 224:20–21; LW 31, 9.

18. "13. This argument is most absurd: A human in error can love a creature above all things, therefore also God. Against Scotus and Gabriel." Ibid., WA 1, 224:28–29; LW 31, 10.

19. "20. An act of friendship is not by nature, but by prevenient grace. Against Gabriel." Ibid., WA 1, 225:7–8; LW 31, 10.

20. "17. Non potest homo naturaliter velle deum esse deum, Immo vellet se esse deum et deum non esse deum" (Humans cannot by nature want God to be God; on the contrary, they want that they are God and that God is not God). Ibid., WA 1, 224:28–225:2; LW 31, 10.

21. Ibid., WA 1, 227:4—5:14; LW 31, 13

of any adequate approach to the understanding of the human and the world is thus heavily emphasized by Luther.

This critique is sharpened and extended even further in the *Heidelberg Disputation* of 1518. This disputation consists of both a theological and a philosophical part.²² The first, theological, part sharpens the critique of the neutrality of the natural by emphasizing that neither God's law nor human works can ever advance a person to justice.²³ Even if the works of humans appear to be good, they are in reality mortal sins; in the same way, God's works may appear to be evil, but they are in reality eternal merits.²⁴ Luther therefore attacks the *via moderna* idea that works without Christ can be dead, but not mortal; this again opens the possibility of a neutral zone that Luther cannot accept.²⁵ The difference between appearance and reality concerning the works of God is further developed as Luther's theology of the cross. In Luther's view one can thus never grasp God's inner essence by exploring his works, the only adequate approach then being to relate to what he has revealed through defeat and death.²⁶

In the second, philosophical, part Luther elaborates his point by maintaining that the errors of late medieval Scholasticism are caused by its dependence on Aristotle.²⁷ Here Luther contends that the Scholastics have not sufficiently freed themselves from the Aristotelian understanding

---

22. The theological theses with arguments and the philosophical theses without arguments are printed in WA 1, 353–74 and LW 31, 39–70; the arguments for the philosophical theses were printed for the first time (with a German translation) in Junghans, "Die probationes zu den philosophischen Thesen den Heidelberger Disputation Luthers im Jahre 1518," and are now to be found in WA 59, 409–26. For a broader presentation of my own reading of the *Heidelberg Disputation* and the relevant literature, see Alfsvåg, *What no mind has conceived*, 181–98.

23. "1. The law of God, the most beneficial doctrine of life, cannot move the human to justice, but rather obstructs this. 2. Even less can the works of humans, frequently repeated by means of natural precepts, do this." Luther, *Heidelberg Disputation*, WA 1, 353:15–18; LW 31, 39.

24. "3. The works of humans always seem to be splendid and good; it is still probable that they are deadly sins. 4. The works of God, which always seem deformed and evil, are still immortal merits." Ibid., WA 1, 353:19–22; LW 31, 39.

25. "9. To say that works without Christ are dead but not mortal (mortua sed non mortalia), seems to show a dangerous lack of fear of God." Ibid., WA 1, 353:31–32; LW 31, 40. On the young Luther's critique of the Ockhamist concept of sin, see further Lohse, *Martin Luther's Theology*, 71.

26. "19. A person is not rightly called a theologian who considers God's invisible character as explorable through actual deeds, (20) but only the one who considers what is visible and posterior in God as explorable through passions and the cross." Ibid., WA 1, 354:17–20; LW 31, 40.

27. The groundbreaking work in terms of Luther's reading of Aristotle is Dieter, *Der junge Luther und Aristoteles*.

of the eternity of the world and the mortality of the human soul, which in Luther's view are both related to Aristotle's inadequate understanding of the infinite. Luther thus finds a continuity between the infinite and the finite in Aristotle's thought that is both philosophically inconsistent—it does not make sense to give an experience-based explanation of the infinite[28]—and makes him an ill-chosen ally for theology. Both the radicality of transcendence and the epistemological humility it entails are, in Luther's view, much better maintained by Plato, whose work thus provides a defense of philosophical unknowability for Luther that opens up the perspective for the realities of revelation in a much better way than Scholastic Aristotelianism does.[29] In the Platonic emphasis on the significance of the One, Luther thus finds a philosophy that closely corresponds to his own emphasis on the theocentricity of the natural,[30] whereas dependence on the Aristotelian understanding of truth as experience does not make sufficient allowance for Scholasticism finding the foundation of its world view in the reality of what is beyond experience and probability.

In my view, there is thus no doubt that Milbank is wrong when he charges Luther with representing a theology of grace without epistemological and philosophical depth. On the contrary, Luther is well aware of the philosophical and anthropological implications of a theology of grace and explores them in detail. His is thus not a theology that philosophically stands in the middle of nowhere; he is clearly aware of where the parting of the ways is located and does not lack either the means or the will necessary for investigating that particular location.

---

28. Here Luther arguably anticipates Hume's critique of the idea of a timeless rationality.

29. "That Plato's philosophy is better than Aristotle's follows from the fact that Plato always works toward what is divine, immortal, separate, eternal, insensible and intelligible, and leaves the singular, individual and sensible behind." (From the explanation to thesis eight in the philosophical part. Luther, *Disputatio Heidelbergae habita*, WA 59, 424:7–11).

30. "9. The way numbers imitate things is asserted in the most ingenious way by Pythagoras, but even better is Plato's doctrine of participation in ideas. (. . .) This second statement follows from what Plato says in the dialogue *Parmenides*, where he in a most beautiful disputation first takes everything off oneness (. . .) and then again dresses it with everything, so that there is nothing left that does not exist as established through oneness, which is both outside everything and in everything." Ibid., WA 59, 425:11–426:7. What Luther has found in Plato is thus a world view that does not allow for an experience-based doctrine of the One (God) while at the same time finding the presence of the One in everything. Luther thus reads Plato as a confirmation of the double emphasis of the theological part of the *Heidelberg Disputation*: no natural theology and no anthropological neutrality.

One may argue, though, that as far as these works are concerned, that is, until about 1518, Luther is much better at deconstructing the contradictions of *via moderna* than at presenting a consistent alternative. He is clearly aware of this problem, too, and his gesture in the direction of Plato can also be seen as an attempt at indicating the contours of the philosophical part of a solution. However, it is still weak theologically, as Luther has not yet given either a precise explanation of how the God-centered life is established or of how it is lived. MacIntyre's critique of the irrationality inherent in Luther's understanding of sin as lack of theocentricity is thus not without relevance in relation to the early Luther, whose pledge that he is not a Manichaeist may seem to be more of an attempt at exorcism than an example of a sound and substantial argument.

LUTHER'S CHRISTOLOGICALLY-INFORMED RATIONALITY

This changes, however, when we come to the work of the mature Luther. He has then reached the conclusion that the re-establishment of the lost theocentricity of the life of the human occurs by humans having the predicates of divinity—justice, power, wisdom and honor are Luther's own examples—transmitted to them through the preaching of the gospel.[31] For Luther the presence of God in the life of humans is uncovered and realized through the power of the biblical message. That puts him at the mercy of rhetoric in a way he clearly acknowledges; for Luther, the significance of language is not to depict reality as experienced, but to create reality by allowing us to see and act on what is otherwise hidden.[32] And it puts him at the mercy of a theology of participation; humans participate in the reality of divinity through the work of the Spirit through the word, without the difference between Creator and creation ever being suspended. The primary manifestation of the unity of the human and the divine for Luther of course being the incarnation of Christ, after the breakthrough Luther's thought is deeply informed by Christology in a way that is only partially glimpsed in the works of the young Luther.[33]

---

31. Luther's own presentation of this change is found in the Luther, *Preface to the Complete Edition of Luther's Latin Works*, WA 54, 179–87; LW 34, 327–38.

32. The work where Luther explores this part of his thought in depth is Anti-Latomus. Luther, *Rationis Latomianae confutatio*, WA 8, 36–128; LW 32, 137–260. For a discussion of its significance, see Alvsvåg, *What no mind has conceived*, 226–38.

33. On the significance of Christology in the thoughts of the mature Luther, see Steiger, "The Communicatio idiomatum as axle and motor of Luther's theology." The development from a world-denying attitude to a Christologically-informed emphasis on worldliness in Luther's thought is observed also in Bayer, "Philosophical Modes of Thought of Luther's Theology as an Object of Inquiry," 19.

The *Disputation on the human* of 1536[34] thus reads as a kind of Christologically-informed revision of the *Heidelberg Disputation* in the sense that it is clearly divided into a philosophical and a theological part, but with the philosophical part now coming first. Here Luther praises reason as something divine and responsible for human knowledge, human society and everything good in the life of humans, such as wisdom, power, virtue and glory, and he explicitly rejects the idea that reason has lost its worldly significance after the fall.[35] There are, however, a number of preconditions for reason to work as intended: one must understand that reason is given for the purpose of ordering life this side of death, and one must acknowledge that reason has no proper understanding of the arguments for its own potency, even if it can somehow grasp it on the basis of the strength of its own achievements.[36] Taking reason as self-sufficient, and Aristotle is again used as an example of such an improper use of reason,[37] one therefore ends up with errors and contradictions.

The complete definition of humans, including their rationality, is therefore only given with the doctrine of justification.[38] This definition places the human within the context of the world as graced, and thus represents the possibility of liberating reason to its true potential. It is therefore completely misguided to build an understanding of restored humanity on what is left within the context of a sinful reality. However, this is what occurs when theologians build a doctrine based on Aristotle's confused understanding of the foundation and potential of human reason.

There is no longer any reason for Luther to pause in order to exorcize the spirit of Manichaeism from his thought, for there is nothing left of it. The reason is that his anthropology is now deeply informed by his appropriation of Chalcedonian two nature Christology; seen through its potential

---

34. Luther, *Disputatio de homine*, WA 39.I, 175–80; LW 34, 137–43. On the significance of this work within the context of Luther's thought, see Lohse, *Martin Luther's Theology*, 196–97.

35. "1. Philosophy, human wisdom, defines the human as a rational, sensitive and corporeal animal. (. . .) 3. But it must be known that this definition defines the human as mortal and within the frame of this life.

4. It is certainly true that reason is the head of all things and comes before all other things pertaining to this life and is something divine. (. . .) 9. And God did not withdraw the majesty of reason after the fall of Adam, but rather confirmed it." Luther, *Disputatio de homine*, WA 39.I, 175:3–21; LW 34, 137.

36. "10. But reason does not know its majesty 'a priore,' only 'a posterior.'" Ibid., WA 39.I, 175:22–23; LW 34, 137.

37. Theses 16 and 28.

38. "32. Paul in Rom 3 (. . .) briefly summarizes the definition of the human, saying: The human is justified by faith." Ibid., WA 39.I, 176:33–35.

for union with the divine and participation in its predicates, the potential of the human nature for knowledge and goodness is virtually limitless. The foundation for the realization of this potential is, however, firmly placed within the realm of the theological; if it attempts to found itself, reason crumbles under the burden of its own inconsistencies.

In the *Disputation concerning the passage "the Word was made flesh"* of 1539, Luther further explores the implications of his Christologically-informed world view.[39] Here his starting point is the fact that the doctrine of the incarnation, which is the very essence of the Christian faith, simply does not make sense outside of this context; what is true in theology, is therefore not true in philosophy.[40] The reason is closely related to the argument of the *Disputation on the human*: in philosophy, words refer to the realities of this life, whereas in theology, this limit is lifted. When it is said that "Christ is human," the reference of the word "human" is thus expanded to include "both the divine and the incarnate God."[41] To deny this possibility is to reject the Christian faith by identifying God with what is logically possible according to the rules of the created world. Luther thus repeats one of the main points from *Disputation against scholastic theology*, emphasizing that methodologically, one has to distinguish between the way one deals with the finite and the way one deals with the infinite. This distinction in itself is, however, perfectly rational.[42]

Luther's defense of the statement that what is true in theology is not true in philosophy has therefore nothing to do with irrationality. On the contrary, it is an argument to the effect that the rationality of reason can only be maintained as long as it is limited to the realm of the finite. Applied to the realm of the infinite, reason itself crumbles to irrationality, as is made clear by the attempts at analyzing the doctrine of incarnation with

39. Luther, *Disputatio de sententia: Verbum caro factum est*, WA 39.II, 3–5 (theses) and 6–33 (arguments); LW 38, 239–77.

40. "2. In theology it is true that the word was made flesh; in philosophy, it is simply impossible and absurd. (. . .) 6. This abominable statement [that truth is the same in philosophy and theology] teaches us to take the articles of faith captive under the judgement of human reason." Ibid., WA 39.II, 3:3–4:3; LW 38, 239.

41. In argument four, Luther discusses the syllogism "every human is a creature, Christ is a human, therefore Christ is a creature" and comments on it in the following way: "In the major premise 'human' signifies a physical human, in the minor another, both the divine and incarnate God." Ibid., WA 39.II, 11:9–10; LW 38, 246. The syllogism is thus invalid because of equivocation between the first and second premise, resulting in what was commonly referred to as a four term syllogism. See further Haga, *Was there a Lutheran Metaphysics?*, 65–67.

42. Cf. argument nine, which rejects the position that philosophy and theology are in contradiction; referring to different realms of reality, they cannot contradict each other. Ibid., WA 39.II, 16:5–15; LW 38, 250.

experience-based univocity. This distinction may not be absolute; referring to Plato and Cicero,[43] Luther entertains the possibility that there may be some understanding of the infinite even in philosophy.[44] On the whole, however, the rationality of reason is conditioned by its ability to keep within its legitimate realm.

The mature Luther thus has a less critical approach to reason than his younger self had. In his early disputations, the only kind of philosophy Luther gives a positive evaluation of is Plato's defense of unknowability. While this emphasis remains,[45] in his later disputations Luther supplements it with a more open attitude towards the positive role of human reasoning. He can do this because he has a better understanding of its proper place. For Luther the understanding of justification as participation in the predicates of the divine thus implies an understanding of divine grace as the foundation from which human reason develops according to its God-given character.

As regards the thoughts of the mature Luther, MacIntyre's critique that Luther's emphasis on grace alone opens the floodgates for irrationality is thus no more relevant than Milbank's. Luther does not abolish reason in his exploration of restored humanity; on the contrary, he considers it as something divine. However, in a way that should be able to find resonance in the thought of both Milbank and MacIntyre, he insists that if not understood as a finite entity, that is, without theology defining its suitable framework, human reason collapses under the pretension of its own absoluteness. Unlike the investigation of the finite, an appropriate exploration of humans' relationship with God must therefore start from the understanding of this relationship as established as a gift through grace. If not, the ultimate contradiction will necessarily occur of the Creator being construed in the image of His creation.

THE PRESERVATION OF DECONSTRUCTION

In spite of the fact that Luther is one of the, if not the single most influential thinkers in Protestant Christendom, his consistent anti-modernity is not an aspect of his thought that has been generally adhered to. Jaroslav Pelikan argued in his 1950 book, which by now is almost old enough to count as a classic in its own right, that to a large extent this is due to the fact that Luther's theological heirs, both in their Orthodox and Pietist variations, were

---

43. On Luther's high regard for Cicero, see further Simpson, "'Putting on the Neighbor': The Ciceronian Impulse in Luther's Christian Approach to Practical Reason."

44. Argument seven, see ibid., WA 39.II, 14:18–15:9; LW 38, 249. The evaluation of Plato, though still positive, is more reserved here than in the *Heidelberg Disputation*.

45. According to, e.g., Lohse, *Martin Luther's Theology*, 199–200.

themselves too heavily influenced by modernity to be able to relate consistently to this part of the Lutheran heritage.[46] The outcome was thus that even within the context of Lutheranism, philosophical critique of modernity became a marginalized project with little influence on the mainstream of theological and philosophical thought.

There have, however, been thinkers who have tried to explore and apply even this part of Luther's thought, thus deepening our understanding of his anti-modernity by referring to him as an important inspiration for their own critical projects. In this respect Pelikan was referring to Søren Kierkegaard, and while this view is certainly commendable, there are other and possibly even better examples. I would therefore like to expand on his perspective by briefly considering two other thinkers who were arguably even closer to Luther's own emphases, thus showing the continuing relevance of his attempts at deconstructing modernity.

Johann Georg Hamann (1730–1788)[47] was an important late eighteenth century critic of the Enlightenment. In his *Socratic Memorabilia* of 1759,[48] he defends the view that human reason at its best will have to admit to its own limits, and in his *Aesthetica in nuce* of 1762[49] he develops the corresponding positive thesis that human exploration of the world originates in God's word of creation. The world can thus only be appropriately conceived as divine revelation. This establishes a parallel with the equally Christologically-informed hermeneutics of both the Bible and of history and nature in general, a perspective Hamann applies as a critique of the one-sidedness of both the mathematization of nature in natural science[50] and of the equally one-sided objectification of history in modern Bible research.[51] In his work *Golgotha und Scheblimini!*[52] of 1784, Hamann expanded his approach as a critique of the alleged natural state of Enlightenment liberal social theory,

---

46. Pelikan, *From Luther to Kierkegaard*.

47. Pelikan's hero Kierkegaard was an avid reader of Hamann and often refers to him, e.g., in *Concluding Unscientific Postscript*. See Kierkegaard, *Skrifter*, vol. 7, 227: "Jeg vil ikke dølge, at jeg beundrer Hamann" (I will not hide that I admire Hamann).

48. Hamann, *Sämtliche Werke*, 2:57–82. The most extensive scholarly discussion of this work is O'Flaherty, *Hamann's Socratic Memorabilia*.

49. Hamann, *Sämtliche Werke*, 2:195–217 (Aesthetics in a nutshell). For a summary of the argument of this work, see Betz, *After Enlightenment*, 123–127.

50. This aspect of Hamann's thought has been explored in detail by Moustakas, *Urkunde und Experiment*.

51. See Bayer, *A Contemporary in Dissent*, 129–143.

52. Hamann, *Sämtliche Werke*, 3:291–320; see further Bayer, *Contemporary in Dissent*, 171–83; Betz, *After Enlightenment*, 258–90. The cryptic word "scheblimini" is a transliteration of the Hebrew text of Psalm 110:1: "Sit at my right hand."

and in *Metakritik über den Purismum der Vernunft*,⁵³ also written in 1784 but not published until after his death, he explores the same perspective as a critique of Kant's *Kritik der reinen Vernunft* of 1781. According to Hamann, reason is never pure in the sense of universal and independent of context; Hamann thus explicitly subscribes to Hume's understanding of any attempt at finding experience-transcendent rationality as pure futility and defends this as the only attitude that corresponds to faith's appropriation of the world as a gift.

As is emphasized by a number of Hamann scholars, Hamann thus anticipates some important postmodern insights; however, in my view it is at least as interesting that he so obviously repeats many of Luther's insights. This is a connection Hamann was well aware of, and he often refers to Luther as an important source of inspiration.⁵⁴

Following this line of thought into the twentieth century, it is tempting to ask whether we do not find a similar emphasis in the work of Dietrich Bonhoeffer. In *Christus, die Wirklichkeit und das Gute*,⁵⁵ a part of his uncompleted work on ethics, Bonhoeffer argues in a similar way to Hamann in *Aesthetica in nuce* that there is only one reality, and that is the world as revealed in Christ.⁵⁶ This certainly does not imply for Bonhoeffer that the church should rule the world, but it does imply that the church has something to say about the Christological framework necessary for the appropriate application of human reason. It is thus the task of the church to protest against what closes the world to the possibility of establishing this framework.⁵⁷ Bonhoeffer finds contemporary theology lacking in this respect in a way that resembles both Luther's and Hamann's critique of their

---

53. Hamann, *Sämtliche Werke*, 3:281–89 (Metacriticism of the purity of reason); see further Bayer, *Contemporary in Dissent*, 156–70; Betz, *After Enlightenment*, 230–57. The word "metacriticism" is Hamann's construction.

54. E.g., in *Aesthetica in nuce*; Hamann, *Sämtliche Werke*, 3:213.1–5. For a summary of Hamann's appreciation of Luther, see, Brose, *Johann Georg Hamann und David Hume I*, 169–78.

55. Bonhoeffer, *Werke*, vol. 6, 31–61 (Christ, reality and the good).

56. "Da aber Gott als letzte Wirklichkeit kein anderer ist als der, der sich selbst bekundet, bezeugt, offenbart, also als Gott in Jesus Christus, so kann die Frage nach dem Guten nur in Christus ihre Antwort finden" (As God as the fundamental reality is no other than the one who manifests, confirms and reveals himself as God in Christ, then the quest for the good can only find its answer in Christ; Bonhoeffer, *Werke*, vol. 6, 33).

57. Cf. the remarks of the polemical use of the Christian against the worldly and, if necessary, vice versa, in Bonhoeffer, *Werke*, vol. 6, 45.

contemporaries; he refers to it as the central theological challenge for his time.[58]

Luther's anti-modernist emphasis may not be the most widely accepted part of his heritage, but to date it has certainly not disappeared.

CONCLUSIONS

There are, in my view, clear parallels between the critique of modernity in Luther, Milbank, and MacIntyre, and the way that this aspect of Luther's thought is received and developed by Hamann, Kierkegaard, and Bonhoeffer confirms and validates this insight. Both Milbank and MacIntyre could thus consider him an ally to a much greater extent than what they so far have been willing to admit. They differ, however, in their constructive alternatives, with both Milbank and MacIntyre emphasizing the significance of Thomas Aquinas in a way Luther, with all his critique of Aristotle, would never have been able to endorse. Wary of the tendency of conflating the temporal and the eternal, which in Luther's view is inherent in all kinds of Aristotelianism, he finds his footing both as a theologian and a philosopher in a much more direct appropriation of the doctrine of the incarnation as interpreted by the Councils of Nicaea and Chalcedon. This allows him to emphasize the discontinuity between sinful and restored humanity without for a moment doubting its inherent goodness and rationality. To the extent that the collapse of self-sufficient reason becomes increasingly visible—and MacIntyre and Milbank are certainly to be commended for their contributions to making this visibility possible—it is thus arguably Luther's incarnational theology that still presents us with a consistent attempt at establishing a sufficiently theocentric anthropology.[59]

It thus does not make sense to see in Luther a theologian of grace who is merely interested in the salvation of the soul, happy to let the world run its own course. On the contrary, he represents a bold attempt to think through the implications of the understanding of the world as carried by God's goodness in a way that both implies a consistent critique of incompatible positions among his contemporaries and has acted as an inspiration for later thinkers to undertake similar critical projects. Admittedly, the objectification of the world made possible by the *via moderna* emphasis on univocity, which he made it his particular challenge to fight, has undoubtedly allowed

---

58. On this way of reading Bonhoeffer, see Johansson, "Med Dietrich Bonhoeffer på väg mot en förnyad evangelisk-luthersk tvårikeslära."

59. For critiques of Milbank and MacIntyre of being less than consistent in their constructive alternatives, see Mattes, "A Lutheran assessment of 'Radical orthodoxy'"; Alfsvåg, "Virtue, reason and tradition."

for scientific and technological progress such as is unprecedented in the history of mankind. It has, however, become increasingly clear that it has also landed us in equally dire problems, and not only in relation to the problem of finding an appropriate approach to the quest for God. Luther as a critic of modernity thus undoubtedly deserves to be heard and to be taken seriously both as a relevant critic in his own right and for his inspiring effect on those who in this respect are to be seen as his followers.

BIBLIOGRAPHY

Alfsvåg, Knut. "Virtue, reason and tradition: A discussion of Alasdair MacIntyre's and Martin Luther's views on the foundation of ethics." *Neue Zeitschrift für systematische Theologie und Religionsphilosophie* 47.3 (2005) 288–305.

———. *What No Mind Has Conceived: An Investigation of the Significance of Christological Apophaticism*. Studies in Philosophical Theology 45. Leuven: Peeters, 2010.

Bayer, Oswald. *A Contemporary in Dissent: Johann Georg Hamann as Radical Enlightener*. Grand Rapids: Eerdmans, 2012.

———. "Philosophical Modes of Thought of Luther's Theology as an Object of Inquiry." In *The Devil's Whore: Reason and Philosophy in the Lutheran Tradition*, edited by Jennifer Hockenberry Dragseth, 13–22. Minneapolis: Fortress, 2010.

Betz, John R. *After Enlightenment: The post-secular vision of J. G. Hamann*. Malden, MA: Wiley-Blackwell, 2009.

Bonhoeffer, Dietrich. *Werke*. Edited by Eberhard Bethge. Gütersloh: Chr. Kaiser Verlag, 1986–1999.

Brose, Thomas. *Johann Georg Hamann und David Hume: Metaphysikkritik und Glaube im Spannungsfeld der Aufklarung*. Vol. I. Frankfurt: Lang, 2006.

Dieter, Theodor. *Der junge Luther und Aristoteles: Eine historisch-systematische Untersuchung zum Verhältnis von Theologie und Philosophie*. Theologische Bibliothek Töpelmann 105. Berlin: Walter de Gruyter, 2001.

Dupré, Louis. "The Dissolution of the Union of Nature and Grace at the Dawn of the Modern Age." In *The Theology of Wolfhart Pannenberg: Twelve American Critiques, with an Autobiographical Essay and Response*, edited by Carl E. Braaten and Philip Clayton, 95–121. Minneapolis: Augsburg, 1988.

———. *Passage to Modernity: An Essay in the Hermeneutics of Nature and Culture*. New Haven: Yale University Press, 1993.

Haga, Joar. *Was there a Lutheran Metaphysics? The interpretation of communicatio idiomatum in Early Modern Lutheranism*. Göttingen: Vandenhoeck & Ruprecht, 2012.

Hamann, Johann Georg. *Sämtliche Werke*, 6 vols., edited by Josef Nadler. Wien: Verlag Herder, 1949–1957.

Heelas, Paul, and Linda Woodhead. *The Spiritual Revolution: why religion is giving way to spirituality*. Malden, MA: Blackwell Publishing, 2005.

Hyman, Gavin. *A Short History of Atheism*. London: I.B. Tauris, 2010.

Hägglund, Bengt. *History of Theology*. St. Louis, MO: Concordia, 1968.

Johansson, Torbjörn. "Med Dietrich Bonhoeffer på väg mot en förnyad evangelisk-luthersk tvårikeslära." *Dansk Tidsskrift for Teologi og kirke* (2014) forthcoming.

Junghans, Helmar. "Die probationes zu den philosophischen Thesen den Heidelberger Disputation Luthers im Jahre 1518." *Lutherjahrbuch* 46 (1979) 10–59.

Kierkegaard, Søren. *Skrifter*. Edited by Niels Jørgen Kappelørn et al., 27 vols. København: Gad, 1997.

Lohse, Bernhard. *Martin Luther's Theology: Its Historical and Systematic Development*. Edinburgh: T. & T. Clark, 1999.

Luther, Martin. *Disputatio contra scholasticam theologiam* (1517), WA 1. Weimar: Hermann Böhlau, 1883; LW 31. St. Louis: Concordia, 1957.

———. *Disputatio de homine* (1536), WA 39, Erste Abteilung. Weimar: Hermann Böhlaus Nachfolger, 1926; LW 34. Philadelphia: Fortress Press, 1960.

———. *Disputatio de sententia: Verbum caro factum est* (1539), WA 39, Zweite Abteilung. Weimar: Hermann Böhlaus Nachfolger, 1932; LW 38. Philadelphia: Fortress Press, 1971.

———. *Disputatio Heidelbergae habita* (1518). WA 59. Weimar: Hermann Böhlaus Nachfolger, 1932.

———. *Heidelberg Disputation* (1518). St. Louis: Concordia, 1957; WA 1. Weimar: Hermann Böhlau, 1883.

———. *Preface to the Complete Edition of Luther's Latin Works* (1545). LW 34. Philadelphia: Fortress Press, 1960. WA 54. Weimar: Hermann Böhlaus Nachfolger, 1928.

———. *Rationis Latomianae confutatio* (1521). WA 8. Weimar: Hermann Böhlau, 1889.

———. Quaestio *de viribus et voluntate hominis sine gratia* (1516). WA 1. Weimar: Hermann Böhlaus Nachfolger, 1883; *Luther deutsch: Die Werke Martin Luthers in neuer Auswahl für die Gegenwart* (LD), vol. 1. Stuttgart: Ehrenfired Klotz Verlag, 1957.

MacIntyre, Alasdair. *After Virtue: A Study in Moral Theory*. London: Duckworth, 1985.

———. *A Short History of Ethics*. New York: Macmillan, 1966.

Mattes, Mark C. "A Lutheran Assessment of 'Radical orthodoxy.'" *Lutheran Quarterly* 15 (2001) 354–67.

Milbank, John. "Knowledge: The theological critique of philosophy in Hamann and Jacobi." In *Radical Orthodoxy: A New Theology*, edited by John Milbank, Catherine Pickstock, and Graham Ward, 21–37. London: Routledge, 1999.

———. *Theology and Social Theory: Beyond Secular Reason*. Oxford: Blackwell, 1990.

Moustakas, Ulrich. *Urkunde und Experiment: Neuzeitliche Naturwissenschaft im Horizont einer hermeneutischen Theologie der Schöpfung bei Johann Georg Hamann*. Theologische Bibliothek Töpelmann 114. Berlin: de Gruyter, 2003.

O'Flaherty, James C., editor. *Hamann's Socratic Memorabilia: A Translation and Commentary*. Baltimore: Johns Hopkins University Press, 1967.

Pelikan, Jaroslav Jan. *From Luther to Kierkegaard: A Study in the History of Theology*. St. Louis: Concordia, 1950.

Simpson, Gary. "'Putting on the Neighbor': The Ciceronian Impulse in Luther's Christian Approach to Practical Reason." In *The Devil's Whore: Reason and Philosophy in the Lutheran Tradition*, edited by Jennifer Hockenberry Dragseth, 31–38. Minneapolis: Fortress, 2010.

Steiger, Johann Anselm. "The Communicatio idiomatum as the axle and motor of Luther's theology." *Lutheran Quarterly* (2000) 125–58.

13

Priesthood of All Believers as Public Opinion

An Unexplored Link between the Lutheran Reformation and the Enlightenment?

URBAN CLAESSON

> Paradoxically Martin Luther equipped both rulers and ruled with, as it would ultimately turn out, effective weapons. The former could use the doctrine of the three estates to keep the subordinated in fear of God and His order. The nineteenth century would clearly reveal that these subjects had long since found the idea of the priesthood of all believers as a strong argument in the battle for political power between Protestants and Protestants anyhow.[1]

Historical research has often focused on how the doctrines of Luther's theology were used by rulers and kings to legitimize power. However, Luther's theology provided tools for men of political power and critics alike. The latter aspect needs to be explored in a more sophisticated fashion. In this chapter I will try to do just that. I will present a case from Swedish church history where Luther's doctrine of the priesthood of all believers seems to have worked as an unexplored precursor of public opinion, and as a new way to legitimize power from below.

---

1. Jansson, *Adertonhundratalets associationer*, 39n46 (my translation).

THE PRIESTHOOD OF ALL BELIEVERS AS A LUTHERAN THOUGHT

The idea of a common priesthood was not invented by Martin Luther. However, his formulation of this doctrine came to give it a strong position within Reformation theology. To introduce his ideas in a simplified way, we can state that Luther believed that all Christians were priests before God. Through their sacrifices the priests of the Old Testament had been able to meet God in the holiest room in the temple of Jerusalem, which was separated from the uttermost holy room by a veil. Luther claimed that all baptized Christians were righteous priests through the sacrifice of Christ. According to the Gospels, the temple veil was torn in two at the very moment Jesus died. From this perspective Luther criticized the medieval perception of the priest as a maker of sacrifices to God. According to Luther, the sacrifice had been completed once and for all. Luther's doctrine of the priesthood of all believers meant that all Christians, as egalitarians, had to admonish and encourage one another to live holy lives, according to what was written in chapter 18 of the Gospel of Matthew. However, for the sake of order and according to the will of God it was important for the church to have ordained priests in place with a particular responsibility for preaching, administration of the sacraments, and the handling of excommunications.[2]

LUTHER'S THEOLOGY IN SEVENTEENTH CENTURY SWEDEN

Lutheran orthodoxy dominated Swedish theology in the seventeenth century. The main focus was on maintaining the correct doctrine, and the priesthood's teaching and preaching were considered crucial. However, this attempt to hold on to the heritage of the Reformation led to a paradoxical overshadowing of elements in Martin Luther's theology. Previous research has shown that Luther's proclamation of the priesthood of all believers was rather forgotten in seventeenth century Swedish theology.[3]

In simple terms, we can say that during the seventeenth century in Sweden other parts of the Lutheran heritage came to be emphasized. For example, Luther's teaching of the three estates came to overshadow the doctrine of the common priesthood. According to Luther, the population was divided along three main functions. The political estate (*status politicus*)

---

2. Goertz, *Allgemeines Priestertum und ordiniertes Amt bei Luther*; Hallgren, *Kyrkotuktsfrågan*, 60–64.

3. Askmark, *Ämbetet i den Svenska kyrkan i reformationens, ortodoxiens och pietismens tänkande och praxis*, 124–202.

consisted of the royals and noblemen, who had to protect and govern the country. The ecclesiastical estate (*status ecclesiasticus*) consisted of priests whose task it was to educate and lead the people in the true faith and a good Christian life. The third, known as the economic estate (*status oeconomicus*), incorporated all the peasants, who were responsible for the production of food. The division between the groups was not static as it was based upon different roles of authority and subordination. A king listening to a sermon in a church was subordinated as part of *status ecclesiasticus* to the priest as his teacher, while at the same time the priest in the role of a secular subject within the *status politicus* was subordinated to the king. The members of the big economic estate were generally situated in subordinate positions. As the doctrine of the three estates came into play in Sweden, the perception of the priesthood of all believers became restricted to the master's duty to keep devotions within his own household, and to teach his family the Christian faith.[4]

The common interpretation of Luther's doctrine of the two regiments of God also tended to overshadow the belief in the priesthood of all believers in seventeenth century Sweden. This doctrine represented a vision of God as working with an arm in each of two regiments. God had created a system of secular rulers in the political estate. Through this "worldly" regiment God maintained the order of society by the sword. God's second arm consisted of a spiritual regiment with free preaching of the Gospel. This spiritual regiment meant that parishioners could be justified before God by grace and through faith alone. Martin Luther included the priesthood of all believers in this regiment, as the members encouraged and admonished one another to lead holy lives based on the word. In Sweden this form of congregational life was not in evidence after the Reformation in the sixteenth century. Even Luther himself gave up his ambition of creating congregations of disciplined and active believers. One reason for this was that he considered common Christians as having too little knowledge of faith. He also became afraid it could lead to sectarianism within the church.[5]

According to *Confessio Augustana* it was important not to confound the worldly and spiritual regiments:

> Therefore, since the power of the church grants eternal things, and is exercised only by the ministry of the Word, it does not interfere with civil government; no more than the art of singing interferes with civil government. For civil government deals

---

4. Stadin, *Stånd och genus i stormaktstidens Sverige*.
5. Bring, *Luther, stat och kyrka*; Törnvall, *Andligt och världsligt regemente hos Luther*; Hallgren, *Kyrkotuktsfrågan*, 47, 72.

> with other things than does the Gospel. The civil rulers defend not minds, but bodies and bodily things against manifest injuries, and restrain men with the sword and bodily punishments in order to preserve civil justice and peace.
>
> Therefore the power of the church and civil power must not be confounded. The power of the church has its own commission to teach the Gospel and to administer the Sacraments. Let it not break into the office of another; let it not transfer the kingdoms of this world; let it not abrogate the laws of civil rulers; let it not abolish lawful obedience; let it not interfere with judgments concerning civil ordinances or contracts; let it not prescribe laws to civil rulers concerning the form of the commonwealth. As Christ says in John 18:36: My kingdom is not of this world; also Luke 12:14: Who made Me a judge or a divider over you? Paul also says in Phil. 3:20: Our citizenship is in heaven. (. . .)[6]

As mentioned above, I will provide an example from Swedish church history of how Luther's doctrine of the priesthood of all believers became highlighted in the same century as it was nearly forgotten. I want to provide a background for how and why this teaching came to be used, and to analyze how this doctrine pointed forward to the Enlightenment. My analysis connects to earlier research that wants to avoid pursuing an uncritical overtaking of the self-understanding of the Enlightenment as something radically new, where religion is stamped out as something of the past, and the secular as something modern. This myth has often obscured the deep roots of the Enlightenment in church history from the past.[7]

TO HIGHLIGHT THE PRIESTHOOD OF ALL BELIEVERS—A SWEDISH CASE

On a dark November evening in 1697 two pastors met in the vicarage in the Swedish copper mining town of Falun. One of the two priests was the vicar of Mora, north of Falun and lake Siljan in the district of Dalecarlia; his name was Jacob Boëthius (1647-1718). The other was Olof Ekman (1639-1713), the pastor of Falun.

The two priests met for talks in troubled times. The previous summers had all been marked by poor harvests and even famine. In 1696 the mine

---

6. *Confessio Augustana*. Article XXVIII: Of Ecclesiastical Power.

7. Beutel, *Aufklärung in Deutschland*, 211-12; Van Horn Melton, "Pietism, Politics, and the Public Sphere in Germany"; Gierl, *Pietismus und Aufklärung*; Claesson, "Habermas, kyrka och offentlighet—ett historiskt perspektiv på religionens återkomst," 49-56.

workers in Falun went on strike as they could no longer support themselves owing to their low wages. Some of these workers had also appealed to the peasants in Mora to join them in order to stage a major uprising. Earlier in 1697 the pious King Charles XI had died of stomach cancer. This particular disease was commonly seen as a bad omen. Shortly afterwards the Three Crowns (*Tre kronor*), the Royal Castle in Stockholm, was burned to the ground. In December 1697, the fifteen-year-old son of Charles XI would claim the crown as Charles XII.[8]

Boëthius and Ekman probably shared feelings of concern about the apocalyptic prophecies of the time. In a letter to Stockholm earlier that same year Olof Ekman had announced that strange symbols in the form of two black crowns, with arrows between them as in a fight, had appeared in the sky in the village of Bjursås outside of the town. Did these appearances mean something ominous in relation to the royal powers? Even worse, Ekman also reported that a lake far south of Falun had turned as red as blood, as was predicted in the Book of Revelation. When the two pastors met in Falun the basic question was: how could you combine the doctrine of the priesthood of all believers with the Swedish system of government that included an autocratic king? Under Swedish law, the king was not answerable to any human being on earth, only to God in Heaven. Absolutism had been introduced under King Charles XI in 1680, which meant that the Swedish parliament had lost its influence. What was known as the sovereignty formula of 1693 allowed the king and his future heirs to reign as autocratic and sovereign rulers. They were not responsible to anyone on earth for their actions, and had received the power to govern as Christian kings and to rule imposing their own will.

Boëthius was full of remorse because he had recently sworn an oath to respect the new Church Law that applied from 1686. He was basically very critical of the new law as it gave the king power over the church. To make things even worse, after his oath he happened to see the formula that the estates in parliament had decided upon in 1693. According to Boëthius the king was not only responsible before God, but was also responsible before his Christian brothers and sisters in the church. Was the new king not a brother who could be reprimanded and criticized by his Christian fellows, especially as the ominous signs were so numerous?[9]

---

8. Berggren, "Jacob Boëthius och hans opposition," 16–19; Ödman, *Kontrasternas spel*, 271–80.

9. Excerpt from a letter from Olof Ekman to Simon Isogæus, 7.17.1697. Palmsköld 165, Uppsala University Library; Berggren, "Jacob Boëthius och hans opposition," 16–19; Boëthius, *Levnadsbilder ur släkten Boëthius levnadshistoria 1520–1731*, 97–98; Petersson, *Prosten i Mora Jacob Boëthius*, 23–24.

Olof Ekman felt that Boëthius was going too far in his interpretation of the priesthood of all believers. According to Ekman, the common priesthood involved one Christian brother admonishing the other if he had committed a sin in public. Ekman did not agree that the priesthood of all believers should be about rebuking rulers. If it became common practice for everyone to be able to criticize (in Ekman's own words: "shoot at") the king, the result would be that the workings of the state would be jeopardized. Unlike Boëthius, Ekman also defended the right of the royal power to decide upon the life of the church. Ekman argued that the prophet Isaiah had referred to the king as the protector of the congregation, and that King David and King Solomon had decided on the content of liturgy and had the right to appoint servants to the temple.[10] Boëthius's argument was that the priesthood of all believers included the right to criticize the king in the same way as all Christians were obliged to pray for him as a Christian brother. According to Boëthius, Ekman finally agreed with that, with the reservation that this criticism must be cautious.[11]

After Boëthius had visited Ekman, he posted two letters. One letter was sent to the king in Stockholm, criticizing the principle of sovereignty, especially the way it had been formulated in 1693. The other letter was sent to the Archbishop of Uppsala, complaining about the royal court and its right to exercise power over the church according to the Church Law of 1686.

On his way home to Mora, Boëthius heard about the strange celestial phenomena that Ekman had written about, which probably assured him that he was right in his criticism.

On the evening before the coronation of Charles XII on December 14, 1697, Boëthius was brutally arrested by police and soldiers after he and his family had gone to bed. Boëthius was then quickly transferred from his home in Mora to imprisonment in Stockholm Palace, and put on trial.

The content of Boëthius's letters was treated as high treason, which meant that the prosecutor Magnus Sternell demanded the death penalty. As a consequence Boëthius wrote a detailed statement of defense around Christmas 1697, in which he claimed that he, as a Christian brother belonging to the priesthood of all believers, and also an ordained priest, was within his rights to put forward demands for change. Boëthius meant he was called to warn the king of the sin of ruling according to his own will. To rule according to your own thinking was not congruent with being a Christian

---

10. Copy of a letter from Olof Ekman to Nils Gripenhielm, 1.7.1698, E 545:g, Uppsala University Library.

11. Copy of Jacob Boëthius's Answer 4.29.1698, N 50, Uppsala University Library.

king. Boëthius compared himself with the prophets of Israel and demonstrated with examples from the Old Testament the disasters that could befall kings who only followed their own human wisdom. Boëthius compared these disasters with what would happen if a simple governor declared himself sovereign ruler, imposing his own will within his province. The king would never accept that. In the same manner, God Almighty was offended that the Swedish king had declared himself sovereign ruler, imposing his own will. Boëthius concluded his statement by urging for his thoughts to be published for ordinary people in general, and also demanded that a national meeting should be called in order for his thoughts to be considered. Finally Boëthius claimed that the king did not actually have any right to interfere in his case, as it came under the spiritual regiment.

In another letter dated January 1698 Boëthius criticized the fact that the young prince Charles had put the royal crown on his own head at the crowning ceremony. Unlike the young king, Jesus had never anointed himself. Boëthius further claimed that the belief that God ordained kings in His place on earth with the right to rule of their own will, was like the papal fallacy. On the contrary, the king should abandon all self-aggrandizement and humbly listen to the messengers that God had sent, opting instead to do penance and repent with all the people. Boëthius requested to meet the new king in person.[12]

After Olof Ekman learned that Boëthius had mentioned him in his statement of defense, he immediately wrote a letter explaining what had been said when the two of them had met at his home in Falun. Ekman concluded his letter by certifying that he had always had reverence for "the high powers" (*höga öfverheten*).[13]

Jacob Boëthius was sentenced to death on July 28, 1698 and first had to witness how his writings were burned by the hangman. However, the sentence was quickly changed to life imprisonment, in the first instance in distant Nöteborg in Finland by the Russian border. In the war that followed, the Russian army released Boëthius from jail. However, he refused to accept this liberation as he had been put in prison by the Swedish state, and not the Russian. After a few years Boëthius was transferred to a prison in Stockholm. He was released in 1710 and died in 1718.[14]

12. Berggren, "Jacob Boëthius och hans opposition," 19–27; Petersson, *Prosten i Mora Jacob Boëthius*, 24–48; Copy of Jacob Boëthius's Exceptio 12.29.1697, N 50, Uppsala University Library; Copy of Jacob Boëthius's Duplique 1.20.1698, N 50, Uppsala University Library.

13. Copy of a letter from Olof Ekman to Nils Gripenhielm 1.7.1698, E 545:g, Uppsala University Library; Berggren, "Jacob Boëthius och hans opposition," 28–29.

14. Berggren, "Jacob Boëthius och hans opposition," 30–32; Petersson, *Prosten i Mora Jacob Boëthius*, 49–72.

BOËTHIUS'S PROGRAM

During his long period in jail Boëthius produced a number of texts. For example, in 1704 Boëthius wrote a long letter, sharply critical of the monarchy, after serious attempts by his wife and others to get him out of jail. His harsh letter deemed the continuing pardon he had been granted to be impossible.[15]

What thoughts did Boëthius develop in his letters and writings during and after his trial? A more systematic account of Boëthius's main arguments follows.

Boëthius belonged to a Lutheran universe of thought. The doctrines of the two regiments and the three estates of society have already been introduced above. Within the Lutheran theological system, Boëthius argued for a reversal of the direction of power. To put it bluntly, he turned it upside down. To understand Boëthius properly, the Church Law of 1686 is the best point of departure. Boëthius's way of thinking was basically a reaction against the power of the king over the church, as was permitted in the new Church Law. According to Boëthius, this Church Law was not in line with the doctrine of the two regiments as it provided the right for the king to rule over the church. It was Christ and not the king who was the head of the church. It was therefore wrong for the king to ordain priests and superintendents. Only the church itself should have the privilege of choosing its own clergy. Boëthius continued this argument by claiming that a free and autonomous sphere of spiritual regiment ought to be normative for the whole of society. In contrast to the worldly power over the church that had been legalized in the Church Law, Boëthius chose to emphasize an opposite model in his interpretation of Lutheran theology, where the spiritual regiment had the upper hand. Boëthius claimed that this sphere ought to be the proper starting point of where the king should acquaint himself with the will of God. Boëthius argued that sovereignty in itself was not capable of keeping a society together—he mentioned that you very seldom found friendship between a master and his servant. According to him, the king's absolute power created fear rather than cohesion. Boëthius claimed that Christ called his faithful believers to become His close friends, while, in contrast, the king treated his subjects as slaves. Christian love could keep a society together much better than the sovereignty of the king. The congregation would thus be held together by a common and free agreement.

In Boëthius we do not find the doctrine of the priesthood of all believers reduced to the master's responsibility for devotions within his own household. Boëthius presupposed a strong link between this doctrine and

---

15. Petersson, *Prosten i Mora Jacob Boëthius*, 52–56.

justification before God. For Boëthius justification was much more than a forensic act. For him it consisted of getting a new and holy life:

> Justification in front of God does not only consist of a renunciation of sins on the outside, but also of a cleansing of the inside (. . .) the gift of righteousness is not something dead or disappearing, as the words and sentences of a worldly judge, but is a living, powerful and always existing work through the Holy Spirit, yes a new life and the seed of God in the justified man, through which our spirit now works with the spirit of God to the hatred of all sins and for the love of God (. . .) renews the man (. . .) to the image of God (. . .)[16]

This way of putting it resembles Martin Luther's *Preface to the Letter of St. Paul to the Romans*:

> Der Glaube is ein göttlich werck in uns, das uns wandelt und new gebirt aus Gott, Johan.i. Und tödtet den alten Adam, machet uns gantz ander Menschen von hertzen, mut, sinn, und allen krefften, und bringet den heiligen Geist mit sich. O es ist ein lebendig, schefftig, thettig, mechtig ding umb den glauben, das unmöglich ist, das er nicht on unterlas sollte guts wircken. Er fraget auch nicht, ob gute werck zu thun sind, sondern ehe man fraget, hat er sie gethan, und ist imer im thun.[17]

According to Boëthius, the priesthood of all believers was responsible for cultivating this holy life. In line with the ideals of Luther, Boëthius wanted church discipline to be in the hands of lay people. Boëthius complained that the Swedish Church Law of 1686 restricted church discipline to the realm of ordained priests, when the pursuing of such a church discipline in the first instance, according to the words in chapter 18 of the Gospel of Matthew, ought to be handled among fellow Christians in the form of free reprimands. All this explains why Boëthius reacted so strongly against the formula of absolutism of 1693. A Christian ruler must be willing to listen to, and to follow, the word as preached by the ordained priests in the *status ecclesiasticus*, and he was also obliged to listen to his Christian fellows in the priesthood of all believers. The reason was that all power emanated from the church as the body of Christ—of which the king was a member together with many others. Boëthius argued that the Principle of Sovereignty was a French invention that should never have been introduced in Sweden. After 1700 Boëthius claimed that Charles XI would have been alive if royal

---

16. Quoted in ibid., 69–70.
17. Luther, *Vorrede auf die Epistel S. Pauli an die Römer*, WA DB 7, 11.

absolutism had never been introduced. He also claimed that the castle of the Three Crowns would not have been destroyed by fire. Boëthius firmly believed he had God on his side.

Boëthius referred to Luther's words in the *Schmalkald Articles*, where Luther complained that the Pope in Rome did not accept the Councils and the will of the church. Boëthius said that the Swedish king was similarly unwilling to be governed by the church. The Swedish king thus became an Antichrist in the same way as the Pope in Rome. Luther's criticism towards papal autocracy was kept within the realm of the spiritual regiment. Boëthius crossed that line.

Boëthius demanded that his criticism of the system should result in a major "National Assembly." This national assembly would consist of pious elders from the parishes, and would give direction to the decisions of the monarch. It would be constituted in a form representing the true Christian spirit and intellect. Similarly, priests would be key advisers to the king, as they had the authority of "Christ inherent in the church." The assembly also had to encourage the Swedish people to turn to a better and more pious life. In a way the point of this national meeting was to express the power of the church against the state, legitimized by the role of the ordained priest within the *status ecclesiasticus*, and the elders as representing to priesthood of all believers.

The term "national assembly" sounds surprisingly modern. Here we find thoughts that resemble perceptions foreshadowing the Enlightenment. Boëthius argued for a free sphere without coercion, which could form the basis for a form of a spiritual public opinion. During the centuries that followed, the political realm would become transformed in accordance with this model. Public opinion would be institutionalized in national parliaments to which the king was responsible.[18]

A NEW PUBLIC OF PIOUS READERS—A KEY TO THE FUTURE?

How was it that Boëthius developed ideas that seemed to foreshadow developments that took place long after he was gone? One explanation is that he was already situated in a context where these developments had fertile ground in which to grow. In his letter to the court after his imprisonment Boëthius referred to the Rostock theologian Heinrich Müller. In his book *Geistliche Erquickstunden*, Müller had argued with a quotation of Luther, that the power to admonish within the priesthood of all believers was so

---

18. Berggren, "Jacob Boëthius och hans opposition," 34–42; Petersson, *Prosten i Mora Jacob Boëthius*, 23–48, 53–58, 64–72.

"great and holy, that even the highest king must remain silent and humble himself, if the meekest peasant or subject admonished him for his sin." Boëthius had tried to persuade Ekman to his view by showing this quote to him, but unfortunately Ekman did not have a copy of *Geistliche Erquickstunden* at his home in Falun. Previous research has confirmed that Müller's book became very widespread and popular in Sweden.[19] Here we have a key to understanding the reason for the priesthood of all believers becoming so relevant. Both Boëthius and Ekman belonged to circles where the new devotional literature of the seventeenth century, such as Müller's book, was read. Johann Arndt had been the great pioneer among these readers. Boëthius mentioned Arndt in his letter of defense. Ekman was so heavily influenced by Arndt that he was called the "alter Arndtius" in a serious poem written in Latin. Arndt was a starting point for Heinrich Müller as well. The Swedish church historian Hilding Pleijel has pointed to the strength of this new public of pious readers. Pleijel has traced 37 editions of Johan Arndt's *True Christianity* in Sweden.[20]

Olof Ekman was known as the author of a reform program that was called "Sjönödslöfte" (*Promise at Sea*) because he had survived almost being shipwrecked on the Baltic Sea while sailing home after fulfilling his duties as a Field Superintendent for the Swedish army in the province of Livonia. Ekman's book was published in 1680, the same year as Charles XI had declared himself sovereign with the right to expropriate property from the Swedish nobility and transfer it to the Swedish state. Ekman's reform program made great demands on the Swedish king and urged the state to introduce Christian education for all subjects in the parishes, which, according to Ekman, would create entirely new Christians within as few as ten to twenty years. Education would help to restore the priesthood of all believers. Members of the congregations could uphold their own church discipline with the right to admonish one another. Ekman's program also advocated deaconesses, missionaries and boarding schools in a way that foreshadowed the pietism that was later developed by August Hermann Francke in Halle. Jacob Boëthius was a great admirer of Ekman's reform program, and wanted to radicalize his thoughts. Church historian Udo Sträter has described the seventeenth

19. Berggren, "Jacob Boëthius och hans opposition," 24n1; Lindquist, *Studier i den svenska andaktslitteraturen under stormaktstidevarvet med särskild hänsyn till bön-, tröste- och nattvardsböcker*, 4.

20. Copy of Jacob Boëthius's Exceptio 12.29 1697, N 50, Uppsala University Library; Pleijel, "Johann Arndt och svenskt fromhetsliv," 326n2. For Ekman, see: Pleijel, *Svenska kyrkans historia. Femte bandet. Karolinsk kyrkofromhet, pietism och herrnhutism 1680–1772*, 145–147. I will soon be publishing a monograph named *Kris och kristnande* (Crisis and Christianity) which will present Olof Ekman as an important pioneer for pietistic ideas in the Swedish Lutheran church.

century as the century of church reform programs. Many different reform programs based on Arndt's new thinking were published during this century.[21] Ekman wrote a program specifically intended to reform the Christian life of Sweden.

Among readers of religious books there was a demand for the activation of the individual's belief and practical piety. In this emerging public sphere the congregation of believers was put forward as the head of the church. Luther's doctrine of the universal priesthood became revitalized in new ways among these critics. With the new religious literature of the seventeenth century the individual and the inner life became the basis of the church. Arndt's writings created a split between the individual and the church. The individual's inner conviction came to form the basis of true Christianity. Private devotion should be cultivated in order to lay the foundation for public life. As far as Arndt was concerned, just going to church, without inner devotion, simply did not count. In this tradition Luther's preface to Paul's letter to the Romans was greatly appreciated. As I have shown, Luther had written inspiringly about the possibilities for a Christian to lead a new holy life.[22]

It is well known that Jürgen Habermas, in his great study of the structural transformation of the bourgeois public sphere, has pointed out that the eighteenth century was characterized by a new form of public opinion. The cultivation of the private became a foundation for life in the public sphere. Reading (newspapers and novels, for example) meant that you did not want to restrict yourself to being a subordinate subject, but rather wanted to develop yourself emotionally and intellectually, and thus manage to establish yourself as a citizen. In a footnote Habermas argues that pietism in Germany prepared for "these forms of secular sentimentality."[23] Habermas is one of those who want to highlight the theological foundations of the Enlightenment.

The cultivation of private emotional life during Enlightenment can be regarded as a secular reflection of the ideals connected to the devotional literature of the seventeenth century.[24] The ideal of a critical public of read-

---

21. Sträter, *Meditation und Kirchenreform in der lutherischen Kirche des 17. Jahrhunderts*.

22. Brecht, "Das Aufkommen der neuen Frömmigkeitsbewegung in Deutschland," 117, 131, 138–39, 142.

23. "In Deutschland hat ohnehin der Pietismus diesen Formen säkularisierter Sentimentalität vorgearbeitet." Habermas, *Strukturwandel der Öffentlichkeit*, 113n51. Also see Nordbäck, *Samvetets röst*, 36–37, 178, 357–62, 409–10, 413.

24. Hansson, *Ett språk för själen*.

ers was foreshadowed by the new pious group of readers in the preceding century.

CONCLUSION

In this chapter I have used the early case of Jacob Boëthius as a vivid example to show how a transition from a subordinate subject to a participant citizen was possible at a time as far back as the late seventeenth century. Johann Arndt had described a tension between the real state of the church and what he modelled as true Christianity. A new basis was created for demanding something more than the established church. Luther's teaching of the common priesthood of all believers could be reactivated in a new public of readers during the late seventeenth century, which pointed towards the new era of Enlightenment and civil society.[25]

SOURCES

Uppsala University Library: Section for Manuscripts and Music.
E 545:g: Copy of a letter from Olof Ekman to Nils Gripenhielm 1.7.1698
N 50: Copy of Jacob Boëthius's Exceptio 12.29.1697
N 50: Copy of Jacob Boëthius's Duplique 1.20.1698
N 50: Copy of Jacob Boëthius's Answer 4.29.1698
Palmsköld 165: Excerpt from a letter from Olof Ekman to Simon Isogæus 7.17.1697

BIBLIOGRAPHY

Askmark, Ragnar. *Ämbetet i den Svenska kyrkan i reformationens, ortodoxiens och pietismens tänkande och praxis.* Lund: CWK Gleerups förlag, 1949.
Berggren, Erik. "Jacob Boëthius och hans opposition." *Kyrkohistorisk årsskrift* (1942) 1–55.
Beutel, Albrecht. *Aufklärung in Deutschland. Die Kirche in ihrer Geschichte,* Band 4, Lieferung O2. Göttingen: Vandenhoeck & Ruprecht, 2006.
Boëthius, Sven Arvid. *Levnadsbilder ur släkten Boëthius levnadshistoria 1520–1731.* Stockholm: Proprius förlag, 1986.
Brecht, Martin. "Das Aufkommen der neuen Frömmigkeitsbewegung in Deutschland." In *Geschichte des Pietismus. Band 1. Der Pietismus vom siebzehnten bis zum frühen achtzehnten Jahrhundert,* edited by Martin Brecht. Göttingen: Vandenhoeck & Ruprecht, 1993.

---

25. As this article has been written as a result of a conference on Lutheran tradition in Sweden, it may be worthwhile to note that the Swedish language in itself has facilitated the analysis of a transition from the priesthood of all believers to the rise of public opinion. In Swedish the common priesthood is commonly referred to as public priesthood (*allmänt prästadöme*), making it easy to associate to public opinion (*allmän opinion*).

Bring, Ragnar. *Luther, stat och kyrka. Luthers syn på de två "rikena" eller "regementena."* Stockholm: Skeab/Verbum, 1979.

Claesson, Urban. "Habermas, kyrka och offentlighet—ett historiskt perspektiv på religionens återkomst." In *Religionens offentlighet. Om religionens plats i samhället*, edited by Hanna Stenström, 47–60. Skellefteå: Artos och Norma bokförlag, 2013.

Confessio Augustana. Online: http://bookofconcord.org/augsburgconfession.php (accessed 12/12/2013).

Gierl, Martin. *Pietismus und Aufklärung. Theologische Polemik und die Kommunikationsreform der Wissenschaft am Ende des 17. Jahrhunderts.* Göttingen: Vandenhoeck & Ruprecht, 1997.

Goertz, Harald. *Allgemeines Priestertum und ordiniertes Amt bei Luther.* Marburger Theologische Studien 46. Marburg: N.G. Elwert Verlag, 1997.

Habermas, Jürgen. *Strukturwandel der Öffentlichkeit. Untersuchungen zu einer Kategorie der bürgerlichen Gesellschaft. Mit einem Vorwort zur Neuauflage 1990.* Frankfurt am Main: Suhrkamp Verlag, 1990.

Hallgren, Bengt. *Kyrkotuktsfrågan. En systematisk studie av kyrkotukten i svensk frikyrklighet och hos Martin Luther.* Stockholm: Svenska kyrkans diakonistyrelses bokförlag, 1963.

Hansson, Stina. *Ett språk för själen. Litterära former i den svenska andaktslitteraturen 1650–1720.* Skrifter utgivna av Litteraturvetenskapliga institutionen vid Göteborgs universitet 20. Göteborg: Göteborgs universitet, 1991.

Jansson, Torkel. *Adertonhundratalets associationer. Forskning och problem kring ett sprängfyllt tomrum eller sammanslutningsprinciper och föreningsformer mellan två samhällsformationer c:a 1800–1870.* Studia historica Upsaliensia 139. Uppsala: Acta Universitatis Upsaliensis, 1985.

Lindquist, Daniel. *Studier i den svenska andaktslitteraturen under stormaktstidevarvet med särskild hänsyn till bön-, tröste- och nattvardsböcker.* Uppsala: Svenska kyrkans diakonistyrelses bokförlag, 1939.

Luther, Martin. *Vorrede auf die Epistel S. Pauli an die Römer* (1546). WA DB 7. Weimar: Hermann Böhlaus Nachfolger, 1931.

Nordbäck, Carola. *Samvetets röst. Om mötet mellan luthersk ortodoxi och konservativ pietism i 1720-talets Sverige.* Skrifter från institutionen för historiska studier 8. Umeå: Umeå universitet, 2004.

Petersson, Lorentz E. *Prosten i Mora Jacob Boëthius. Lefnadsteckning, mest efter otryckta källor.* Stockholm: Albert Nilson, 1878.

Pleijel, Hilding. "Johann Arndt och svenskt fromhetsliv." *Svensk teologisk kvartalskrift* (1938) 319–32.

———. *Svenska kyrkans historia. Femte bandet. Karolinsk kyrkofromhet, pietism och herrnhutism 1680–1772.* Stockholm: Svenska kyrkans diakonistyrelses förlag, 1935.

Stadin, Kekke. *Stånd och genus i stormaktstidens Sverige.* Lund: Nordic Academic Press, 2004.

Sträter, Udo. *Meditation und Kirchenreform in der lutherischen Kirche des 17. Jahrhunderts.* Beiträge zur historischen Theologie 91. Tübingen: Mohr Siebeck, 1995.

Törnvall, Gustaf. *Andligt och världsligt regemente hos Luther. Studier i Luthers världs- och samhällsbild.* Lund: Håkan Ohlsson, 1940.

Van Horn Melton, James. "Pietism, Politics, and the Public Sphere in Germany." In *Religion and Politics in Enlightenment Europe*, edited by James E. Bradley and Dale K. Van Kley, 294–333. Notre Dame, IN: University of Notre Dame Press, 2001.

Ödman, Per-Johan. *Kontrasternas spel. En svensk mentalitets- och pedagogikhistoria. Del I.* Stockholm: Nordstedts förlag AB, 1995.

14

Luther's Interpretation of the *Magnificat* and Latin American Liberation Theology

ELINA VUOLA

In most Lutheran churches today, the Mother of God is absent—in prayers, liturgy, theology, and spirituality. At the same time, there are ecumenical grass-roots movements such as the Taizé movement, in which the Virgin Mary is more present. There is a noteworthy theological silence about Mary in the Lutheran tradition, even though the first two Marian dogmas of the early church and Luther's thought provide much more common ground for an ecumenical Mariology than we might think.

A Mariology based on the historical and biblical Mary of Nazareth as well as the need and yearning felt for a deeper Marian spirituality among contemporary people, possibly among women in particular—in the Lutheran churches as well—could draw from liberation theology and feminist theology. An especially clear example is the biblical *Magnificat*, which Luther deals with extensively and which is a particularly important biblical passage about Mary in liberation theology.

My long-term research on the figure of the Virgin Mary, especially in the Catholic context, and lately, in the Finnish Orthodox tradition,[1] has made me think about the dearth—if not absence—of Marian theology and Mariology in Lutheran churches. At the same time, I have paid attention

---

1. My current research project, funded by the Academy of Finland, which is ongoing, includes interviews with Finnish Orthodox women on their relationship to the Virgin Mary.

to some similarities between Luther's thought and liberation theology concerning Mary.

An important part of my research has focused on Latin American liberation theology—or theologies in the plural, since I include Latin American feminist, indigenous, black (Afro Latin American), and ecological theologies in the term liberation theology, thus understood in a broad sense. On the one hand, there are important contemporary Marian interpretations in Latin American liberation theology—primarily but not exclusively Catholic—as it has been developed since the 1960s and 1970s onwards, and on the other, in feminist theology, globally and ecumenically.

In this chapter I will compare Luther's commentary on the *Magnificat* with some (Catholic) Latin American liberation theologians' contemporary interpretations of the Mother of God. Luther both agrees with pre-Reformation ecumenical Mariology and has Mariological interpretations of his own. The latter is especially clear in his commentary of the *Magnificat*.

My interest in comparing Luther's thoughts on Mary with liberation theology is twofold. First, the silence about Mary and her absence in the Lutheran tradition need to be rethought in relation to Luther's own texts. Thus, my chapter is a critical reflection on one specific aspect of Luther's theology, which could also make it more relevant for contemporary discussions about gender and social justice on a broader basis. Secondly, a more practical interest is based on thinking about Mary and Mariology as contributions—and not obstacles—to ecumenical relationships.

LUTHER'S COMMENTARY OF THE MAGNIFICAT

The commentary of the *Magnificat* is the only systematic and broad Mariological text by Luther. In addition to it, he deals with Mariological themes in his sermons and elsewhere, but not as systematically as in his long commentary on the *Magnificat*, which runs to over 60 pages.[2]

The *Magnificat* is a biblical text to be found in Luke 1:46–55. The young Mary has found out that she will be the mother of Jesus. She visits her cousin Elizabeth, the mother-to-be of John the Baptist—an often depicted scene called *Visitatio* in Western and Byzantine art. During this encounter, Mary breaks out in praise of God:

> My soul magnifies the Lord,
> and my spirit rejoices in God my Saviour,
> for he has looked with favour on the lowliness of his servant.
> Surely, from now on all generations will call me blessed;

---

2. Luther, *The Magnificat*, LW 21, 296–358.

> (...)
> He has shown strength with his arm;
> he has scattered the proud in the thoughts of their hearts.
> He has brought down the powerful from their thrones,
> and lifted up the lowly;
> he has filled the hungry with good things,
> and sent the rich away empty.
> He has helped his servant Israel,
> in remembrance of his mercy.

I will not go through Luther's interpretation in detail. It is verses 52–53 in particular that are important, both in Luther and liberation theology—for obvious reasons for the latter, known as theology of the poor.

The main themes that are to be found in Luther's commentary are the following. First, according to Luther, the Virgin Mary is speaking on the basis of her own experience. Luther starts his commentary with the following words:

> In order properly to understand this sacred hymn of praise, we need to bear in mind that the Blessed Virgin Mary is speaking on the basis of her own experience, in which she was enlightened and instructed in the Holy Spirit. No one can correctly understand God or His Word unless he has received such understanding immediately from the Holy Spirit.[3]

Secondly, because of this experience and the wisdom transmitted by it, Mary sets an example to others. She "teaches us, with her words and by the example of her experience, how to know, love, and praise God."[4] This view of Mary as a teacher is repeated throughout Luther's text.[5]

Thirdly, another leitmotif in Luther's text is the understanding of Mary as an ordinary human being, an ordinary woman, including her being of poor and humble origin. Luther writes, for example:

> (...) we must believe that she came of poor, despised, and lowly parents. (...) Even in her own town of Nazareth she was not the daughter of one of the chief rulers, but a poor and plain citizen's daughter, whom none looked up to or esteemed. To

---

3. Ibid., LW 21, 299.
4. Ibid., LW 21, 301.
5. For example, ibid., LW 21, 325, 331.

her neighbors and their daughters she was but a simple maiden, tending the cattle and doing the housework (...).⁶

Fourthly, in spite of her lowliness and ordinariness, Mary is the Mother of God, *Theotokos*, worthy of devotion:

> The 'great things' are nothing less than that she became the Mother of God, in which work so many and such great good things are bestowed on her as pass man's understanding. For on this there follows all honor, all blessedness, and her unique place in the whole of mankind, among which she has no equal (...).⁷

The editor of the text, Jaroslav Pelikan, comments in this context that throughout his life and theological development, Luther continued to ascribe the title *Theotokos* to the Virgin Mary, as well as calling her blessed in every sense of the word.⁸ According to Luther, calling Mary the Mother of God is the greatest thing one can say of her or to her, and it "needs to be pondered in the heart what it means to be the Mother of God."⁹ According to my understanding, this points to a deep Marian spirituality in Luther. Certain things, including Mary and her role as the Mother of God, can primarily be understood by the heart, not by the intellect.

Fifthly and finally, in spite of Mary's unique place and her being an example for the rest of humankind, Luther quickly—and consistently with his overall theology—reminds us of the danger of idolatry, including in the case of the Mother of God. Mary is not to be seen as a goddess or an idol, nor even as the Queen of Heaven,¹⁰ the latter being the standard understanding in Catholic Marian teaching and devotion.

By and large, it can be said that Luther's relationship to the Virgin Mary is positive, even warm and affectionate. There is a Marian spirituality and importance given to Mary in Luther's thinking, which later largely disappeared from the Lutheran tradition, both theologically and in practice. It is probably the Marian spirituality that is so poorly understood in Lutheran churches, and often even seen as something heretical. This is also the most important difference between the Lutheran and Orthodox churches concerning Mary. The differences are not so much dogmatic, since, like Protestant churches, Orthodox churches have not approved the two later Marian dogmas of the Catholic Church (*Immaculata Conceptio* 1854 and *Assumptio*

---

6. Ibid., LW 21, 301.
7. Ibid., LW 21, 326.
8. Ibid., LW 21, 326n26.
9. Ibid., LW 21, 326.
10. Ibid., LW 21, 327.

1950). Rather, the differences relate to ecclesiology, liturgy, and spirituality: the central place of the Mother of God in Orthodox understanding of the Church, its liturgy, and its spirituality, has no equivalent in the Lutheran churches.

According to the Finnish Luther scholar Anja Ghiselli, Luther's overall Mariology can best be understood in the context of Christology, especially the theology of the cross.[11] This is also the context of much of liberation theology's Mariology. Ghiselli stresses that Luther agrees with the two Marian dogmas of the early church, as do Lutheran churches to this day, namely calling Mary the Mother of God, *Theotokos* (Ephesus, 431) and Mary's perpetual virginity (Constantinople, 681). Consistently with his overall theology, Luther stresses Mary's exemplary faith in God: the entire *Magnificat* is about praising God's glory and goodness. It is God-centered. Mary's humility—which Luther so much underlines—is not so much about Mary herself as it is about the critique of power and self-centeredness. God chose her as someone who had no power in human terms. Mary's humanity, even when praised as exemplary, does not make her divine. There is a place for Marian spirituality and devotion in Luther, but not for her divinization.[12]

The Danish Luther scholar Else Marie Wiberg Pedersen has argued that Luther's ambivalent and torn ("between bad anthropology and good theology") view of women is reflected in his Marian interpretations. However, it is precisely Luther's commentary on the *Magnificat* that has clear social implications. It is a political program, talking about real and concrete poverty and oppression, but it is first and foremost a theological program: true Mariology is about humanizing the human world. Mariology is, thus, an integral part of Luther's "democratic" theology.[13]

Luther is consistent in seeing Mary as a human being, even if an exemplary one. Mary's humanity is also about her being ordinary and poor. Nevertheless, as was said above, Mary is worthy of praise and devotion. As Kirsi Stjerna proposes, Luther's spirituality and theology of the cross are also a basis for his social critique.[14] Since these elements are so tied together in his commentary on the *Magnificat*, it is interesting to ask whether Luther's Mariology is in fact representative of how spirituality, theology of the cross, and social critique are interrelated in his thought. The combination of spirituality, social critique, and theology is also at the core of liberation

---

11. Ghiselli, *Sanan kantaja. Martti Lutherin käsitys Neitsyt Mariasta.*
12. Ibid.
13. Wiberg Pedersen, "A Man Caught Between Bad Anthropology and Good Theology?" 197.
14. Stjerna, "For the Sake of the Future."

theology, often misunderstood as lacking spirituality in favor of mere social critique.

LATIN AMERICAN LIBERATION THEOLOGY

Practically all texts by Catholic liberation theologians contain some reference to Mary, not necessarily as an alternative interpretation, but rather as an indication of Marian devotion. Of the Latin American male liberation theologians, it is Leonardo Boff from Brazil who pays most attention to Mary and Mariology. His most important Mariological works are *O rostro materno de Deus* (1979, in English, *The Maternal Face of God*, 1988) and *A Ave Maria. O feminino e o Espírito Santo* (1980, in English, *Ave Maria*, 1990).[15]

Most feminist liberation theologians deal with the figure of Mary for the same reason as feminist theologians elsewhere. Feminist theological interest in the most important female figure of Christianity and dogmatic interpretations of her are an ecumenical phenomenon. Of the Latin American feminist liberation theologians, I will refer primarily to the English translations of the book by Ivone Gebara and María C. Bingemer, titled *Mary, Mother of God, Mother of the Poor* (1989), and the doctoral dissertation of María Pilar Aquino, *Our Cry for Life. Feminist Theology from Latin America* (1993).[16]

Leonardo Boff ties his Mariological interpretations to his view of women. According to Boff, the Virgin Mary is simultaneously the archetype of the feminine and a dimension of God, the "maternal face of God." Mary has a special relationship to the Holy Spirit, which represents the feminine principle of the Trinity. Thus, Boff locates Mary in a very important, even central, place in the history of salvation.[17] Mary is not merely her Son's collaborator, but together with him is the absolute *Mediatrix*, mediator or intercessor. In a way, Boff deifies Mary as much as Latin American popular devotion does.

For Boff, this deified Mary has the anthropological implication of women being bearers of divinity. In a way, he radicalizes the traditional

---

15. I use the Spanish translations of both books, see bibliography. All direct translations from Spanish to English are mine.

16. The Portuguese original of the book by Gebara and Bingemer is called *Maria, Mãe de Deus e Mãe dos Pobres* (1987) and the Spanish original by Aquino *Nuestro clamor por la vida: teología latinoamericana desde la perspectiva de la mujer* (1992). In the latter, the English translation has parts which are not included in the original Spanish edition.

17. Boff, *El Ave María*; Boff, *El rostro materno de Dios*.

Catholic view of Mary, affirming theologically the divine character she actually has in popular piety, and, to some extent, in theology as well.

Boff has sensitivity towards what he calls "the feminine." His starting point for both Mariology and his dealings with gender issues in general is an understanding of sexuality and sexual difference as ontological structures of the human being. His Jungian-based theological anthropology defines femininity and masculinity as two different poles or dimensions of human existence. The first expresses "the obscurity and night, mystery and profoundness, interiority, earth, sentiment, receptivity, the generating power, human vitality," whereas the latter expresses "the light, time, impulse, the provoking power, order, exteriority, objectivity and reason." The feminine character entails "repose, immobility, darkness that defies curiosity and investigation, the immanence, the longing for the past." In contrast, the masculine entails all that is "transformative dynamism, aggressivity, transcendence, clarity able to distinguish and separate, the capacity to order and project towards the future."[18]

Nevertheless, it is precisely his starting point, the exaltation of the feminine in the figure of Mary, that turns out to be problematic. Boff's perception of Mary as the archetypal mother, as *Theotokos*, is based on his view of human motherhood:

> The maternal potentiality impregnates all the fabrics of a woman's life. This is the dimension of receptivity, care and of being protected at home. Even if a woman were to have no children, every woman is a mother, because it belongs to her to nurse and gestate (. . .)[19]

Gender essentialism and a certain kind of romanticism concerning women in Boff have been criticized by Latin American feminist theologians. Most feminist liberation theologians diverge from Boff, at least implicitly, in the exaltation of the feminine at the cost of real women and bodily womanhood. This devaluation of all other women except Mary—of those who cannot be like her—is one of the consequences of classical Mariology. According to a feminist theological understanding, a simple and clear affirmation of human

---

18. Boff, *Testigos de Dios en el corazón del mundo*, 163. See also Boff, *El rostro materno de Dios*, 67–68; and Boff, *El Ave María*, 17, 47. In the latter, there are more characteristics such as tenderness, delicacy, profundity, interiority, sentiment and donation for the feminine, as well as mystery. For a more detailed analysis of Boff's understanding of gender see Vuola, *Limits of Liberation*, chapter 3.3.2.

19. Boff, *El Ave María*, 47.

bodiliness, especially in its female form (in the Mariological context) makes the separation of Mary from all other women unnecessary.[20]

Thus, feminist liberation theological Mariology implies a critique of an (excessively) high Mariology in liberation theology. Since Boff in particular takes femininity as the starting point for his Mariology, the critique from his feminist colleagues has centered on this notion of femininity as abstract and essentializing as well as in the placing of Mary against other women. Constructively, a feminist Mariology has its starting point in giving value to human motherhood, sexuality, birth, and bodiliness, not in abstract femininity. The option for the poor needs to be translated into an option for poor women. Women's own—possibly gendered—experiences and interpretations of the Virgin Mary and their often intimate relation to her need to be taken into account.

LIBERATION THEOLOGY AND MAGNIFICAT

Both male and female liberation theologians, but especially the former, have a more historical interpretation of Mary in the context of the *Magnificat*. As soon as their interpretation is not guided by "the feminine principle," Mary becomes more concrete, more real and less isolated from human experience. When interpreting Mary of the *Magnificat* as "the liberating mother" and "a prophetess committed to liberation,"[21] Boff is also more in tune with the overall theological method of liberation theology, giving priority to historical realities and praxis.[22]

Thus, in the context of liberation theology, Mary of the *Magnificat* is a prophet and universal liberating mother, who commits herself to justice and the announcement of the Kingdom of God. She is *persona ecclesiae*, the personification of the church of the poor and marginalized. Mary herself is poor and ordinary, a *campesina* woman, but chosen by God. This is the God-centered understanding of the option for the poor: it is the God of the poor who opts for them. Because of Mary's faithful and courageous response to God's call, she becomes the paradigm of faith and solidarity.

According to María Pilar Aquino, in the base communities Mary is thought of not as an object of worship but as an active participant in liberation processes.[23] The stress is not on Mary's individual virtues but on her solidarity with the common project to create a new order. She is not seen exclusively in terms of her role as the mother of Jesus but in relation to God's

---

20. Vuola, *Limits of Liberation*, 172.
21. Boff, "María, Mulher Profética e Libertadora."
22. Vuola, *Limits of Liberation*.
23. Aquino, *Our Cry for Life*, 173–74.

reign that is bursting into history.²⁴ Aquino also stresses the same element in Mary that several other feminist theologians do, based on the actual experiences of ordinary women: Mary is not a heavenly creature but a woman like themselves who shares their lives as a comrade and sister in struggle.²⁵

THE VIRGIN MARY IN LUTHER AND LIBERATION THEOLOGY

In what follows, I will make a comparison between Luther and liberation theology in relation to the *Magnificat*. First, I will draw attention to some important similarities.

Luther stresses how Mary came of poor, despised, and lowly parents. Her humility and poverty are real, "disregarded, despised and lowly estate" meaning poverty, sickness, hunger, being imprisoned, suffering, and death.²⁶ One central, maybe the most important, tenet in liberation theology's Mariology is to consider her as "one of us," a *campesina*, an ordinary, poor woman, which is why she can be so easily identified with by the poor and marginalized of today. Similarly, as in Luther, humility is an outcome and expression of sickness, hunger, suffering, and poverty. The larger context of theology of the cross is present in both Luther and liberation theology.

Humility is nothingness, true lack of many things, and it is important to differentiate between true and false humility. For Luther false humility is pride. It is God alone who knows humility.²⁷ Artificial humility for Luther is being fixed on the rewards and results of one's humility, whereas "the truly humble look not to the result of humility but with a simple heart regard things of low degree and gladly associate with them."²⁸ Luther's distinction between pride and humility, on the one hand, and true and false humility, on the other, can also be found in liberation theology. False humility is closely related to power.

According to Ivone Gebara and María Clara Bingemer,

> the central core, which in summary form we call incarnation, is the basis around which Luke's text is organized, and it is also the source of the new power that the old poem taken from the ancient traditions of the people and from the prophetesses of the Old Testament assumes on Mary's lips. (. . .) Mary's joy

---

24. Ibid., 175–76.
25. Ibid., 176–77.
26. Luther, *The Magnificat*, LW 21, 301, 313, 317.
27. Ibid., LW 21, 313–14.
28. Ibid., LW 21, 315.

> expresses the joy of the people that lives and proclaims the wonders of the presence of God who looks down on that people and brings about justice in the people's midst. (. . .) Mary's song is a war chant, God's battle song enmeshed in human history, the struggle to establish a world of egalitarian relationships, of deep respect for each individual, in whom god-head dwells. That is why there is mention of confounding the proud, of deposing the mighty (. . .)[29]

According to Leonardo Boff, in accordance with probably all liberation theologians,

> it has been the task of our time to elaborate an image of Mary as a prophet, as a determined and strong woman, committed to the messianic liberation of the poor from their socio-historical injustices.[30]

As has been said, for Luther Mary is also an exemplary Christian and teacher. She teaches us a twofold lesson: first, every one of us should pay attention to what God does for us rather than to others, because this is the only way to avoid false humility through works. The second lesson Mary teaches us is that everyone should strive to praise God by pointing to the works God has done for us, and only then by praising God's works towards others. Mary confesses that the foremost work God did for her was that He bestowed regard upon her, which is the greatest of God's works. This is why she is called blessed.[31]

In liberation theology, there is the classical Catholic emphasis on Mary as an exemplary Christian and teacher, a model and example to follow. In fact, this is not a specifically liberation theological view but something that all Christian churches share: Mary as the paragon of faith and an exemplary Christian.

Furthermore, throughout his commentary, Luther stresses Mary's confidence in God, her God-centeredness. She should not be made an idol or a divine being. Here Luther's critique of the Mariology and Marian practices of his time is clearly visible. According to him, the proper understanding of the *Magnificat* is in its (Mary's) God-centeredness.[32] Praising Mary as blessed is based on God bestowing regard upon her. Showing her honor

---

29. Gebara and Bingemer, *Mary, Mother of God, Mother of the Poor*, 72.
30. Boff, *El rostro materno de Dios*, 220–21.
31. Luther, *The Magnificat*, LW 21, 301, 318–19, 321.
32. Ibid., LW 21, 322.

and devotion—that are her due, according to Luther—is not to make her an idol.³³ This could be called Luther's low Mariology.

Similarly, in liberation theology, it is God who opts for the poor, and who is God of the poor; this opens up a horizon of confidence and utopia. God opts for the poor and lowly to show human beings that it is only with this attitude that we can attain the right Christian attitude towards God, ourselves and our fellow human beings. The emphasis on Mary's ordinariness—as critique of a distant Queen of Heaven—is an element of low Mariology in liberation theology as well.

Both Luther and liberation theologians thus see Mary primarily as an ordinary human being, chosen by God. Any Marian devotion is based on her closeness to God, as *Theotokos* and exemplary human being. Marian spirituality is not about making her a goddess.

The ordinariness of Mary is concretely expressed by Luther: when she learns of her pregnancy, Mary

> conducts herself as before, when she still had nothing of all this; she demands no higher honors than before. She is not puffed up, does not vaunt herself or proclaim with a loud voice that she is become the Mother of God. She seeks not any glory, but goes about her usual household duties, milking the cows, cooking the meals, washing pots and kettles, sweeping out the rooms, and performing the work of maidservant or housemother in lowly and despised tasks, as though she cared nothing for such great gifts and graces. She was esteemed among other women and her neighbors no more highly than before, nor desired to be, but remained a poor townswoman, one of the great multitude. (. . .) How many came in contact with her, talked, and ate and drank with her, who perhaps despised her and counted her but a common, poor, and simple village maiden, and who, had they known, would have fled from her in terror.³⁴

María Pilar Aquino states simply that the prophetic proclamation of *Magnificat* has become a key source for the spiritual journey and practice of Latin American women.³⁵ The connection between Mary and the base communities is central to Latin American women's thinking about her. Mary is thought of not as an object of worship but as an active participant in liberation processes.³⁶ Poor women see Mary not as a heavenly creature

---

33. Ibid., LW 21, 322, 327.
34. Ibid., LW 21, 329.
35. Aquino, *Our Cry for Life*, 172.
36. Ibid., 174.

but as someone who shares their lives as a sister in struggle. Her solidarity and prophecy become a program for these women and the communities themselves.[37]

Another similarity between Luther and liberation theology is the image of God, who—according to Luther—comforts those who suffer injury and evil, and are oppressed. God destroys and puts down the mighty and the great who vent their pride on their inferiors, who suffer at their hands. God

> comforts those who must suffer injury and evil. And as much as He comforts the latter, so much He terrifies the former. (. . .) The oppressed are raised up, also without any sound, for God's strength is in them, and it alone remains when the strength of the mighty has fallen.[38]

The term God of the poor (*el Dios de los pobres*) has become known as *the* image of God in liberation theology. The poor means not just the economically or materially poor, but all the oppressed and marginalized—for other reasons than material poverty as well, such as ethnicity and gender.[39]

Similarly, Luther says that "those of low degree are not the humble, but all those who are contemptible and altogether nothing in the eyes of the world."[40] God

> lets them be exalted spiritually, and in God, and be judges over seats and power and all might, here and hereafter; for they have more knowledge than all the learned and the mighty. (. . .) All this is said for the comfort of the suffering and for the terror of the tyrants.[41]

We may want to compare this view of Luther's with liberation theology's epistemological claim about the primacy of the poor. As a truth claim, the viewpoint of the poor can be problematized, but what liberation theologians[42] mean by epistemological rupture (*ruptura epistemológica*) is primarily an ethical perspective of the poor and the oppressed which enables us to

---

37. Ibid., 176–77.
38. Luther, *The Magnificat*, LW 21, 343–44.
39. See Vuola, *Limits of Liberation*, for a critical analysis of "the poor" in liberation theology.
40. Luther, *The Magnificat*, LW 21, 345.
41. Ibid.
42. See for example Sobrino, "El conocimiento teológico en la teología europea y latinoamericana," 200–202. See Vuola, *Limits of Liberation*, for a critical evaluation of the concept of praxis and praxis-related truth claims in liberation theology.

perceive the moral dimensions of oppression. Theologically, this perspective is closely related to our image and understanding of God.

There is thus a clear and noteworthy critique of wealth and abuse of power in Luther's commentary. The socio-political aspect of the *Magnificat* is shared by Luther and liberation theologians. Critique of richness and material wealth is at the core of liberation theology's critique of domination, money as idolatry and false god, and the poor as non-persons. For example, Gustavo Gutiérrez says that liberation theologians' "interpellator is the poor, the 'non-person', that is, someone who is not valued as a human being with all rights."[43] The challenge to Christian faith, in a continent like Latin America, does not come principally from the non-believer, but from these non-persons who call into question not so much the religious world as the economic, social, political, and cultural world.[44] The emphasis on idolatry rather than faith versus atheism has been a consistent theme in liberation theology.

Interestingly, Luther says that we must learn by experience what poverty and hunger are. We must not only think and speak of a low estate but actually come to be in a low estate and caught in it.[45] This is close to what liberation theologians mean by the option for the poor (*la opción por los pobres*), and the need for the church to become a church of the poor. Both Luther and liberation theologians stress that it is not only an ethical option but the only way to understand who and what God is.

DIFFERENCES BETWEEN LUTHER AND LIBERATION THEOLOGY

There are more similarities than differences between Luther's and liberation theologians' interpretation of the *Magnificat*, in my view, even though too direct a comparison between texts from such different historical times and contexts should not be drawn. However, there are also some important differences.

Even in the commentary on the *Magnificat*, Luther has a section that is strongly anti-Semitic. His critique of the Jews is tied to his interpretation of spiritual pride ("he has scattered the proud in the thoughts of their hearts"), relating it to the rejection of Christ by the Jews and their "perverse hypocrisy."[46] As far as I can tell, there is not one liberation theologian who would express an anti-Semitic attitude. On the contrary, there is a critical

---

43. Gutiérrez, *Teología de la liberación*, 31.
44. Gutiérrez, *La fuerza histórica de los pobres*, 77.
45. Luther, *The Magnificat*, LW 21, 347–48.
46. Especially ibid., LW 21, 342–43.

attitude towards anti-Semitism in all liberation theologies, consistent with the critique of oppression on the basis of ethnicity, race, religion, or gender. Rather, in the context of Mariology, liberation theological view of Mary is based on her being an ordinary woman of her time, including her being a Jewish woman.

Another difference between Luther and liberation theology is in what was presented above as Luther's critique of "high Mariology"—Mary becoming the Queen of Heaven, an idol and even a sort of goddess. Luther combines this Mariological critique with his overall critique of some Catholic practices of his time:

> Alas, the word "service of God" has nowadays taken on so strange a meaning and usage that whoever hears it thinks not of these works of God, but rather of the ringing of bells, the wood and stone of churches, the gold, silver, and precious stones in the vestments of choirboys and celebrants, of chalices and monstrances, of organs and images, processions and churchgoing, and, most of all, the babbling of lips and the rattling of rosaries. (. . .) We chant the Magnificat daily, to a special tone and with gorgeous pomp; and yet the oftener we sing it, the more we silence its true music and meaning.[47]

Even though the emphasis on low Mariology is to be found in both Luther and liberation theology, the important role and place of Mary in Catholic theology and devotion is central for liberation theologians. In this sense, Catholic liberation theological Mariology is also a combination of "high" and "low" Mariology. For Luther, Mary has no importance in herself. In Latin American Catholicism, Mary has a unique and central status, especially in everyday religion and popular religiosity (*religiosidad popular*), which draws from both mainstream Catholic teaching and the lasting presence of pre-Colombian female deities, never fully eradicated, but rather infused with specific features in a syncretistic Marian devotion in different countries of Latin America. The sphere of everyday religion is especially important for women.[48]

Luther's emphasis on Mary as an ordinary woman is thus shared by liberation theology, although in the latter Mary's status as a powerful and divine woman, and as a prophet, is also strongly accentuated. Mary's role as

---

47. Ibid., LW 21, 350.

48. For Latin American women's popular Marian piety see Vuola, "*La Morenita* on Skis"; Vuola, "Seriously Harmful for Your Health?"; Vuola, "Patriarchal Ecumenism, Feminism and Women's Religious Experiences in Costa Rica."

a prophet, announcing the Kingdom of God, is especially clear in liberation theologians' interpretation of the *Magnificat*.

And finally, Leonardo Boff in particular links the Virgin Mary strongly with the Holy Spirit, though not exactly in the context of the *Magnificat*. For him, Mary more than any other human being, and the woman Mary more than any man, is the image of the Holy Spirit. She incarnates the feminine in God and God in the feminine.[49] As has been said, this mysterious relationship between Mary and the Holy Spirit is strongly linked to how Boff perceives "the feminine." Mary is also the feminine face of God—again, reflecting Boff's intent to give more importance not only to "the feminine" and to women, but also his image of God.[50] For Boff, Mary is the mediator, together with Jesus,[51] something which obviously Luther does not agree with. The link of Marian spirituality to the image of God and the Trinity, especially the Holy Spirit, seems to be something that can be found in both Luther and liberation theology, but in somewhat different ways.

MARY: ECUMENICAL BRIDGE, RATHER THAN OBSTACLE?

The double emphasis on Mary as the ordinary, even "lowly," woman and as the paragon of faith, are to be found in both Luther and liberation theology. The context of Luther's theology of the cross also brings his Mariology close to liberation theology. Nonetheless, there are important differences. However, the similarities may point to the possibility of an ecumenical Mariology, which starts with the experiences of ordinary Christians. This starting point does not concentrate on later Catholic Marian dogmas, of which Lutherans do not approve, but instead presents the ordinary human Mary of Nazareth, and her role as the defender of the oppressed, as a possible ecumenical bridge, rather than as its obstacle.

Both liberation theology and feminist (liberation) theology are ecumenical by nature. Thus, a possible ecumenical Mariology is not merely about a dialogue between Protestant and Catholic theologians but, within the larger liberation theological context, it is ecumenical already at its roots.

In that process, Lutheran theologians may need to ask what the relationship between Luther's Mariology and Luther*an* Mariology is. It is obvious that Luther's Mariological thought and devotion have not been developed in Lutheran churches, but rather, they have been obscured, forgotten or even (wrongly) seen as an ecumenical obstacle.

---

49. Boff, *El Ave María*, 46. The qualifying subtitle of this book is "The feminine and the Holy Spirit."

50. Boff, *El rostro materno de Dios*.

51. Ibid., 212.

Luther's emphasis in the ordinariness of Mary comes close to the attention paid in the feminist study of religion to everyday religion or lived religion, a sphere dominated by women, excluded from formal positions of representation and power. In the case of Mary, special attention needs to be given to women's identification with Mary *qua women*, her being "like myself" and not different, and a source of empowerment, especially for women.

What is to be found in Luther, liberation theology and in feminist theology is what I call low Mariology, the emphasis on the humanity of Mary. Thus, it is an obvious source for an ecumenical Mariology. However, the high(er) Mariology of the Catholic tradition sees Mary as worthy of devotion. This is a point of potential difference and conflict between Protestant and Catholic Mariology. However, according to my analysis of Luther's interpretation of the *Magnificat*, he too has a space for this kind of relationship to the Mother of God. Again, it is the later Lutheranism which has come to see all devotional practices relating to Mary as idolatry and deification of a human being. Yet, as we could see, Luther himself has an aspect—even a central one—in his interpretation of Mary of the *Magnificat* which is best understood as Marian spirituality, including its devotional aspects. Finally, the critique of power and pride in the *Magnificat*, together with the notion of Mary's exemplary faith, are sources of social change, found in Luther, liberation theology and feminist theology.

If such a possibility for an ecumenical liberation theological Mariology exists, what are the necessary steps towards it? In other words, how would it be possible? I am not claiming that such a project is necessary or even possible. Rather, I am arguing that a closer reading of Luther's Mariological thoughts reveals that there are many more such possibilities than contemporary Lutheran churches and theologians may think.

Based on the above, I think at least the following issues are necessary for the kind of Mariology that could be genuinely ecumenical. First, Mary's exemplary humanity should be taken seriously. It is a central Marian theme in all Christian churches, including the Lutheran tradition. Secondly, it is important to pay attention to the fact that Mary seems to have specific importance for women in all Christian churches. This does not mean the mostly Catholic emphasis on Mary as a specifically female ideal, impossible as such, as many feminist theologians remind us. Rather, her exemplary humanity is female humanity, and thus has connotations that may be gender-specific. I have called this female Marian piety and devotion *imitatio*

Mariae—Mary as a divine mirror reflecting human womanhood and thus validating it.[52]

Thirdly, Mary's importance for the poor and marginalized is highlighted, particularly in the context of the *Magnificat*. There is the possibility of a Marian spirituality, related to the understanding of her as an exemplary human and paradigm of faith, which points to social change and critique of structures of power. Here, too, it may be possible to talk about *imitatio Mariae*, not necessarily in a gender-specific form, but considering Mary simultaneously as a prophet and an ordinary, even poor and insignificant, person, chosen by God. Mary is both like her people (deeply human) and something more (a prophet and powerful figure).

This relates to the fourth point concerning Mary's role in lived religion and popular piety. I argue that it is exactly this dual role of hers which is so central in *religiosidad popular*, including in some of its gender-specific forms. Historically, the cult of the Virgin Mary in the Americas has had this role since the very beginning of the Conquest, Mary forming the cultural bridge between the European and the American, between the white and the indigenous, resulting in a unique form of Marian piety even within the Catholic Church.

Fifthly, as we have seen, there is the possibility of a Marian spirituality even in Luther. Mary's importance in the Catholic and Orthodox churches is best understood from the perspective of spirituality. The Lutheran churches share the two ecumenical dogmas with other Christian churches, but instead of the deep Marian spirituality, liturgy and devotion of the Catholic and Orthodox churches, there is an emptiness and a vacuum in the Lutheran tradition.

The idea of Mary as *Mediatrix*, mediator and intercessor, is central in Catholic Mariology and popular devotion. At the same time, it is exactly this role that raises suspicion in the Lutheran tradition. In his commentary on the *Magnificat*, Luther seems to be ambivalent about it. On the one hand, all his theology revolves around the idea that there is no other mediator besides Christ. On the other hand, the last sentence of his commentary points to a more devotional understanding of Mary that does not exclude the possibility of Mary having some kind of active role: "May Christ grant us this [a right understanding of the *Magnificat*] through the *intercession* and for the sake of His dear Mother Mary."[53] It is clear in the overall context of Luther's theology that this does not mean Mary acting as some kind

---

52. Vuola, "Patriarchal Ecumenism, Feminism and Women's Religious Experiences in Costa Rica," 229; Vuola, "*La Morenita* on Skis," 516–18.

53. Luther, *The Magnificat*, LW 21, 355, emphasis EV.

of *co-redemptrix* beside her son or having some salvific power in herself. Understanding Mary's mediating and intercession rather as a bridge—to God and to Christ, to fellow human beings, between women and men, between cultures—means taking her role in the other Christian churches seriously as well as opening up a space for a Lutheran Marian spirituality.

Finally, this role of hers as a bridge and example to follow (*imitatio*) can be relevant not only in ecumenical but also in interfaith contexts. Mary is important in Islam and the Qu'ran where she is in fact mentioned by name more often than in the New Testament. There is an entire sura of Mary in the Qu'ran. She is not venerated as the Mother of God but as the mother of the prophet Jesus.

Whatever kind of Marian theology and spirituality there is in the Christian churches, it is important to remember that Miriam of Nazareth was a Jewish woman, also by religion. She was raised as a Jew, she lived as a Jewish woman of her time, and she died as a Jew. Mary has been used as a weapon both in Christian anti-Semitism and Jewish anti-Christianity. However, it is Mary and her body that form the bridge at the crossroads of the three Abrahamic religions.

BIBLIOGRAPHY

Aquino, María Pilar. *Our Cry for Life: Feminist Theology from Latin America*. Maryknoll, NY: Orbis,1993.
Boff, Leonardo. *El Ave María. Lo femenino y El Espíritu Santo*. Bogotá: Indo-American Press Service, 1980.
———. *El rostro materno de Dios. Ensayo interdisciplinario sobre lo femenino y sus formas religiosas*. Madrid: Ediciones Paulinas, 1987.
———. "María, Mulher Profética e Libertadora. A Piedade Mariana na Teologia da Libertação." *Revista Eclesiástica Brasileira* 49 (1978) 59–72.
———. *Testigos de Dios en el corazón del mundo*. Santander: Sal Terrae, 1985.
Gebara, Ivone and María Clara Bingemer. *Mary, Mother of God, Mother of the Poor*. Maryknoll, NY: Orbis, 1989.
Ghiselli, Anja. *Sanan kantaja. Martti Lutherin käsitys Neitsyt Mariasta*. Helsinki: Suomalainen Teologinen Kirjallisuusseura, 2005.
Gutiérrez, Gustavo. *La fuerza histórica de los pobres*. Salamanca: Sígueme, 1982.
———. *Teología de la liberación. Perspectivas*. 14 ed. Salamanca: Sígueme, 1990.
Luther, Martin. *The Magnificat* (1521). LW 21. St. Louis: Concordia, 1956.
Sobrino, Jon. "El conocimiento teológico en la teología europea y latinoamericana." In *Liberación y cautiverio. Debates en torno al método de la teología en América Latina*, 177–207. México: Comité Organizador, 1976.
Stjerna, Kirsi. "For the Sake of the Future." In *Lutheran Identity and Political Theology*, edited by Carl-Henric Grenholm and Göran Gunner. Eugene, OR: Pickwick, 2014.
Vuola, Elina. "*La Morenita* on Skis. Women's Popular Marian Piety and Feminist Research of Religion." In *The Oxford Handbook of Feminist Theology*, edited

by Sheila Briggs and Mary McClintock Fulkerson, 494–524. Oxford: Oxford University Press, 2011.

———. *Limits of Liberation: Feminist Theology and the Ethics of Poverty and Reproduction*. London: Sheffield Academic Press, 2002.

———. "Patriarchal Ecumenism, Feminism and Women's Religious Experiences in Costa Rica." In *Gendering Religion and Politics: Untangling Modernities*, edited by Hanna Herzog and Ann Braude, 217–38. New York: Palgrave MacMillan, 2009.

———. "Seriously Harmful for Your Health? Religion, Feminism, and Sexuality in Latin America." In *Liberation Theology and Sexuality*, edited by Marcella Althaus-Reid, 137–62. London: Ashgate, 2006.

Wiberg Pedersen, Else Marie. "A Man Caught Between Bad Anthropology and Good Theology? Martin Luther's View of Women Generally and of Mary Specifically." *Dialog: A Journal of Theology* 49:3 (2010) 190–200.

15

"Satis est" (CA 7)

The Confessional Unity of the Church and the Augsburg Confession Today

HENNING THEIßEN

This chapter provides a rereading of the ecclesiological key article of the Augsburg Confession, preceded by some reflections on why present-day theologians still consider the confessional writings from the Reformation period to be meaningful for their work in the early twenty-first century. In doing so, they seem to subscribe to a *historical* view of the Reformation as a model for interpreting the present. This is what may at first sight seem odd in the *doctrinal* approach I will be following in these pages, since that view is somewhat in danger of overestimating the normative role of the confessional writings (*norma normata*) in comparison with the biblical writings (*norma normans*).[1]

I will not dwell on the issue of Scripture and Confession here, but content myself with a precursory remark. It deserves note that common understandings of the relationship between the two pose serious problems in terms of logic. Once we concede that the confessional writings have an edge over the Bible *hermeneutically* in that they offer a model interpretation of it, we cannot escape the conclusion that the normative character of the Bible is a product of interpretation and the Bible itself embedded in the

---

1. I am indebted to Ramona Schließer for her editorial support in the work with this chapter.

tradition from which that interpretation springs, i.e. the ecclesial tradition.[2] Obviously this argument dissolves the Reformers' categorical differentiation between scripture and tradition. To be sure, it is true that the Bible is a product of tradition just like the confessional writings are, but the doctrinal relationship between these two is not. There is no linear development leading from the Bible to the writings of the Reformers, so the latter do not directly interpret the Bible, but only the faith it provokes. Consistently, the theological dignity of the Bible as Word of God[3] is not in prompting confessional writings, but in provoking people to believe.[4]

Therefore, to consider the Reformation a model for interpreting the present does not mean to revisit the *fundamentals of faith* (word and sacrament), but rather to renovate the edifice of *life in faith* that is built on these fundamentals. In order to express the difference between the two, theological consultations within the Leuenberg Church Fellowship have suggested refining the Reformers' doctrine of the *notae ecclesiae* by making a distinction between *marks of the church* and *marks of Christian life*.[5] I will come back to this distinction in the course of my chapter, but will be defining the latter in the sense of Christian values. Since values are always controversial in a secular and pluralist society, my approach to the model character of the Reformation through the Leuenberg doctrine of the *notae ecclesiae* embraces a twofold thesis about the transition the Lutheran tradition is about to face in the not too distant future.

In order to interpret the present through the lens of the Reformation, (1) Lutherans will have to engage both with the Leuenberg model of

---

2. This conclusion has been drawn explicitly in a number of ecumenical convergence documents between Protestant and Roman Catholics in Germany. Cf. a document issued by the Ecumenical Working Group of Protestant and Catholic Theologians (ÖAK): *Verbindliches Zeugnis III. Schriftverständnis und Schriftgebrauch*, 361 (§ 184). A similar argument can be found in a joint declaration by the United Evangelical Lutheran Church in Germany (VELKD) and the Catholic Conference of Bishops in Germany (DBK): *Communio Sanctorum. Die Kirche als Gemeinschaft der Heiligen*, 34–35 (§ 53–54).

3. For a comprehensive discussion of the problem of the theological status of the Bible as Word of God, cf. the masterly Ph.D. thesis by Michael Coors, see Coors, *Scriptura efficax. Die biblisch-dogmatische Grundlegung des theologischen Systems bei Johann Andreas Quenstedt*.

4. That God's word provokes belief is a fundamental line of argument in Luther's teaching on the sacraments, cf. Luther, *De captivitate Babylonica ecclesiae praeludium*, WA 6, 543:31–543:33. It is particularly important for Luther's defense of infancy baptism, since if faith is provoked by God's word and baptism is, according to Luther, nothing but God's word embracing water, then personal belief is not a prerequisite for baptism, but its result.

5. Cf. *The Church of Jesus Christ*, 96–97.

ecumenism and with the values of secular modernity like individuality and pluralism. (2) In return, the Lutheran understanding of word and sacrament will provide a theological argument as to why and how this engagement should be put into practice.

These precursory remarks give an idea of the consequences that might ensue from considering the Reformation a model for interpreting the present. Logically, prior to this is the question as to what presuppositions such an understanding of the Reformation makes. I will turn to these now, presenting the presuppositions first and then a few brief remarks on the possible corollaries for the model character of the Reformation. The second section of my chapter will follow the same substructure with a discussion of CA 7 first, and then some reflections on its significance for interpreting the present.

PRESUPPOSITIONS FROM REFORMATION THEORY

As recent debates among Reformation theorists in Germany[6] indicate, the problem with the alleged model character of the Reformation is about the unity of the Reformation. In terms of Reformation theory, this unity covers both confessional and territorial units, but what is controversial is how far their respective range is. In a doctrinal perspective, the easiest way to settle such controversies is to define Reformation unity by the unity of the true church. This is also what can be found in the debates themselves.

The most recent of these debates was launched in 2005 when Gunther Wenz made a case for the Augsburg Confession as an expression of confessional unity within the Evangelical Church in Germany (EKD), arguing that it was the Augsburg Confession that explained the Leuenberg-based concept of church fellowship among the EKD member churches.[7] The Theological Board of the EKD disapproved Wenz's proposal in 2009 claiming that Wenz mistakenly reduced the ecclesial quality of the EKD to a mere church fellowship rather than a church in its own right.[8]

6. Cf. the debate about Gunther Wenz's proposal (2005) to agree on the Augsburg Confession as a common confessional writing for all member churches of the Evangelical Church in Germany, Wenz, "Die Confessio Augustana als evangelisches Grundbekenntnis? Ein Beitrag zur Strukturdebatte der EKD [2005]," 19–30.

7. Cf. ibid., 25: "Der gemeinsame Bezug auf die Confessio Augustana— welcher der Leuenberger Konkordie jenes inhaltliche Format zu verleihen vermag, das sie für sich genommen nicht hat—kann, so mein ceterum censeo, einer solch kommunikativen Wahrnehmung evangelischer Einheit in hohem Maße dienlich sein."

8. Cf. *Soll das Augsburger Bekenntnis Grundbekenntnis der Evangelischen Kirche in Deutschland warden?*, 11: "Und ebenso wie alle ihre Gliedkirchen am Leib Christi teilhaben, hat auch deren Gemeinschaft daran teil. (. . .) In diesem Sinne hat auch die EKD kirchlichen Charakter und ist Kirche."

The whole incident takes us back to an open question from earlier theological debates: what is the range of an ecclesial unit that is based on confessional unity? It is a question characteristic of Reformation theory, as can be learned from the following rough estimate. *Before* the Reformation it was not a question at all, since in those days there was (at least officially) no need to reflect on confessional diversity in a Europe that considered itself a homogenous Christian body (even if this body had two heads: the Emperor and the Pope). *After* the Reformation at the beginning of the confessional age in Europe our question was no longer a question, since the Peace of Augsburg (1555) at least in theory (*cuius regio, eius religio*) divided Europe into confessionally homogenous principalities, thus only transposing the pre-Reformation ideal of coextension between territory and confession to a smaller scale. However, for the time of the Reformation itself, our question turns out to be crucial. I will approach this problem in three steps to show that when Dorothea Wendebourg's writing gave rise to a vivid dispute among church historians in 1992, the controversy was basically about the range of confessional unity in Reformation churches.

a) Wendebourg argued (particularly against her Göttingen colleague Bernd Moeller) that the unity of the Reformation was only *extrinsically* constituted.[9] Her point was that to articulate the common theological grounds for the different strands of the Reformation presupposed an external standpoint, which was *not* on that same common ground. In historiographic terms, so Wendebourg argued, it was the Catholic Reform that constituted the unity of the Reformation. This openly provoked churches that consider themselves to live in *unity* with the Reformers' tradition, but it has prodded others to consider the constructive corollaries of Wendebourg's thesis as well. Berndt Hamm of Erlangen has argued in favor of the internal diversity of the Reformation as an expression of its liberating potentials.[10] The *Augsburg Confession*, we might then say, alluding to Ernst Käsemann's canon theory, does not account for the confessional unity of the Reformation, but for the diversity of its interpretations.[11] To interpret the present in the light of the Reformation would thus foster pluralism and *diversity* within the church and outside of it.

---

9. Wendebourg, "Die Einheit der Reformation als historisches Problem," 34–35: "Zu kaum einem der umstritenen Topoi gab es damals bereits eine verbindlich definierte Doktrin: Weder war die Lehre von Rechtfertigung, Gnade und Glauben dogmatisch festgelegt (. . .)."

10. Cf. Hamm, "Die Einheit der Reformation in ihrer Vielfalt. Das Freiheitspotential der 95 Thesen vom 31. Oktober 1517."

11. Cf. Käsemann, "Begründet der neutestamentliche Kanon die Einheit der Kirche? [1952/53]."

b) A closer look at the debate reveals that the problem with the model character of the Reformation cannot be settled in a rather harmless interplay between unity and diversity, but touches upon the contradiction between true and false church. The reason why Wendebourg says there is only an extrinsic unity of the Reformation is that there was no formal doctrine of justification before the Council of Trent, which the Reformers' criticism could have addressed.[12] This suggests that the unity of the Reformation is primarily a doctrinal unity. Even if Wendebourg emphasizes that the Reformation denotes a whole "way-of-life," its cultural or social factors appear subordinated to its religious and spiritual moments.[13] Thus Wendebourg's argument seems to provide a dogmatic analogy for the historiographical thesis of an extrinsic unity of the Reformation: the object of doctrine, the Word of God, too, is extrinsic to the Reformation (*extra nos*).

c) However, this analogy is dubious. Following Wendebourg's opponent in the Göttingen debate, Bernd Moeller, Thomas Kaufmann argues that the cities that adopted the Reformation in the sixteenth century must be considered "small corpora christiana" (Moeller). Here the Reformation established a homogenous cultural paradigm, which reached far beyond the intellectual sphere of theological doctrine into people's everyday life to create an intrinsic (not extrinsic, as in Wendebourg) "confessional cultural" unity of the Reformation in terms of architecture, craftsmanship, music, arts, and education alike.[14] If anyone considered this sort of confessional culture to weaken confessional unity, such an objection would reveal a rather narrowed idea of confession in the sense of a written statement. Against such an idea, it is worthy of note that some of the papers delivered to the Theological Board of the EKD during the debate about Wenz's aforementioned proposal stressed a wider meaning of the term "confession." For example, Wolf-Dieter Hauschild emphasized that the Augsburg Confession has always had a political function in identifying those religious groups or units that enjoyed protection by the Habsburg emperors.[15]

Comparing this with Wendebourg's and Kaufmann's argument, it turns out that their dissent is not essentially about the status of doctrine in comparison with other factors of Christianity, but about the range of confessional units in the Reformation era. While Wendebourg considers

12. Cf. Wendebourg, "Die Einheit der Reformation als historisches Problem," 34–35.

13. Ibid., 37; Wendebourg, "Replik," 135 ("way-of-life"), 133.

14. Cf. Kaufmann, "Das Bekenntnis im Luthertum des konfessionellen Zeitalters," 298–300.

15. Cf. Hauschild, "Die Geltung der Confessio Augustana im deutschen Protestantismus zwischen 1530 und 1980 (aus lutherischer Sicht)."

the Reformation on a rather large scale, measuring its confessional unity by its external counterpart in the Catholic Church, Kaufmann focuses on the much smaller cities. In a way, this controversy will remain open, since it can hardly be denied that there have been examples of confessional unity in either range.

What may take us further forward here is to turn from these historical reflections to a doctrinal perspective, which reveals an interesting affinity between Wendebourg and Kaufmann. As Wendebourg's opponent and Kaufmann's teacher, Bernd Moeller, has noted in the Göttingen dispute, arguments like those of Wendebourg define the unity of the Reformation in retrospect[16] by placing the unity of the Reformation in sharp contrast to the Catholic Church. This contrast marks a threshold between a reform (within the Catholic system) and a Reformation that trespasses the system boundaries of the Catholic Church.[17] This system-theory-based differentiation seems to have been consensual in the debate, but it means doctrinally that the unity of the Reformation, whether extrinsic or intrinsic, is always the *unity of the true church* in *opposition to the false church*. This does not only apply to Wendebourg's findings, but also to Kaufmann's. Wendebourg argues that the distinction between the true and false church is inherent in the visible (!) church.[18] Kaufmann is more hesitant, but provides historical evidence that where the cultural paradigm of the Reformation was imposed on particular cities, it turned into a hegemonic paradigm, including coercive measures against dissenters.[19]

Summarizing these debates, it can be argued that the historical phenomena of confessional unity in the Reformation, whether on a larger or smaller scale, presuppose the doctrinal understanding of unity in the sense of the true church in opposition to the false church.

---

16. Cf. Moeller, "Replik," 55–56.

17. At least this is what Berndt Hamm's contribution to the debate suggests, cf. Hamm, "Einheit und Vielfalt der Reformation—oder: was die Reformation zur Reformation machte," 64–66.

18. Wendebourg, "Kirche," 412: "Schließlich gibt es in der sichtbaren Kirche noch einen dritten Unterschied, der bei der verborgenen Kirche ausgeschlossen ist, die Differenz zwischen 'wahrer' und 'falscher' Kirche (ecclesia vera et falsa)."

19. Kaufmann, "Das Bekenntnis im Luthertum des konfessionellen Zeitalters," 290–91 says with reference to Eike Wolgast that under these circumstances "Verzicht auf Glaubenszwang bedeutet nicht Verzicht auf religionspolizeiliche Maßnahmen überhaupt."

A MARKET OF TRUTHS?

How do these presuppositions influence the model character of the Reformation? If the Reformation represents the true church, interpreting the present through its lens expresses the demand to live in truth. Such life in truth seems impossible without demarcation from that which is false. Demands for truth can be addressed to others, but must always be applied to the one who utters them as well, and will then turn into truth claims. Such claims need not necessarily lead to intolerance, either in theory or in social practice, but at least in social life they will endorse clearly defined institutions that allow for deciding whether a given social life form is good or not, and whether it is just or unjust. One might therefore expect that to interpret the present through the lens of the Reformation favors a competitive society, but if so, then also a society where different religious, moral, and political convictions coexist and compete—and in this respect such a view of the Reformation would also lead to a society of freedom and market.

The overall picture of such a society is pluralist, but to what degree, exactly? Its pluralism is certainly not for ignorance of truth claims, but will be a pluralism of truth-seeking communities. This means that the "freedom" and "market" aspects of such pluralism will primarily apply to religious convictions. In a societal framework of functional differentiation such as exists in a system-theoretical approach, such religious pluralism will also be less likely to entail pluralist demands on other segments of society like the economic sector.[20] In return, an understanding of religious pluralism that includes particular corollaries for political or economic power to be pluralized is unlikely to subscribe to a system-theoretical background.[21]

TOWARDS A LUTHERAN STANCE ON MODERNITY

The above conclusions from current Reformation theory are only conjectural unless put to the test of an actual reading of the Reformation's self-understanding. Therefore, I now turn to the central ecclesiological article

---

20. E.g., Herms, *Gesellschaft gestalten. Beiträge zur Sozialethik*, 248, conceives of Lutheran social ethics as a system-theory-based pluralist theory of institutions that sketches religious pluralism as a sort of market for the different religious institutions, although the overall impression is certainly that of reluctance to accept the present day prevalence of the economic sector (260–65; 360–61). This would be unthinkable unless the different societal systems are considered more or less segregated from one another.

21. A good example from a Lutheran background is Geyer, "Wahrheit und Pluralismus," 294–305, who draws precisely the socio-ethical conclusions mentioned in the text. However, his basic argument is a dogmatic one. Following Geyer, the basic Christian conviction of loving one's enemy is the only way of representing God's omnipotence in the world which demands that all earthly powers be pluralized.

of the Augsburg Confession, CA 7, and its concept of the true unity of the church (*vera unitas ecclesiae*). The unity of the church, according to CA 7, is its *truth*.

> CA 7,1: *Item docent, quod una sancta ecclesia perpetuo mansura sit.*

While most of the doctrinal articles of the Augsburg Confession begin with "*Item/de (. . .) docent*" and thus echo the "*Ecclesiae magno consensu apud nos docent*" (CA 1), only CA 5, 8, and 20 directly continue the articles that precede them. In the case of ecclesiology, this enclitic structure has contributed to the influential assumption that the Lutheran doctrine had a twofold concept of the church, one in faith (dealt with in CA 7) and one in experience (dealt with in CA 8). How else could the *ecclesiae* from CA 1 (i.e. the territories supporting the Confession at the Diet) teach that there was only one *ecclesia*? However, the point which CA 7,1 makes here is different, pointing less to the oneness (*una*) than to the holiness (*sancta*) of the church and interpreting the latter as perpetuity (*perpetuo mansura*). In a preparatory study for his great historical commentary on the Augsburg Confession, Wilhelm Maurer has argued that this perpetuity in the sense of temporal universality expressed a consensual attitude between Protestants and Roman Catholics and thus contributed a lot to the irenic character of the Augsburg Confession. Following Maurer, the real ecclesiological controversy in the days of the Reformation was about the alternative understanding of universality in spatial terms since to claim such universality was to openly defy Roman "catholicity."[22] However, I wonder if there is not already an unmistakably Protestant point in the teaching of the *ecclesia perpetuo mansura*.

This point, I suppose, is that the demarcation line between holy and profane is not the line of death, but the line between God and man, which runs right through the church. This makes it difficult—if not impossible—to draw a clear-cut distinction between true and false church. Unlike the Roman Confutation of CA 8, which considers the church of the saints (*congregatio sanctorum*) a purely otherworldly community of people who have passed away in a state of personal holiness, the Reformers attest sanctity to living sinful people merely due to what God effects in them. The further development of CA 21 speaks volumes in this respect. While in 1530 King David's warfare appeared as an example of holiness,[23] the Apology turned to

---

22. Cf. Maurer, "Ecclesia perpetuo mansura im Verständnis Luthers," 68–69. Unsurprisingly, for Maurer the two lines of understanding the universality of the church also make the difference between Luther (68) and Melanchthon (69n23).

23. *Die Bekenntnisschriften der evangelisch–lutherischen Kirche*, 83b.

Peter's renouncement, forgiven by Jesus,[24] and the variant of CA 21 (1540) returned to David's holiness again, but this time to his confession of sins before Nathan.[25]

> CA 7,2: *Est autem ecclesia congregatio sanctorum, in qua evangelium pure docetur et recte administrantur sacramenta.*

In its grammatical structure, this sentence looks like an Aristotelian definition with the congregation of saints as generic term and the gospel and sacraments as specific difference of the church against other congregations of saints. However, if the Reformers only draw the line of holiness between God and man, as CA 7,1 revealed, any congregation of saints will by definition be identical with the church. Therefore, the relative clause about good practice in gospel teaching and administering of sacraments does not provide any criteria to sever true church from false church, nor do the attributes of "pure" gospel teaching and "right" administering of sacraments, and this also applies to the following core sentence of CA 7—the famous *satis est.*

> CA 7,3: *Et ad veram unitatem ecclesiae satis est consentire de doctrina evangelii et de administratione sacramentorum.*

In his Apology (1531), Melanchthon referred to gospel and sacraments as "marks" of the church (Latin: *notae*).[26] This again suggests a demarcation line between true church and false church and has led to the question as to what further criteria are required to decide whether a given Christian community teaches the gospel purely and administers the sacraments rightly. Many suggest that the *satis est* expresses only a "minimum definition" of confessional unity,[27] which needs supplementary criteria or a third *nota*

---

24. Ibid., 317–18.

25. *Evangelische Bekenntnisse. Reformatorische Bekenntnisschriften und neuere Theologische Erklärungen*, 1:57.

26. *Die Bekenntnisschriften der evangelisch-lutherischen Kirche*, 238:22–23. "Et addimus notas: puram doctrinam evangelii et sacramenta."

27. In this respect, a 1967 article by contemporary church historian Klaus Scholder proved very influential at least in Germany: Scholder, "Die Bedeutung des Barmer Bekenntnisses für die evangelische Theologie und Kirche." Scholder's overall thesis was that it was not until the Declaration of Barmen that the Protestant churches had a theological definition of the church—the minimum criteria given in CA 7 were obviously insufficient, according to Scholder. His argument does not only attribute great ecclesiological value to the German Church Struggle in general, but particularly to the third thesis of the Barmen Declaration, which we will see contains all the elements of the church contemporary Protestant ecclesiology has suggested to amend CA 7.

ecclesiae like a formal consent in doctrine[28] or the ordained ministry[29] or the experience of communion[30] in the communities. It seems that most of these proposals are in one way or another inspired by ecumenism—be it in the sense of interconfessional relations or of international, worldwide relations of the church. The dogmatic problem with these ecumenical amendments to the Reformers' doctrine of the *notae ecclesiae* is, in my opinion, that they operationalize the doctrinal function of the *notae* for the purposes of the ministry issue.

While it is true that Melanchthon, both in the Augsburg Confession and its Apology, conceives of the *notae* as criteria for the unity of the church, Luther's use of them is methodologically far less strict, which accounts for the much higher number of *notae* in Luther: whereas Melanchthon restricts the *notae* to word and sacrament, Luther offers lists of seven[31] or even ten[32] *notae*. For Luther, the *notae* seem to have a pastoral function rather than a doctrinal one since he introduces them as a helpful device for perplexed Christians to detect the church in circumstances where Christ's presence with his people has been dissimulated. "Woher wil oder kan doch ein armer irriger Mensch mercken, wo solch Christlich heilig Volck in der welt ist?"[33]

Recognizing these internal differences in the two Wittenberg Reformers' understanding of the *notae* can help avoid at least two of their most common operationalizations. First, it would be unwise to use a list of

---

28. It seems that this is still in the background of Wenz's aforementioned thrust for the Augsburg Confession, since his basic argument is that any concept of the church needs doctrinal expression in order to be implemented in an ecumenical discourse.

29. The issue of ministry has certainly been the most prominent in ecumenical discourse ever since the Reformation. It was already included in Robert Bellarmin's doctrine of the three bonds (*tria vincula*) holding the church together (1590).

30. That a full Protestant understanding of the church requires the experience and notion of communion in the sense of brotherhood has been a characteristic idea of numerous Pietist arousals, but has also proved influential on ecclesiologies in the Moltmannian vein that have an affinity to grassroots processes in worldwide church life, cf. Weth, "Theologische Ekklesiologie nach 1945 im kritischen Horizont des Barmer Bekenntnisses (Barmen III) [1980]," 156.

31. Luther, *Von den Konziliis und Kirchen*, WA 50, 628:29–643:26. 1. "Gotteswort" (628:30), 2. "Sacrament der Tauffe" (630:22), 3. "Sacrament des Altars" (631:7), 4. "schluesseln" (631:37), 5. "empter" (632:36), 6. "gebet" (641:21), 7. "Kreutz" (. . .) (642:1).

32. Luther, *Wider Hans Worst*, WA 51, 479:4–485:7, 1. "Tauffe" (479:5), 2. "sacrament des altars" (480:3–480:4), 3. "schlussel" (480:14), 4. "predigampt und Gottes wort" (481:7–481:8), 5. "Symbolon" (481:17), 6. "gleich gebot dasselb vater unser" (482:8), 7. "weltliche herrschafft ehren" (482:15), 8. "Ehestand loben" (483:9), 9. "leiden" (484:1), 10. "[Er]dulden" (485:4).

33. Luther, *Von den Konziliis und Kirchen*, WA 50, 628:19–21.

pastoral criteria (Luther) to amend a set of *doctrinal* criteria (Melanchthon). Against this background it seems safer to me to refrain from the entire issue of a third (or fourth, fifth (...)) *nota* besides word and sacrament. Secondly, it would be equally unwise to conclude that since the *notae* fulfill different functions in the two Reformers, they needed to be allocated to different groups of people within the church: word and sacrament to the ordained ministry, but such *notae* like intercession and self-surrender to the priesthood of all believers. If the different *notae* are allocated in this way, they will not serve confessional unity (which they ought to do according to CA 7), but detach it from the priesthood of all believers, which is not explicitly mentioned in the Lutheran confessional writings.[34] Thus detached, the freedom ministers enjoy in public will be transformed into an *external* ('public') representation of the church while according to the doctrine of the *notae* this public freedom is an *internal* freedom of conscience in that ministers moderate and integrate the different forms of Christ's presence with his people.[35]

Either of the aforementioned problematic operationalizations can be avoided if the common ground between Luther's and Melanchthon's doctrine of the *notae* is respected. They disagree on the number of the *notae*: while Melanchthon confines them to two, Luther's divergent statements preclude a comprehensive list. At the same time, Luther does not extend the list arbitrarily, but arranges the *notae* he suggests concentrically around Melanchthon's exclusive list of two. This suggests that there is an implicit distinction in the two Reformers between that which is at the heart of the life of the church and its rather peripheral aspects. Periphery here does not evoke lesser importance, but only that which the terms denote literally: those aspects of the church where it comes into touch with the world outside the church. It is therefore in the line of the Reformers' argument to make a distinction between *notae* in the sense of "marks of the church" and *notae* in the sense of "marks of Christian life," which is actually what the Community of Protestant Churches in Europe has suggested in its aforementioned theological consultations on the doctrine of the *notae*. Before

---

34. The papers delivered at the ecclesiological symposium of the German *Luther-Gesellschaft* in 2005 (cf. Theißen, "'Ich glaube die heilige christliche Kirche'") provide an excellent overall picture of the type of Lutheran confessional culture that relates to this kind of argument. Meanwhile, the papers have been published outside the journals affiliated with the *Luther-Gesellschaft*. The most prominent of these is Müller, "Das Kirchenverständnis der lutherischen Reformation."

35. In a different context, I have argued in detail for this understanding of the ordained ministry: Theißen, "Bekenntnis und Bekennen als Fixpunkte kirchlicher Orientierung und Erfahrung," 218–25.

turning to the dogmatic significance of this distinction, I would like to stress that it may help settle the ecumenical debate about their number.

How hazardous this debate is dogmatically can be seen on a meta level. The mere fact that the churches involved in this debate disagree about what is a mark of the church and what is not turns these marks into something negotiable among churches. It turns pure gospel and right sacraments into requirements the churches have to meet in order to establish ecclesial unity. In logical terms, it turns criteria into necessary conditions (*conditio sine qua non*). However, the logical status of CA 7,3 is different. The famous "*satis est*" indicates that these conditions are not necessary, but sufficient (*conditio per quam*).[36] In contrast to necessary conditions, sufficient conditions of something denote that which constitutes that something. Thus the point in CA 7,3 is that gospel and sacrament are constitutive for the church and cannot therefore be negotiable in any discourse on ecclesial unity. In dogmatic terms, *pure* gospel and *right* sacraments are *God's work in the church*. It is pointless to seek an ecclesial unity fuller than that which God works; such efforts have no influence on the true church, CA 7 concludes, thus emphasizing the contrast between human and divine institutions.

> CA 7,4: *Nec necesse est ubique similes esse traditiones humanas seu ritus aut ceremonias ab hominibus institutas; sicut inquit Paulus: Una fides, unum baptisma, unus Deus et pater omnium* etc.

Essentially, CA 7 is not an Aristotelian definition of the church, but a description of God's work in the church. Consistently following its concept of sanctity as God's work in man, the Augsburg Confession also confines its ecclesiological articles to the divine factors of the church. This ecclesiology is a bulwark against any attempt to demarcate true church from false church. The corollaries this has for an understanding of the true church are far-reaching when we only consider CA 8 and its idea of the church as an entity made up of good and of evil. As Wilhelm Maurer has pointed out in his historical research on the Augsburg Confession,[37] this article deals with the problem of Donatism (not of Novatianism, as parallels in Luther's Confession of 1528 do) and thus points in particular to ministers who do not administer the sacrament rightly, but consider it a human sacrifice before God (*sacrificium missale*). The acceptance of these "*mali admixti*" (CA 8,1) is not due to an embarrassment before the Reformers ordained their

---

36. Cf. Kambartel, "Bedingung," 762–65.
37. Cf. Maurer, *Historischer Kommentar zur Confessio Augustana*, vol. 2, 165.

own ministers,[38] but rather the ultimate consequence of their ecclesiological focus on God's work in the church, which can even be effected through unworthy or heterodox ministers.

A WEB OF TRUTH

Turning finally to the current significance of my proposed reading of CA 7, we have to ask: what remains of the model character of the Reformation if even ministers who do *not* administer the sacraments rightly are included in the church of "pure" gospel and "right" sacraments? While our first impression was that a Reformation-oriented understanding of the present led to a pluralistic and competitive coexistence of disparate truth-seeking communities and their relating institutions, our rereading of CA 7 offers a different picture where even contradictory convictions about what is "true" and "right" are suspended in the hope of God's work in the human community. The theological nature of this argument is obvious, and its optimistic attitude towards the reconciliation of opposing convictions seems plausible in an age when either side of the emerging confessional discord in Europe pleaded the truth of Christendom, which alone allowed for an inclusive line of argument such as in CA 8. But nowadays the Reformers' focus on God's work seems to disregard modern achievements like individualism and secularism, which openly defy the idea of a common truth. At the same time, it leaves those who still believe in such truth defenseless against obvious distortions of their belief.

Faced with these problems, present-day reaction to the Reformation should emphasize that the Reformers' understanding of the "true church" in CA 7 does not suspend the true/false dichotomy altogether, but reworks it from an outwardly-directed demarcation into a *self-differentiation* between word and sacrament as an *act of the church* and as *God's work*. To be the true church is thus not a possession of the church, but a challenging gift. In the light of such self-differentiation, to interpret the present following the model of the Reformation would not lead to a competitive "market of truths," but rather to a "web of truth," within the texture of which each truth-seeking community depends on the truth understanding of the others in order to fully express their own truth claim. This implies that the unity of God's work cannot be represented in the unity of a single unit and its truth claim in this "web," but only in the diversity of the fullness of the "web."

---

38. On this issue, cf. the Berlin Ph.D. thesis by Krarup, *Ordination in Wittenberg*, 100–104, who argues that there were Protestant ordinations well before the close of the Diet in 1530.

The proposed concept of truth as a "web" in which different communities interact is not meant to turn truth into a secular value whose authority is rooted in the interaction of societal powers. What it does do, however, is give a hint as to how the truth of the gospel (representing the "marks of the church") relates to the values of modernity (being the "marks of Christian life"). I would like to conclude with some reflections on the relationship between truth and values.

There is a widespread Protestant reluctance to accept values, which is probably to a considerable extent fuelled by Eberhard Jüngel's influential criticism of the "tyranny of values" (an expression borrowed from a joint publication with Carl Schmitt). Jüngel argues that the *theological* authority of the gospel as a mere request and invitation to *truth* and reconciliation[39] is in itself irreconcilable with the authority of *values* which regularly require the exercise of *political* authority. Perhaps there is an even more fundamental opposition beyond that between theological and political authority, and that is Jüngel's struggle with atheism and secularism.

In this respect Jüngel's juxtaposition of truth and values has also been a reply to the challenges atheist philosophers such as Jürgen Habermas in particular have posed for theology. However, Habermas' position has developed further since the late 1970s, when Jüngel published his essay *Wertlose Wahrheit*. In particular, Habermas' speech delivered on receiving the German Booksellers' Peace Award in 2001 makes some important changes to his earlier statements.[40] Up until then Habermas used to emphasize the need for religious convictions to be translated into arguments of public reason. In his 2001 speech, which was given only a few weeks after 9/11, Habermas reckoned with a peculiar rationality in religion, too, which was not to be fully transformed into secular values. Public discourse therefore had to accept and learn the terms and logic of this religious rationality.

The change in Habermas' argument has widely been considered to open up a new access for religion to public discussion in a secular society. Since 2001, religious motivations for decision and policy making seem to have gained more and more significance—in fact, more than the "overlapping consensus" which Habermas' intellectual opponent from the 1980s, John Rawls, had already conceded in 1993: the possibility of arguing for *secular* values from the background of the divergent "comprehensive doctrines" of religious convictions.[41] After Habermas' Peace Award address, genuinely *religious* values appeared on the stage of public discourse. Scholars like Hans

---

39. Cf. Jüngel, "Die Autorität des bittenden Christus," 179–88.
40. Cf. Habermas, *Glauben und Wissen*.
41. Cf. Rawls, *Political Liberalism*, 58–66, 133–68.

Joas, who has given a genetical account of the indispensable role different religious convictions have played in producing the values expressed in the General Declaration of Human Rights,[42] give an example of this.

However, it would be misleading to tell this story as a contest between secular and religious values. At least Joas' argument is far more complex. The "generalization of values" he has in mind takes place when a rational discourse between opposing value systems incites either party to modify and renew their own tradition.[43] The renewals and modifications achieved in this mutual process will constitute values on a level beyond the parties' traditional ones as they will have to be *common values* between *opposing value systems*. Joas borrows the theoretical background of such a "generalization of values" from Talcott Parsons[44] and applies it to the genesis of the General Declaration of Human Rights, but it is perfectly possible to quote further examples of generalized values from religious traditions.

For example, if the theological value of the Sabbath and Sunday had not been controversial among the early Christians in their Jewish surroundings, there would probably be no Judaeo-Christian value of a weekly day off work that covers both the Jewish Sabbath and the Christian Sunday. Even though this example may be an oversimplification, it shows clearly the theoretical claim Joas makes when drawing on Parsons' "generalization of values." He certainly does *not* take a step *back behind* the difference between religious and secular values, but rather a step *forward beyond* it, since that common Judeo-Christian, thus religious, value is only established by mutual acceptance of the other's opposing value as literally of equal value to one's own. This pushes either party beyond the limits of their own value system. It would even constitute a preliminary, merely technical definition of religious values to consider them at the more generalized level that value controversies reach through mutual communication of their opposing values.

Following this line of argument, Habermas' modified position from 2001 cannot be considered to renounce secularization, nor can a theological adoption of his Peace Award address claim religious values by either shrinking back from secular values or skipping over them with a post-secular attitude. Quite the opposite: religious values would not emerge at all if it were not through controversy about other values. What theology and religion may therefore justifiably expect of those other values is that they can be

---

42. Cf. Joas, *Die Sakralität der Person. Eine neue Genealogie der Menschenrechte*.

43. Cf. ibid., 264: "Erneut zeigt sich, daß das Resultat einer gelingenden Kommunikation über Werte mehr oder weniger ist als das Resultat eines rationalen Diskurses: zwar kein voller Konsens, aber eine dynamische wechselseitige Modifikation und Anregung zur Erneuerung der je eigenen Tradition."

44. Cf. ibid., 261 et passim.

acquired in a religious way. This criterion precludes what are merely economic values from religious values, but leaves enough room for many other modern values like secularization itself, or pluralism.

My conclusion is that even the Lutheran tradition is particularly well-prepared for this kind of engagement with modernity and its values. The incessant controversy about values, which is so typical of modern pluralist societies, requires precisely the kind of communication Lutherans are perfectly acquainted with owing to what has earlier in this chapter been called the freedom of conscience in Protestant ministry. That is to say that there are no moral constraints for ministers to propagate some ecclesial belief publicly in the pulpit, which they would not be willing to confess privately according to their conscience. In their public proclamation of the gospel, ministers are not supposed to preach their individual convictions at all, but to hold together and even integrate divergent, perhaps opposing forms of confessing the truth of the Christian faith. It is particularly this integrative task of "unity in reconciled diversity" that requires theological expertise, and this is something that Lutherans, as is well known, have—at least in the second half of the twentieth century—been experts at.[45]

Public communication of values in a pluralist society requires the same type of freedom, but not the same type of expertise, for unlike the proclamation of the gospel, such a public discourse does not aim at the unity of God's work. Values do not belong to the *notae ecclesiae* in the sense of word and sacrament but in the sense of 'marks of the Christian life,' and as such they address every Christian, not just ordained ministers. However, their expertise in 'unity in reconciled diversity' can offer a model for every Christian who is called to contribute to the societal task of generalizing values. It will require of Lutherans to engage with the modern values of secularization, individualization, and pluralism on the one hand, but engaging with the controversies about them will also open up opportunities for Lutherans to detect their religious values anew.

BIBLIOGRAPHY

The Church of Jesus Christ. The Contribution of the Reformation towards Ecumenical Dialogue in Church Unity. Edited by Wilhelm Hüffmeier. Leuenberg Texts 1. Frankfurt, 1995.

Communio Sanctorum. Die Kirche als Gemeinschaft der Heiligen. Bilaterale Arbeitsgruppe der Deutschen Bischofskonferenz und der Kirchenleitung der Vereinigten Evangelisch-Lutherischen Kirche Deutschlands. Paderborn: Bonifatius 2000/Frankfurt: Lembeck, 2000.

---

45. The phrase "unity in reconciled diversity" is widely considered to originate in the 4th General Assembly of the Lutheran World Federation in Dar es Salaam (1977).

Coors, Michael. *Scriptura efficax. Die biblisch-dogmatische Grundlegung des theologischen Systems bei Johann Andreas Quenstedt. Ein dogmatischer Beitrag zu Theorie und Auslegung des biblischen Kanons als Heiliger Schrift*. Göttingen: Vandenhoeck & Ruprecht, 2009.

Die Bekenntnisschriften der evangelisch-lutherischen Kirche. Herausgegeben im Gedenkjahr der Augsburger Konfession 1930. Göttingen: Vandenhoeck & Ruprecht, (1930) 1998.

Evangelische Bekenntnisse. Reformatorische Bekenntnisschriften und neuere Theologische Erklärungen, vol. 1, edited by Rudolf Mau. Bielefeld: Luther-Verlag, 1997.

Geyer, Hans-Georg. "Wahrheit und Pluralismus." In *Andenken: Theologische Aufsätze*, edited by Hans Theodor Goebel, Dietrich Korsch, Harrtmut Ruddies, and Jürgen Seim, 294–305. Tübingen: Mohr Siebeck, 2003.

Habermas, Jürgen. *Glauben und Wissen. Rede zum Friedenspreis des Deutschen Buchhandels 2001*. Frankfurt: Suhrkamp, 2001.

Hamm, Berndt. "Die Einheit der Reformation in ihrer Vielfalt. Das Freiheitspotential der 95 Thesen vom 31. Oktober 1517." In Berndt Hamm and Michael Welker. *Die Reformation—Potentiale der Freiheit*, 29–66. Tübingen: Mohr Siebeck, 2008.

———. "Einheit und Vielfalt der Reformation—oder: was die Reformation zur Reformation machte." In Berndt Hamm, Bernd Moeller, and Dorothea Wendebourg. *Reformationstheorien. Ein kirchen-historischer Disput über Einheit und Vielfalt der Reformation*, 57–127. Göttingen: Vandenhoeck & Ruprecht, 1995.

Hauschild, Wolf-Dieter. "Die Geltung der Confessio Augustana im deutschen Protestantismus zwischen 1530 und 1980 (aus lutherischer Sicht)." *ZThK* 104 (2007) 172–206; (EKD-Texte 103 (2009)) 31–58.

Herms, Eilert. *Gesellschaft gestalten. Beiträge zur Sozialethik*. Tübingen: Mohr Siebeck, 1991.

Joas, Hans. *Die Sakralität der Person. Eine neue Genealogie der Menschenrechte*. Frankfurt: Suhrkamp, 2011.

Jüngel, Eberhard. "Die Autorität des bittenden Christus. Eine These zur materialen Begründung der Eigenart des Wortes Gottes. Erwägungen zum Problem der Infallibilität in der Theologie." In *Unterwegs zur Sache. Theologische Bemerkungen*, edited by Eberhard Jüngel, 179–88. BEvTh 61. München: Kaiser, 1972.

Käsemann, Ernst. "Begründet der neutestamentliche Kanon die Einheit der Kirche? [1952/53]." In *Exegetische Versuche und Besinnungen*, 1:214–23. Göttingen: Vandenhoeck & Ruprecht, 1960.

Kambartel, Friedrich. "Bedingung." In *Historisches Wörterbuch der Philosophie*, vol.1 edited by Joachim Ritter, 762–65. Basel: Schwabe & Co, 1971.

Kaufmann, Thomas. "Das Bekenntnis im Luthertum des konfessionellen Zeitalters." *ZThK* 105 (2008) 281–314.

Krarup, Martin. *Ordination in Wittenberg. Die Einsetzung in das kirchliche Amt in Kursachsen zur Zeit der Reformation*. BHTh 141. Tübingen: Mohr Siebeck, 2007.

Luther, Martin. *De captivitate Babylonica ecclesiae praeludium* (1520). WA 6. Weimar: Hermann Böhlau, 1888.

———. *Von den Konziliis und Kirchen* (1539). WA 50. Weimar: Hermann Böhlaus Nachfolger, 1914.

———. *Wider Hans Worst* (1541). WA 51. Weimar: Hermann Böhlaus Nachfolger, 1914.

Maurer, Wilhelm. "Ecclesia perpetuo mansura im Verständnis Luthers." In *Luther und das evangelische Bekenntnis*, edited by Ernst-Wilhelm Kohls and Gerhard Müller, 62–75. Kirche und Geschichte 1. Göttingen: Vandenhoeck & Ruprecht, 1970.

———. *Historischer Kommentar zur Confessio Augustana*. Vol. 2. Gütersloh: Mohn, 1978.

Moeller, Bernd. "Replik." In Berndt Hamm, Bernd Moeller, and Dorothea Wendebourg. *Reformationstheorien. Ein kirchen-historischer Disput über Einheit und Vielfalt der Reformation*. Göttingen: Vandenhoeck & Ruprecht, 1995.

Müller, Gerhard. "Das Kirchenverständnis der lutherischen Reformation." *LKW 54* (2007) 199–216.

Rawls, John. *Political Liberalism*. The John Dewey Essays in Philosophy 4. New York: Columbia University Press, 1993.

Scholder, Klaus. "Die Bedeutung des Barmer Bekenntnisses für die evangelische Theologie und Kirche." *EvTh* 27 (1967) 435–461.

Soll das Augsburger Bekenntnis Grundbekenntnis der Evangelischen Kirche in Deutschland werden? Ein Votum der Kammer der Evangelischen Kirche in Deutschland für Theologie. EKD-Texte 103. Hannover, 2009.

Theißen, Henning. "Bekenntnis und Bekennen als Fixpunkte kirchlicher Orientierung und Erfahrung. Systematisch-theologische Näherbestimmung am Beispiel von Apostolikumstreit und Barmer Theologischer Erklärung." In *Preußische Union, lutherisches Bekenntnis und kirchliche Prägungen. Theologische Ortsbestimmungen im Ringen um Anspruch und Reichweite konfessioneller Bestimmtheit der Kirche*, edited by Jürgen Kampmann and Werner Klän, 213–31. Oberurseler Hefte Ergänzungsband 14. Göttingen: Edition Ruprecht 2013

———. "'Ich glaube die heilige christliche Kirche.' Bericht vom Luther Seminar in Coburg am 16./17. September 2005." *Luther 77* (2006) 113–16

Verbindliches Zeugnis III. Schriftverständnis und Schriftgebrauch, edited by Wolfhart Pannenberg und Theodor Schneider. DiKi 10. Göttingen: Vandenhoeck & Ruprecht; Freiburg: Herder, 1998.

Wendebourg, Dorothea. "Die Einheit der Reformation als historisches Problem." In Berndt Hamm, Bernd Moeller, and Dorothea Wendebourg. *Reformationstheorien. Ein kirchen-historischer Disput über Einheit und Vielfalt der Reformation*. Göttingen: Vandenhoeck & Ruprecht, 1995.

———. "Kirche." In *Luther Handbuch*, edited by Albrecht Beutel, 403–14. Tübingen: Mohr Siebeck, 2005.

———. "Replik." In Berndt Hamm, Bernd Moeller, and Dorothea Wendebourg. *Reformationstheorien. Ein kirchen-historischer Disput über Einheit und Vielfalt der Reformation*. Göttingen: Vandenhoeck & Ruprecht, 1995.

Wenz, Gunther. "Die Confessio Augustana als evangelisches Grundbekenntnis? Ein Beitrag zur Strukturdebatte der EKD [2005]." In *Soll das Augsburger Bekenntnis Grundbekenntnis der Evangelischen Kirche in Deutschland werden? Ein Votum der Kammer der Evangelischen Kirche in Deutschland für Theologie*. EKD-Texte 103. Hannover, 2009.

Weth, Rudolf. "Theologische Ekklesiologie nach 1945 im kritischen Horizont des Barmer Bekenntnisses (Barmen III) [1980]." In *"Barmen" als Herausforderung der Kirche. Beiträge zum Kirchenverständnis im Licht der Barmer Theologischen Erklärung*, edited by Rudolf Weth, 83–159. TEH, NF 220. München: Kaiser, 1984.

www.ingramcontent.com/pod-product-compliance
Lightning Source LLC
Chambersburg PA
CBHW050345230426
43663CB00010B/1996